Public Law within Government

Public Law within Government

Sustaining the Art of the Possible

T. P. B. Rattenbury

palgrave
macmillan

First published 2008 by
PALGRAVE MACMILLAN
Houndmills, Basingstoke, Hampshire RG21 6XS and
175 Fifth Avenue, New York, N.Y. 10010
Companies and representatives throughout the world

PALGRAVE MACMILLAN is the global academic imprint of the Palgrave Macmillan division of St. Martin's Press, LLC and of Palgrave Macmillan Ltd. Macmillan® is a registered trademark in the United States, United Kingdom and other countries. Palgrave is a registered trademark in the European Union and other countries.

ISBN 978-1-349-36281-3 ISBN 978-0-230-58362-7 (eBook)
DOI 10.1057/9780230583627

This book is printed on paper suitable for recycling and made from fully managed and sustained forest sources. Logging, pulping and manufacturing processes are expected to conform to the environmental regulations of the country of origin.

A catalogue record for this book is available from the British Library.

Library of Congress Cataloging-in-Publication Data

Rattenbury, T. P. B., 1952–
Public law within government : sustaining the art of the possible / T. P. B. Rattenbury.
p. cm.
Includes bibliographical references and index.

1. Public law–Great Britain. 2. Administrative law–Great Britain. 3. Local finance–Law and legislation–Great Britain. 4. Public law. 5. Administrative law. 6. Local finance–Law and legislation. I. Title.

KD3930.R38 2008
342.41–dc22 2007052979

10 9 8 7 6 5 4 3 2 1
17 16 15 14 13 12 11 10 09 08

Transferred to Digital Printing 2011

To Diana, with love and enormous appreciation.
To Jay and Carrie, with love.
And to the countless public officials, elected and unelected,
who do their honest best.

Contents

Preface

Students and scholars of public administration and public law are often frustrated by the lack of solid information about the workings of public law within government. That these are important is attested to by the steady stream of judicial review cases, sometimes of great political, social or human significance, in which particular acts or decisions are held up to close judicial scrutiny and rulings are made about whether or not, in the circumstances, public authorities have overstepped their bounds. Thus much is learned about the substance of public law.

Far less is learned, though, about how it works, and the latter is the focus of this book. My aim has been to examine public law in its natural setting, as an everyday part of government operations, and there to explore the variety of its contributions to the political process.

As source material I have taken a particularly interesting chain of events, full of legal and political variety, that unfolded in the recent past of English local government, when the Thatcher government tried to restrain local authority spending, and some local authorities did not like it one little bit. Public law was central to their responses. I have been fortunate that one of the local authorities involved has assisted by allowing access to its internal documents and to the former senior officials most closely involved. This has made the study far richer than it could otherwise have been.

Huge thanks are due to the local authority concerned, as well as to the three officials – 'the Treasurer', 'the Solicitor' and 'the Deputy Solicitor' – whose assistance has been invaluable. 'The Treasurer', in particular, has spent many hours meeting with me, and many more reviewing rough and less rough drafts of the text.

Also huge are the thanks I owe my wife, who has read and reread, encouraged and suggested, and now knows far more about the *ultra vires* rule than should be expected of any self-respecting professor of English.

Others who have provided valuable support or comment at critical times include Keith Hawkins, John Goodrich and the reviewers of both my proposal and the typescript. Thanks also to the editorial and production staff at Palgrave Macmillan, who have been efficient and accommodating.

If, despite the accumulated efforts of all the above, errors or infelicities remain ... I blame my wife, naturally!! (Just kidding, dear.)

1 Introduction

Not so long ago, in a Labour-controlled local authority somewhere in England, there was a problem. The council had ambitious plans to tackle the serious social deprivation in its area, but plans like these cost money, and the central government in London, Conservative at the time, thought that local authorities should be spending less money, not more. This was not just a polite difference of opinion. The local authority, and others like it, had strong views about what they should be doing for their areas. The government's views were also strong, but were very different. The government, however, had the power to convert its wishes into laws that the local authorities would have to obey; it was to use this power repeatedly. Faced, then, with what was to become a 'sustained battery of legislative and fiscal measures aimed at securing their compliance with the wishes of central government' (Carmichael 1995: 292), what, if anything, could the council do to realize its own ambitions for its area? It all depended on the *ultra vires* rule.

The words *ultra vires* ('beyond the powers') and expressions like the *ultra vires* 'rule', 'doctrine' or 'principle' are found in the public law of many countries and are central to this book. 'Public law' (or 'administrative law': writers use both terms and they are interchangeable for present purposes) is concerned with what governments do and how they do it, and within that context an *ultra vires* act or decision is one that is beyond the legal authority of a particular government entity. Thus at the local government level in America, 'contracts entirely beyond the municipal jurisdiction are *ultra vires* ...' (Valente 1980: 699). At both the provincial and federal levels in Canada, a statute that is 'outside the powers conferred upon the enacting body' is 'ultra vires and for that reason invalid' (Hogg 1997/current: 5–27). At the national level in unitary New Zealand there are also 'ultra vires challenges' to the executive (McLean 2006: 140–1). Cooley (2001: 69), writing in relation to Sri Lanka, lists in a chapter heading the wide range of authorities to which 'the *ultra vires* concept or, what is the same thing, the nullity question' (vii) has been applied there:

(1) Parliament / House of Representatives of Ceylon
(2) Sovereign / Governor / Governor General of Ceylon
(3) President of Sri Lanka
(4) Cabinet Ministers
(5) Heads of Government Departments
(6) Local Authorities / Statutory Bodies
(8) Miscellaneous.

For local governments, both in England and elsewhere, the *ultra vires* rule has a special resonance. For many of them the foundational principle of public law is that local authorities are the creatures of statute and can only do what statute permits. They have, in other words, no inherent power of action; their powers are the ones that legislatures confer, and everything else is *ultra vires*. Humes and Martin (1969: 183), in their comparative survey of 81 countries, describe this as being true of 'almost all local governments in English-speaking countries', though one must also mention constitutions as a source of local government powers in some American states (McCarthy and Reynolds 2003: 22) and, for example, Malawi (Kaunda 1999: 124–7). In a more recent comparative collection Denters and Rose (2005c: 251) still comment that local government autonomy is comparatively limited in the United Kingdom, Australia and New Zealand under the 'long-standing tradition of *ultra vires*', though they note that in all three places broad new powers have recently been added.

The essays in Reddy (1999) reveal a similar picture in a number of Southern African states. Mauritius is clearly stated to be subject to the *ultra vires* rule (Dukhira 1999: 135), and Lesotho appears to have enshrined it in its constitution (see Wallis 1999: 98). Pasteur's review of eight countries singles out Uganda for its 'departure from the *ultra vires* tradition' through its enactment of a 'power of general competence' (1999: 43). In South Africa, Smith (2006) writes that 'One of the debates that flowed from the new constitutional status of local government was the idea that perhaps the *ultra vires* doctrine did not apply any more.' However, 'Close examination of the constitutional provisions and the provisions in other legislation shows that the *ultra vires* doctrine is alive and well. If a municipality cannot point out the statutory authority to do something it cannot do that.'

Two important points must be added immediately to this whirlwind tour of the universe. The first is that when local authorities or other governments exercise their statutory powers they must comply with public law rules about how statutory powers should be exercised. These rules, which require things like procedural fairness and disregarding 'irrelevant considerations', are themselves component parts of the *ultra vires* rule, using that term in what Commonwealth writers like Craig (2003: 5, UK), Jones and de Villars (2004: 133–5, Canada), Sarma (2004: 13, India) and Head (2005: 92, Australia) refer to as its broad or extended sense. The equally important other side of the coin, however, is that if the local authority complies with all of those rules, and therefore remains within its powers (or *intra vires*), neither the courts nor any other level of government has any inherent right to tell it what to do. Any such right would itself need to be created by legislation. It is because local authorities are, in principle, autonomous within the limits of their statutory powers that these powers are rightly described as important 'resources' that are at the disposal of local authorities in their dealings with central government and others (Rhodes 1999: 78–81). They were certainly essential resources in the tale told in this book.

The book is a study of the *ultra vires* rule in action, of public law at work *within* government. This internal perspective is very different from that of writers like Head (2005: 1), who says that 'Administrative law is about challenging government power'. Seen from within, administrative law is not about challenging government but about sustaining it, about providing the legal underpinnings that support valid decision-making at all points of the administrative/political spectrum and without which decisions may be vulnerable if challenged by those whom they displease. If politics is, in that well-worn expression, 'the art of the possible', then public law *within* government is about sustaining the art of the possible. It is an ever-continuing process of providing legal inputs so that outputs can be legal.

This process of sustaining the art of the possible will be explored in detail in this study. The immediate context is English local government, where the aim is to contribute another 'modest step in investigating and trying to make sense of the relationship between Administrative Law and Public Administration at the local level', as Bridges *et al.* (1987: vii) described their own objective in studying the aftermath of *Bromley LBC v GLC* (1981), a controversial House of Lords decision that struck down the Greater London Council's 'Fares Fair' transport subsidy policy. Through its local government example, however, the book aims to advance understanding of the functioning of public law within government generally, whether at local, intermediate or national levels. This may seem a large ambition for a thoroughly local study, especially since local government is often considered a 'junior' form of government, but the local political process shares enough common features with other levels of government that the principal themes of this study can be widely generalized, as long as this is done carefully. Strong-willed politicians and diligent bureaucrats are stock characters of the political drama everywhere, working together to achieve policy goals. Elections, local and general, frame the political horizons. Budgetary cycles like the ones to be described in this book revolve, raising all the time the question of what a government will spend and how it will pay for it, and governments of many kinds are constrained by legislation restricting their taxing or spending powers, as was the local authority whose experiences will be examined here. Furthermore, the public law described in this book is anything but parochial. Delaney (2001: vii), comparing the law of Ireland, the United Kingdom, Canada, Australia and New Zealand, finds 'a surprising amount of common ground', and even in the United States, where constitutional and statutory formulas such as 'due process' and 'arbitrary, capricious, an abuse of discretion, or otherwise not in accordance with law' unavoidably frame the exposition, Warren (2004: 27) writes that 'probably more than 90 percent of administrative law is derived from common law', and Schwartz and Wade (1972: 207) consider that English and American courts produce 'much the same results' even while they 'often seem to be talking different languages'.

In addition, the process of working with statutory powers towards public policy ends, which is the focus of this book's attention, is a basic and widespread feature of government operations. In their recent comparative collection Craig and Tomkins (2006b: 7) point out that 'in many of the jurisdictions here the most significant source of executive power is legislation'. Carter and Harrington (2000: 124), after reviewing some of the implications of constitutional theory for American administrative law, turn their attention to

> the more common, if mundane, problem of figuring out what a statute actually commands an agency to do. ... As the later cases in this section show, the problems for courts and agencies do not usually arise because the authorizing statute violates separation of powers or delegation rules or other constitutional provisions. The most common problem in this field is simply that no-one can tell with precision what the statute means in the first place.

That American observation is loudly reaffirmed by the study in this book.

Combined with these similarities, of course, there are also many differences between governments, and from a public law perspective there are three that stand out as deserving immediate comment because of the additional dimensions they might provide to studies in other specific settings.

The first is that some governments do have the inherent capacity for action that the local governments of 'English-speaking countries' typically lack. Classic examples are the national and intermediate governments that are quaintly but conveniently referred to as 'the Crown' in the public law of the United Kingdom, Canada, Australia and New Zealand (see Craig and Tomkins 2006a). State and federal administrations in the United States seem to fall somewhere between the two extremes of 'inherent capacity' and 'purely statutory' governments, with the federal government, in particular, being one of 'limited, enumerated powers' (Rosenbloom 2003: 31), where, Warren (2004: 20) writes, 'Congress has created virtually every department, agency, commission, board, and so on and assigned their administrators the task of performing their regulatory mandate in a manner consistent with the public interest'. There are also governments like the Scottish Executive, whose executive authority is not necessarily dependent on legislation but is nevertheless tied to 'devolved matters' (see Himsworth 2006).

The second obvious point of public law difference relates to governments' varying capacities to legislate. Well endowed (though a gradually diminishing breed) is the archetypal Westminster-style government commanding a legislative majority in a unitary state without a Bill of Rights. Towards the other end of the range is a local government like the one described in this book, with only limited by-law making powers, none of them relevant to the situation at hand, and without the benefit of a home rule provision of the kind that, in some American states, gives municipalities a degree of immunity from state legislative interventions (Valente *et al.* 2001: 265–9). In between there are various elements – Bills of Rights, separations of powers, European Community law and federal or devolved distributions of legislative competence, for example – that mean governments will have some, but probably not all, of the legislative authority they might want.

The third obvious area of public law difference relates to the formal legal structures of governments. Here again one may contrast the traditional Westminster-style government, separate from Parliament but operating through a cabinet appointed from among the majority party, with the traditional English local government model, where the government is a collective corporate entity made up of *all* elected members, of any political party or none, and officials serve the council as a whole rather than just the executive branch. Other possibilities include, of course, things like directly elected presidents, governors and mayors, not to mention the odd framework of 'executive arrangements' grafted onto the formal structures of most English local authorities by the *Local Government Act 2000*. Each of these structures sets up its own framework of loyalties and responsibilities, and will affect the functioning of public law.

There are several reasons why these obvious differences do not detract from the similarities, outlined earlier, that allow a study grounded in English local government to illustrate themes that can be widely generalized. One is that additional public law resources such as an inherent capacity to act and legislative authority are, indeed, just that: *additional* resources. Both of them (if I may comment as a lawyer employed initially in English local government, but for the past 24 years by the province of New Brunswick, Canada, a government which enjoys them both) are valuable, but neither of them alters the essential nature of working with public law rules, as described in this book. The inherent capacity to act offers the possibility of an alternative justification for some government actions when no relevant statute is available – Harris (2007: 236) calls it the 'third source' of authority for government action, the others being statute and the unique prerogative powers of the Crown – but it operates much like a statutory power from a public lawyer's point of view. It is subject to its own restrictions and it cannot be exercised inconsistently with legislation, so interpreting statutory powers is often an integral part of determining whether or how the inherent capacity can be deployed. As for the ability to legislate, it, too, is an important public law resource, and it certainly improves the prospects that a government's legal powers will be the ones it wants. However, there are no guarantees. There may be constitutional limits to a government's legislative capacity. Or a government may decide to live with legislation it does not like, perhaps because of the time or the political costs involved in changing it (Daintith and Page 1999: 331). Alternatively, a government may legislate but do so unwisely – at least in the eyes of the bureaucrats affected, some or all of whom may have advised the government not to do as it did, but who still have to live with the consequences. In all cases, though, whether a government has created its legislation or not, and whether it likes the legislation or not, it still has to work with its laws in the ways described in this book.

As for the differences in governments' legal structures, these are of great importance, and are exactly the kind of thing to which careful attention must be paid when applying the themes of this book in differing contexts. Formal structures will determine, for example, such major points of public law practice as whether legal advice is given behind closed doors to the government only, or in public forums such as council or committee meetings with the opposition present and able to raise questions.

Even so, the themes of this study are not confined by their local government source material. In part this is because sustaining the art of the possible is, in everyday terms, primarily a matter of bureaucrats dealing with bureaucrats within a given context of substantive law, knowing (or sometimes not knowing) the general direction in which their political masters wish to go. This process will occur in any government. In part, though, it is also because the themes of this book expressly emphasize the importance of both formal and informal government structures – *organization*, as these will be known – to the functioning of public law. This essential point of variation is therefore already taken on board as part of the analysis. The analysis, moreover, though elaborated here through a local government example, is also silently informed by many years of personal experience and observation in a Westminster-style government. Readers who step back from the specifics of the narrative and disaggregate it into its component elements will readily see that most of the scenarios examined here, with their ever-evolving blends of change and stability in laws, policies, politics and administrations, fall squarely within the common ground of democratic governance, however unique the example that illustrates them.

Bridges *et al.*, in their exploration of the impact of *Bromley LBC v GLC* (1981), refer to two related objectives: 'investigating' and 'trying to make sense of' the relationship between administrative law and public administration. This book addresses both. As to 'investigating', it returns to a time and a policy arena, local authority spending in 1980s England – the turbulent Thatcher years – that is of unusual interest both politically and from the point of view of the *ultra vires* rule. The events of the day provided a 'morbid' but 'fascinating' spectacle, 'the twentieth century equivalent of throwing Christians to the lions' (Rhodes 1986a: 231) – one that, if the abiding interest in the 'Poplarism' of the 1920s is anything to go by (see for example, Keith-Lucas 1962; Branson 1979; Griffith 1993, ch. 1), may guarantee the 1980s their own special place in the annals of local government scholarship. At the same time, however, much of what occurred was prosaic, and it is this rare opportunity to study not only ordinary events, but also wholly extraordinary ones in conjunction with them, that makes the period a particularly rich source of material. To see the *ultra vires* rule in action in as varied a range of situations as possible, sifting and comparing both exceptional and unexceptional events alike for whatever general lessons they contain, one could hardly hope for better subject-matter than financial decision-making in the 1980s. Since then, of course, the legislation around which those decisions revolved has been largely replaced, more than once in some cases, and many other changes in the powers, structures and operations of English local authorities have occurred. Throughout it all, however, the *ultra vires* rule, as a body of judge-made law about how statutory powers are to be exercised, remains relatively constant, and the process of working with statutes on the terms that the *ultra vires* rule establishes is a perennial one, shared by many governments and administrative agencies alike. This book is, above all, a study of that process and of the rich variety of its manifestations.

What the book will 'investigate', to use Bridges *et al.*'s term again, is the part that the *ultra vires* rule played in the ten budget-making exercises that a particular local authority carried out from 1979 to 1990, first under the shadow, then under the reality, of the *Local Government, Planning and Land Act 1980*. The period has a nice symmetry, beginning with the introduction of new legislative provisions and ending with their abolition; it displays, therefore, the operation of the *ultra vires* rule through all the various phases of a particular statutory régime. The events that are to be described will contain some familiar elements. Several authors have discussed the political and financial aspects (Duncan and Goodwin 1987; Elcock *et al.* 1989; Lansley, Goss and Wolmar 1989; Butcher *et al.* 1990; Midwinter and Monaghan 1993), and Loughlin's *Legality and Locality* (1996), in particular, has dealt with the law, presenting it in its external dimension as a key feature of a troubled central-local government relationship.

What this book adds is an internal legal dimension, an examination of the workings of public law *within* a local authority, and of how and why it was that, within the confines of the *ultra vires* rule, a particular local authority was able to take the kinds of decisions that enabled the overall central-local conflict to unfold as it did. The council involved has made this unusual perspective possible by allowing generous access to relevant files and extensive discussions with the senior officials of the day, who have also commented on drafts of the resulting chapters. Thus the vantage point of the study is a legal one, with internal sources, both human and documentary, adding context and depth to the parts of the story that are in the public domain. The gathering of raw material began in 1989, at the very tail end of the events described here, and though it has taken time for the study to develop from preliminary research to finished product, the early start does mean that most of the input from officers was provided while the events were still relatively fresh in their minds. They have since had the opportunity to add further comment with the benefit of hindsight. The result is that the book goes deep into the 'black box' of government decision-making, reaching unusually close to what Sunkin (2004: 62) describes as 'the heart of the relationship between law and bureaucracy', where 'some of the most difficult but most interesting research issues arise' but where 'the problems of researching and identifying impacts of judicial review [the legal procedure for challenging the *vires* of government actions] grow, principally because few of us will have an insider's knowledge or experience of the system and access may give rise to problems'. In this case, however, the problems have been overcome: access has been allowed, and the insiders with the most intimate knowledge have been willing to contribute it.

The focus throughout the study will be on the relationship between law and action within this local authority – or more accurately, perhaps, on the variety of the relationships, for what is most clearly demonstrated by the ten-year study, which follows the single policy process of budget-making through multiple annual repetitions, is that the relationship between law and action is far from constant. Even within a single local authority, where the actors, the issues and much of the law remained largely the same from year to year, the ways in which the *ultra vires* rule contributed to the political process were noticeably different.

This, then, leads us to the second of the two objectives that Bridges *et al.* described: 'trying to make sense of' the relationship between administrative law and public administration. Bridges *et al.* restricted their own attention to one very small part of that subject, namely 'the response which local authorities have made to recent judicial decisions' (1987: 119). Halliday (2004) takes things further. Though he, too, focuses on 'the influence of judicial review judgments' (9), he is less concerned with the immediate response than with understanding 'the conditions and factors which mediate the influence of judicial review judgments on administrative behaviour' (3–4). In doing so he identifies several factors which, despite the intended focus on judicial review judgments, spill over into the broader topic of the relationship between law and practice in a government setting. These include 'the reception of legal knowledge' (ch. 2), which refers to the process by which administrators come to know about the relevant law, and 'legal conscientiousness' (ch. 3), which is concerned with the degree to which they apply their legal knowledge to the full range of tasks they perform.

Halliday's observations will be seen in this book to be accurate. However, as the present enquiry extends beyond the influence of judicial review judgments to the workings of public law in general, some of the terms that Halliday proposes need to be adjusted to fit their broader context, and others need to be added. There being no well-established framework of terminology that can be borrowed from other studies in the field, this book will propose, and organize its findings around, two inter-connecting sets of expressions. One is abstract and capable of being applied in many decision-making contexts; the other is concrete and designed to bring the abstract terms into focus as elements of the actual decision-making scenarios that are to be discussed here.

The abstract terms are *disposition, information, latitude, autonomy* and *consequences*. These represent five key variables in the workings of public law; differences in outcomes and behaviours can be explained by reference to these five variables and the factors that influence them. *Disposition* relates to what the key actors want to do and how badly they want to do it. Halliday's 'legal conscientiousness' is one possible *disposition*, but by no means the only one. *Information* refers to how much the key actors know about the relevant law. Halliday's 'reception of legal knowledge' is all about how people obtain *information*, but the expression is a little unwieldy, and for the broader purposes of this study it seems preferable to differentiate the *information* itself from the process of reception. *Latitude* describes how much room for manoeuvre the law allows in any given situation, whether by means of a deliberately created statutory discretion or as the unintended consequence of uncertainties as to how an Act is to be interpreted. Some writers apply the word 'discretion' not only to the former of these but also to the latter (see, for example, Hutter 1997: 12; Galligan 1986 describes several senses of the word), but that usage will not be followed here; discretion has too many shades of meaning, and it seems an unnatural word to apply to the second of the scenarios just mentioned, when a statute is imprecise and people are simply doing their best to determine what it means. *Autonomy* relates to the extent to which a decision-maker can achieve his or her ends without the intervention or assistance of others. *Autonomy* is high where a decision-maker has the legal authority and the practical ability to act alone, as when an individual official exercises delegated statutory powers. It is lower where, for example, an effective decision requires internal or external consensus, or where there is an active regulator in the field.

Consequences, finally, deal with the assessments of risk that are often a part of decision-making. Whether consciously or sub-consciously people sometimes ask: 'If I do this and it's *ultra vires* what is the worst that can happen?' In the technical sense the consequence of an act being *ultra vires* is that it is invalid and can be quashed in proceedings for judicial review. In different factual situations, however, what flows from an action being *ultra vires* may be anything from minor inconvenience, such as the need to take a decision again but properly, to major problems such as the multi-million pound restitutionary claims that were before the English courts through the 1990s and beyond after the House of Lords held in *Hazell v Hammersmith and Fulham LBC* (1991) that local authority interest rate swap transactions were *ultra vires*.

It is useful to provide immediately some illustrations of the five terms set out above, applying them to material drawn from the 'small number of studies which have empirically examined the difficult question of the relationship between judicial review and administrative decision-making' (Halliday 2000: 110). Some of those studies deal with local government, some with other administrative settings.

The local government examples would include Loveland's comparison of the operation of the homelessness legislation in three local authorities (Loveland 1995) and Obadina's examination of gypsy camp site provision (Obadina 1998). Loveland highlights three different approaches his local authorities took towards the discharge of their statutory duties – these would be differences of *disposition* – and traces them back primarily to the differences in housing supply available. Over time, *dispositions* and approaches tended to converge as housing supply became tight for all three authorities. Loveland also describes clear differences in *information*, with the housing officers of one authority being more legally aware than those of the others, and thus more technically accurate in the discharge of their functions. Obadina's work on gypsy site provision is clear in its illustration of *latitude, autonomy* and *consequences*. The councils studied recognized that they had a statutory duty to provide camp sites, but interpreted the legislation as leaving considerable *latitude* as to how and when they performed it. Their *autonomy* was reinforced by the fact that the courts had held that this was a duty that could only be enforced by the Minister, and the Minister showed no inclination to intervene. For the same reason the likely *consequences* if they were in fact failing in their duty seemed insubstantial. This changed a little when new case-law decided that the courts might hold local authorities to be acting *ultra vires* in some circumstances; as a result, one would suggest, their *autonomy* lessened a little, and *consequences* gained more significance, but still the interpretational *latitude* remained considerable.

For examples of *disposition* and *information* in administrative settings other than local government, one may look to Buck's discussion of the Social Fund and its Independent Review Service (Buck 1998b). In what Buck describes as the 'Consolidation' phase of the Service's activities, the principal objective – or *disposition* – was to ensure that the Social Fund inspectors' decisions were not held *ultra vires* in judicial review proceedings. The means adopted to achieve this was to improve the legal *information* available to them. A change of Commissioner then ushered in a 'Customer Focus' phase – in other words, a change of leadership led to a change in organizational *disposition* – and a conscious decision was taken that inspectors should perform their functions less legalistically, though in a way that was certainly still intended to produce *intra vires* decision-making. (Sunkin and Pick 2001 offer a similar presentation of the same events.) An illustration of *latitude*, or more specifically of its reduction, would be McCrudden's reference to the 'substantive super-mandates' (in other words, overriding limitations) that were created for all regulators when the *Human Rights Act 1998* obliged them to discharge their statutory responsibilities in accordance with the European Convention on Human Rights (McCrudden 1999b: 290). Merry, as legal adviser to the Director General of the Office of Water Services, is reflecting on the Office's *autonomy* when he says, in relation to the exercise of the Director General's discretionary power to release prejudicial information, that 'this type of judgment is one about which a court would be very slow to "second guess" the regulator concerned' (Merry 1999, 186–7). *Consequences*, meanwhile, are the key factor in the various references that exist to administrative agencies declining to exercise the powers they think they have because they are aware that if their action is challenged in the courts, and the courts do not agree with the agencies' interpretations, far more will be lost overall than would be gained by the exercise of those powers in the individual situation in question. McBarnet and Whelan's discussion of the Financial Reporting Review Panel is a case in point (McBarnet and Whelan 1999a: 73; 1999b: 87).

Disposition, information, latitude, autonomy and *consequences* are terms that will be used regularly throughout this book as ordering concepts that help to 'make sense of' the relationship between public law and government action. In order, though, to link these terms more closely to the events that are to be described, a second and more concrete set of terms will also be employed: *policy, organization* and *law*. These are readily recognizable descriptions of the three main forces that will be seen to be continually at play as this study unfolds. The impact of the *ultra vires* rule will be presented as being the product of a continuing interaction between *policy* and *law* in the contexts determined by *organization*.

Policy is the natural word to use to describe the collective *disposition* of a local authority or any other government. It refers to what that government wants to do and how badly it wants to do it. There are other settings in which *policy* would not be the right word, for example when the relevant *dispositions* are those of individual officials as they exercise delegated statutory powers. In the particular situations described in this book, though, it was the council's *policy* in the ordinary sense of the word that drove all major issues of *disposition*.

Policy affects the impact of the *ultra vires* rule in numerous ways, some more subtle than others. For now, suffice it to say that a government's *policies* will determine which legal issues it must confront and whether it finds its legal powers in any particular context to be adequate or constraining. Where *policy* – what a government wants to do – coincides with its legal powers, *law* will have a lesser perceived impact than where the two collide. Invariably, however, the law leaves choices. In some cases this is because there is a discretion as to how a particular power is to be used. But even where there is no discretion, and it is absolutely clear what must or must not be done, there will always be a choice as to what else to do at the same time. Elcock *et al.* (1989: ch. 3) have used the terms 'compliance', 'shadowboxing' and 'brinkmanship' to describe three different policy orientations that local authorities could adopt in response to the financial controls of the 1980s. The choice that each authority took would propel it into different frameworks of powers and obligations, and of course new issues of *vires*. The council described in this book adopted all three of them at different times.

Organization, meanwhile, has to do with who takes what decisions and in consultation with whom. 'It is the structure that determines the bringing together, or separation, of various concerns and considerations, at different hierarchical levels' (Egeberg 1999: 157). It is therefore the key to *autonomy*, at least so far as concerns the internal aspects of a government's decision-making. It is also one of the keys to *information*, since who knows what about a government's *vires* in any particular context is at least partially determined by who has to deal with whom for that purpose. The relevance of *organization* is readily understood with the assistance of Schattschneider's 'famous passage', as Newton (1976: 217) describes it: 'organisation is the mobilisation of bias. Some issues are organised into politics while others are organised out'. The *ultra vires* rule, whether deliberately or not, is organized into some decision-making contexts and organized out of others. Its impact will vary accordingly. The *ultra vires* rule was clearly 'organized into' most of the decisions that will be discussed in this book, though at some times more actively than others, and with a few interesting, and sometimes surprising, exceptions.

Compared to the readily understood notions of *policy* and *organization, law* requires a little more explanation. It is well recognized by administrators as well as legal practitioners and commentators that what the law is can often be the subject of debate: 'judgements always have to be made about both the meaning of the legal rule and its applicability to the problems encountered by officials' (Hutter 1997: 80). From a practical point of view, there are really two separate dimensions of *law* that can be differentiated. This book will name them *given law* and *operative law*. *Given law* consists of the clearly articulable legal propositions that apply to a situation; it is the law as enunciated by the law-givers. For local authorities, since they can only do what statute permits, the words of a particular statute will always be a key element of the *given law*. Added to this will be the more detailed requirements that the *ultra vires* rule provides as to the way in which statutory powers are to be exercised: that procedures must be fair, that irrelevant considerations must be disregarded, that discretion must not be fettered, and so forth. Chapter 2 explains those rules more fully. At times there may also be relevant case-law to be considered. *Given law* consists of the objective legal propositions that can be clearly stated when a government begins the process of considering an exercise of its powers. Sometimes *given law* may clearly point to a particular outcome. Often, however, it will not.

Operative law is located at the opposite end of the decision-making process. *Operative law* is the law as it is understood when decisions are actually taken. At this time the facts have been analysed, the questions left unanswered by the *given law* have been addressed as best they can be, and a legal conclusion has been reached that is *operative* in the sense that it is the one that will actually inform a government's conduct. *Operative law* is the final statement of what the applicable law in a particular situation is understood to be. Depending on the circumstances, *operative law* may be more or less clearly dictated by the *given law*. In cases where the words of a statute are clearly determinative of the action to be taken, there will be little space between them. In other circumstances, however, *given law* may provide at best some general signposts, and the *operative law* will be determined through the exercise of professional judgment.

It is in this interval between *given law* and *operative law* that *latitude* resides, both the *intended latitude* of deliberately-created discretion and the *unintended latitude* that results from the uncertainties of statutory interpretation. Here *policy* interacts with *law* to produce outcomes that are a balance between the strength of the *disposition* and the scope of the available *latitude*. This is the basic equation that determines the boundaries of the possible.

It should not be thought, of course, that *policy* is always strong or clear. Sometimes it is confused or non-existent. Nor should it be thought that the interaction between *law* and *policy* follows a single pattern, for there are different modes of engagement. There are times, for example, when the impact of the *ultra vires* rule may be *subliminal*, affecting people's conduct without their knowing it; this may be because they have internalized its requirements or because it is being fed into procedures and processes in ways that they do not notice. At other times the law may be *peripheral* to decision-making; people may be aware that it applies to their conduct, but it is not a major influence, probably because all of the options among which they are deciding are comfortably *intra vires*. In other cases again, the law will be one among many *explicit* factors that people take into account as they reach their decisions, and sometimes it may even be wholly or partially *determinative* of their actions. This, though, will often not be a problem because the decision-makers are prepared to do whatever the law says; they simply want to know what that is. Finally there are cases where the impact of the law is *contested*, where the decision-makers have a very clear view of what they want to do and they are prepared to argue about the substance of a legal opinion that could make a particularly cherished objective *ultra vires* and unattainable. One must add that these various manifestations of the law – as *subliminal*, *peripheral*, *explicit*, *determinative*, or *contested* – will sometimes all exist simultaneously, depending on whose eyes one is seeing things through. An example would be when officers or departments disagree vigorously as to what a report should say about the *vires* of a proposal, but eventually a compromise is reached and the final text is entirely anodyne. To the officers concerned, the impact of the *ultra vires* rule may have been vigorously *contested*. Yet to the politicians it might be *peripheral* at best, or perhaps even *subliminal*: they might simply never know that an issue of *vires* existed and had determined the nature of the options with which they were presented.

A final operational distinction that must be blended into the mix is that the *ultra vires* rule may be applied in any particular situation with different degrees of intensity. Writers on administrative law often use the word 'intensity' to describe the varying degrees of rigour that the courts demand when applying the principles of the *ultra vires* rule in different contexts (Black and Muchlinski 1998: 9–11; Craig 2003: 552). Similar variations can be seen in government practice. The intensity ranges from what may be called *intuitive* decision-making at one end of the scale, through *reasoned* decision-making in the middle, to *meticulous* decisions at the other end. *Intuitive* applications of the *ultra vires* rule are those that people do not have to think about. They simply know what the law is (rightly or wrongly, it may sometimes turn out). *Reasoned* applications involve applying logic to the *given law* in order to work out what the *operative law* should be. Often, though not always, this is because the particular situation or the particular law in question is unfamiliar. *Meticulous* applications of the *ultra vires* rule are the ones where every legal angle is covered carefully. This may well be because the stakes are high and mistakes must be avoided, but as this study will show, even high profile decisions are sometimes determined by *intuitive* legal advice, and matters of no great moment are sometimes dealt with *meticulously*. What is *intuitive*, moreover, can and does change. In the practice of law, as in other professions no doubt, moods shift, patterns of thought develop, the climate of professional opinion evolves, and sometimes it turns out, perhaps even after the event, that the boundaries of the possible have been unconsciously re-drawn. Intangibles such as these form an important part of this book and of the workings of public law within government.

Events have moved on, of course, in local government since the last of the budget-making exercises described here, and much new legislation has come and gone. The more important pieces will be discussed in the appropriate places. Throughout all of these legislative changes, however, the process of working with statutory powers on the terms established by the *ultra vires* rule remains. This study seeks to illuminate the subtleties of that process, using material drawn from the particular experiences of local government but developing ideas that can be applied in other administrative and governmental settings as well. By taking the single policy sequence of local authority budget-making, and superimposing the annual repetitions of this sequence upon each other through the complete ten-year life cycle of a particular statutory régime, this book seeks to highlight and explain not only the consistent features of the workings of public law within government, but also the variety and the unpredictability of their interaction.

2

The *Ultra Vires* Rule: Its Substance and Significance

To understand the relationship between public law and government practice, one must know something of the law. This chapter, accordingly, describes the substance and significance of the *ultra vires* rule in enough detail to enable readers to follow the legal threads of the study that follows. Fuller expositions of the substance can be found in the texts of local government law (such as Elias and Goudie 2004/current; *Cross* 2004; Sharland 2006) or general administrative law (such as *de Smith* 1999; Craig 2003; Wade and Forsyth 2004) and their equivalents in other countries. Explanations of its significance, however, are thinner on the ground, which is unfortunate, because its implications run both wide and deep.

Halsbury's Laws of England (2001/current), the classic multi-volume compendium of English law, provides a conveniently compact introduction to the *ultra vires* rule as applied to local government, but substantially the same description holds good for other statutory agencies, as well as for the Crown when exercising statutory powers. A comparable but less precise set of rules applies when the Crown employs its non-statutory authority (*R (Bancoult) v Secretary of State for Foreign and Commonwealth Affairs* 2007); key similarities and differences will be pointed out as the discussion progresses. *Halsbury* explains:

> **408. Local Authorities as statutory bodies.** The local authorities in England and Wales are, with few exceptions, corporations created by statute, and as such they may do such things only as are expressly or impliedly authorised by statute or by subordinate legislation. ...
> **409. The doctrine of ultra vires.** The rules which require statutory corporations to act intra vires and which are applied by the courts to local authorities consist not only of the limitation of powers but extend also to matters concerning the manner of exercise of a

discretion or duty and the procedure adopted. The following matters are among the relevant considerations in deciding whether any action of a local authority which is subject to challenge in the courts is lawful or is ultra vires:

(1) whether the action of the local authority is expressly or impliedly authorised or is within the general subsidiary powers of the authority;
(2) whether the action challenged has been exercised in good faith and for the purposes for which the power was conferred;
(3) whether the decision challenged was influenced to a significant extent by relevant considerations not being taken into account or by irrelevant considerations being taken into account;
(4) whether the decision reached was manifestly unreasonable in the sense that it could not have been reached by any reasonable body;
(5) whether the decision challenged was accompanied by a failure to comply with mandatory procedural requirements or other mistake of law;
(6) whether a discretion has been exercised or a duty executed;
(7) whether a discretion has been fettered by an improper application of general rules for policy established by the local authority;
(8) whether the action taken by an appropriate authority, committee or person has been taken by an authority, committee or person with the powers for that purpose lawfully entrusted and exercised, or whether a lawfully entrusted authority, committee or person was correctly constituted when it decided the matter;
(9) whether, in exercising powers or duties of a semi-judicial or judicial character, a local authority (or its authorised committee, sub-committee or officer) followed procedure contrary to the rules of natural justice.

Halsbury's two-part formulation matches the association that Commonwealth writers often make between *ultra vires* in the narrow sense, which, like para. 408, relates to governments' capacity to act, and *ultra vires* in the broad or extended sense, which, like para. 409, relates to the proper exercise of that capacity. In the United States this formulation can usefully be compared with the short statement by McCarthy and Reynolds (2003: 267) that:

> ... local governing powers ... must find their source either expressly or by implication in state authorization through constitutional home rule clauses and specific or general statutory provisions.

> Exercise of the powers will also be subject to state and federal constitutional protections and to the limitations in the local governing entity's charter.

The first sentence deals with capacity. The second deals with the proper exercise of that capacity, and turns out, as one reads in McCarthy and Reynolds of the kinds of 'public purpose', 'due process' and 'rationality' elements embodied in the constitutional protections and charter limitations that they mention, to bear many resemblances to the substance of *Halsbury*, para. 409.

From a local authority's point of view, the key lesson to be drawn from this is of just how comprehensively the *ultra vires* rule regulates its conduct. There are two major aspects to the rule. First there is the underlying principle that local authorities may only do what statute permits. Then there are a number of specific rules that say how statutory powers are to be exercised. These two aspects feed into each other. Since local authorities can only do what statute permits, every act of every local authority must be in some way an exercise of a statutory power. And since every act must be an exercise of statutory power, every act is subject to the specific rules about how statutory powers are to be exercised. The local authority must satisfy all of them simultaneously, furthermore. Breach of any one of them will make an action *ultra vires*, even if all of the others have been observed.

The specific rules can sound disjointed when presented in a list like the one in *Halsbury*. In fact, however, they form a coherent whole. Analysed in functional terms, they bear on four key elements of local authority decision-making: *what* is done, *why* it is done, *who* does it and *how*. These elements – the four 'W's of the *ultra vires* rule, as they will be named here in honour of the famous three 'R's of reading, 'riting and 'rithmetic – blend different items on the *Halsbury* list. Thus *Halsbury's* reference to 'whether the action of the local authority is expressly or impliedly authorised' in para. 409(1) relates to *what* may be done. The reference to 'whether the action challenged has been exercised in good faith' in para. 409(2) relates to *why*. The reference to an 'action taken by an appropriate authority, committee or person' in para. 409(8) is concerned with *who*. The reference to a 'failure to comply with mandatory procedural requirements' in para. 409(5) deals with *how*. Some of the specific rules sometimes overlap more than one of these headings. For example, 'irrelevant considerations being taken into account', para. 409(3), may sometimes raise issues of motive, of *why* a decision is reached, and sometimes of process, or *how*. The specific rules of the *ultra vires* doctrine have, therefore, a certain fluidity of function. Taken together, however, they provide a comprehensive framework for the legal regulation of the activities of local government, and they have, as will be demonstrated later in this chapter, a strong consistency of theme. The remainder of this chapter will provide more information about each of these four 'W's, adding some comments about their wide-ranging significance for local government generally and their various contributions to the story that is to follow. It will close by offering some preliminary observations about the relationship of public law with local government practice and about the unavoidable ambiguities involved in any analysis of that subject.

A. *What?*

i. The underlying principle

What local authorities can do, the first 'W' of the *ultra vires* rule, starts with the underlying principle that local authorities may only do what statute permits. This is a judge-made rule, based on the inference that 'where there is an Act of Parliament creating a corporation for a particular purpose, and giving it powers for that particular purpose, what it does not expressly or impliedly authorise is to be taken to be prohibited' (*A-G v Great Eastern Railway Co.* 1880: 481). Legal texts normally describe this rule as emerging in the late nineteenth century, originally in relation to commercial entities rather than governmental ones, and it does still have some relevance in corporate and commercial law. For statutory local authorities, however, it has been settled since at least the House of Lords's decision in *LCC v A-G* (1902) that the same rule applied. This appears to be about the same time that, in the United States, the *ultra vires*-like 'Judge Dillon's Rule ultimately won out against Judge Thomas Cooley's assertion of an inherent right to local self-government' (McCarthy and Reynolds 2003: 18–19). Dillon's Rule is that:

> A municipal corporation possesses and can exercise only the following powers: (1) those granted *in express words*; (2) those *necessarily or fairly implied* in or incident to the powers expressly granted: (3) those *essential* to the accomplishment of the declared objects and purposes of the corporation – not simply convenient, but indispensable. (Valente *et al.* 2001: 252)

For many years after *LCC v A-G*, however, there were also a number of municipal corporations in England that had been created by non-statutory means, mostly by royal charter, and the prevailing legal wisdom is that these non-statutory local authorities had, at least in theory, the capacity of common law corporations to do whatever individuals could. (See, for example, Hart 1968: 289–300). In Canada Rogers (1971/current: para. 63.34, n. (g)) identifies the city of Saint John, New Brunswick, as being one of the few that fall in the same category. The non-statutory corporations in England, though, ceased to exist in the local government reorganizations of the 1960s and 1970s, and although *Halsbury* (2001/current: para. 408 and n. 2) mentions in passing that there are exceptions to the general statement that local authorities are corporations created by statute, what it offers as examples are some rather unusual bodies: the Common Council of the City of London, the Sub-Treasurer of the Inner Temple and the Under-Treasurer of the Middle Temple.

There has long been debate about whether the underlying principle that local authorities can only do what statute permits is a satisfactory groundrule for English local government. (Similarly in America 'local governments have sought to undo Dillon's Rule virtually from the time Judge Dillon articulated it' – Valente *et al.* 2001: 253.) Finer (1933: 171–94) provides an early discussion, and Robson (1954: 227–9) describes the unsuccessful attempts in the 1930s to enact broadly stated Local Authorities (Enabling) Bills. Since the report of the Committee on the Management of Local Government (1967) much of the discussion about an alternative groundrule has been expressed in terms of the committee's recommendation (para. 286) that local authorities should be given a 'general competence' to do whatever is in their opinion in the best interests of their area or their inhabitants. That particular proposal was not accepted (Rattenbury 1984: ch. XI describes the government's deliberations in detail), but recent years have seen broad powers of various sorts enacted in some countries. These will be returned to below. In England the current version of a general power is s.2 of the *Local Government Act 2000*, which permits local authorities to do anything that they consider will improve or promote the 'economic ... social ... [or] environmental well-being of their area'. The government has taken pains to point out, however, that although s.2 is broad and flexible, local authorities can still 'only do what they are empowered to do by statute, and any other action would be considered by the courts to be *ultra vires*. The new power does not change this situation' (Department of the Environment, Transport and the Regions 2001: 15).

This underlying principle of the *what* of the *ultra vires* rule has many consequences for local authorities. Obviously it affects their freedom of action, and makes it hard to accept, as a matter of pure legal analysis, the otherwise attractive proposition that local authorities are more than the sum of their statutory parts. From a legal point of view, the sum of their statutory parts is precisely what local authorities are. As Béar bluntly puts it: 'From a public lawyer's perspective, local government can be defined as a collection of powers and duties, defined by Parliament, and exercisable for the benefit of the public, but in a particular area' (*Butterworths* 2002/04: para. A[2]).

In an empirical study such as this one, though, the main point that must be made about this underlying principle is that it is, indeed, an *underlying* principle rather than something that one can expect to see permanently on display. It sets the stage for the observable action, establishing that *policy* must always be sustained by *law*, yet it seldom needs to be discussed, or even referred to, in its own right. Since local authorities know that they can only do what statute permits, what they do in practice is get on with the business of applying their statutory powers. Thus the local authority described in this book, as it deals with rents, rates, budgets, many kinds of property transactions and a whole host of other issues, will continually be seen relating its *policy* back to the *given law* contained in its statutory powers. In doing so it is responding to the *what* of the *ultra vires* rule in the only way it can. Explicitly, it is exercising the powers it has. Implicitly, it is giving effect to the underlying principle that it can only do what statute permits.

ii. Moderating principles

The *what* of the *ultra vires* rule starts, therefore, with the idea that *what* local authorities can do depends entirely on legislation. Local authorities have the *duty* to do what legislation says they must, and they have the *power* to do what legislation says they may. There are, though, two legal principles that moderate the sharp outlines of this picture. First, in relation to duties, some are considered 'directory' rather than 'mandatory'. This distinction is sometimes thought misleading, but in general, if a duty is directory, non-compliance must be substantial in itself or in its effects before it will be held to make conduct *ultra vires* (see *Cross* 2004: 24–30). Second, in relation to powers, there is the comparable moderating principle that 'whatever may fairly be regarded as incidental to or consequential upon those things which the Legislature has authorised, ought not (unless expressly prohibited) to be held to be ultra vires' (*A-G v Great Eastern Railway Co.* 1880: 478).

In the abstract, both of these principles have the potential to add flexibility at the margins of the *ultra vires* rule. In practice, however, they add very little, though there was a time – actually, the exact period covered by this book – when the principle relating to incidental powers became significant for a while.

In relation to directory duties, one reason why the moderating principle has modest effects is that the kind of duties that are found to be directory tend to be technical or procedural in nature. Flexibility in relation to duties of this sort will obviously not greatly affect local authorities' capacity for action, though it is sometimes useful after the event, when mistakes have been made and actions are challenged. The more general reason, though, is that in practice directory duties have to be taken seriously. It is hard to know in advance whether a court will consider a duty directory, and harder still to know in advance whether a breach will cause prejudice. 'Public authorities therefore have to assume that all procedural requirements are mandatory and do their best to comply with all of them' (Kay 1999: 34). There were certainly no examples during the ten budget-making exercises described in this book where the local authority considered disregarding a statutory duty on the ground that the duty might be directory rather than mandatory. What will be seen more often, in fact, is the opposite tendency: to infer obligations even when Acts did not expressly create them, and to follow statutory duties closely out of concern that non-compliance with even technical or procedural obligations might unnecessarily undermine *policies* that the council might otherwise lawfully attain.

The doctrine of 'incidental powers' requires fuller discussion, not for the law itself, which receives surprisingly lengthy treatment in texts such as *Cross* (2004: 11–22) and Sharland (2006: 79–91), but for the lessons it teaches about the relationship between *given law* and *operative law*, about legislative good intentions gone awry, and about the way in which, especially in a statutory body such as a local authority, huge consequences can sometimes hinge on the most nondescript of statutory words.

The central feature of the *given law* here is s.111 of the Local Government Act 1972:

> (1) Without prejudice to any powers exercisable apart from this section but subject to the provisions of this Act and any other enactment passed before or after this Act, a local authority shall have power to do anything (whether or not involving the expenditure, borrowing or lending of money or the acquisition or disposal of any property or rights) which is calculated to facilitate, or is conducive or incidental to, the discharge of any of their functions.

This section, a statutory rendering of the common law rule on incidental powers, came into being as part of the Ministry of Housing and Local Government's response to the Committee on the Management of Local Government's criticism of the *ultra vires* rule as being unduly restrictive of local government (1967: para. 283). Ministry officials felt, according to one of them (at interview) who was closely involved, that if the *ultra vires* rule was indeed a source of problems, part of the reason was that local authorities were unduly cautious in interpreting their statutory powers, and wrongly blamed the *ultra vires* rule when they wrongly decided that particular actions were beyond their powers. The main purpose of s.111, therefore, was to stiffen the sinews of local authority lawyers, to provide them with an explicit statutory basis for providing more robust, and in the Ministry's view more reasonable, interpretations. The Ministry's lawyers, according to this official, thought that the section was redundant: that it only said what the common law already said, and therefore did not need saying. The Ministry decided, nonetheless, that whether or not s.111 was *legally* necessary there was a useful *practical* function for it to perform.

Initially, the *operative law* of s.111 did not respond. Arnold-Baker, for example (1973: 104), commented dismissively that the section merely 'states in statutory form a proposition of common sense' that had already been accepted in the case-law. As the 1970s unfolded, however, some local authorities and some Counsels' opinions started looking more favourably on the section, and through the 1980s, the period covered in this book, this *operative law* continued to evolve; s.111 gained increasing acceptance in local government circles as a statutory power with some substance.

In 1991, however, the bubble burst, in a very big way. The auditor for Hammersmith and Fulham LBC had challenged the council's activities in the interest rate swaps markets, and by the time the dispute reached the House of Lords in *Hazell v Hammersmith and Fulham LBC* (1991), the fate of interest rate swaps involving, according to Loughlin (1990: 403), 'a principal sum of between £5 and £10 billion' hung on the nondescript words 'function' and 'incidental' in s.111. If 'debt management' was a 'function' many of these swaps (though not all of Hammersmith and Fulham's) would be *intra vires*, because they were 'incidental to debt management'. But if 'functions' meant 'statutory powers and duties', all swaps would be *ultra vires*, since the council was unable to identify a specific power or duty that interest rate swaps were 'calculated to facilitate, or ... conducive or incidental to'. The House of Lords adopted the latter interpretation, setting off a chain reaction of financial and legal controversy that extended well into the new millennium (*Kleinwort Benson v City of Glasgow Council* 2002).

This ruling on the meaning of 'function' constituted new *given law* on s.111, which reined in the *operative law* that had been developing. For several years afterwards the story of s.111 was largely of its failure to provide the statutory support that local authorities had thought it did. Examples include *Allsop v North Tyneside MBC* (1992: enhanced redundancy payments) and *Crédit Suisse v Waltham Forest LBC* (1996: loan guarantees). Later cases, though, such as *Newbold v Leicester CC* (1999: payment under a redeployment agreement), *R v Broadland DC, ex parte Lashley* (2000: operation of a standards committee) and, most significantly, the House of Lords in *Akumah v Hackney LBC* (2005: a parking control scheme) have readjusted the balance. *R (Comninos) v Bedford BC* (2003) suggests that an important element of the narrower interpretations in earlier cases was that councils were attempting to use s.111 to circumvent limitations on their other powers.

One consequence of this cycle of growth and retraction in both the *operative law* and the *given law* of s.111 is that the section plays a different part in the events described in this book than might have been expected at other times. Things that, either before or after this particular period, might have been carefully analysed in relation to s.111 were more easily accepted as being *intra vires*. In some cases people might reflect consciously, but probably briefly, before reaching the *reasoned* conclusion that s.111 was the source of the necessary statutory authority. In other cases that conclusion might have been so *intuitive* as hardly to receive conscious attention at all. It seems fair to suggest that the *operative law* of s.111 as it existed shortly before *Hazell v Hammersmith and Fulham LBC* was a far better reflection of what the Ministry of Housing and Local Government had in mind in developing s.111 than the post-*Hazell* situation became. What the future holds remains to be seen, but now that the *given law* of *Hazell* has been counterbalanced by the new *given law* of *Akumah*, we are, perhaps, at least back to where we started before the Ministry provided the intended helping hand of s.111.

iii. The general power

Counteracting somewhat the restrictions described so far is another significant feature of the *what* of the *ultra vires* rule: local authorities' once narrow, now broad, statutory power to take unspecified action for the benefit of their areas. The original version was s.6 of the *Local Government (Financial Provisions) Act 1963*, which permitted local authorities to 'incur expenditure ... for the benefit of their inhabitants or their areas' on items that fell beyond the limits of their other statutory powers, but only up to a specified financial limit: the product of a rate of one (pre-decimal) penny per year for the main authorities, and one-fifth of that for parish councils. S.6 was a stopgap power, designed to enable local authorities to do things that were inoffensive but happened not to be otherwise authorized by statute. Its wording was actually very broad, but s.6 was nevertheless, as a file note prepared in the Ministry of Housing and Local Government in 1969 put it, 'a little section tucked away in a little Act. It would be unreasonable to regard this as introducing some dynamic new principle in local government' (see Rattenbury 1984: 344).

In partial response to the Committee on Management's advocacy of a 'general competence', s.6 was later revised and re-enacted as s.137 of the *Local Government Act 1972*. The section remained a stopgap power, only available where other powers did not exist, but the financial limit was raised to 2p (decimal) – a large increase for the main authorities and an enormous one for the parishes – and some significant technical relaxations were also made. In later years, following, and largely despite, the recommendations of the Widdicombe Committee of Inquiry into the Conduct of Local Authority Business (1986: paras 8.33–35), the section was tightened up somewhat, and the financial limit was recast as a prescribed sum per head of population. This time the motivating force was the government's concern that s.137 allowed local authorities too free a rein at a time when, in the government's view, local government had become too political. Information on the use that local authorities made of s.137 can be found in studies such as Crawford and Moore (1983), Thompson and Game (1985), the Widdicombe Committee (1986), and Mason *et al.* (1999).

For the major local authorities, s.137 has now been replaced by s.2 of the *Local Government Act 2000*:

> Every local authority are to have power to do anything which they consider is likely to achieve any one or more of the following objects –
> (a) the promotion or improvement of the economic well-being of their area,
> (b) the promotion or improvement of the social well-being of their area, and
> (c) the promotion or improvement of the environmental well-being of their area.

Local authorities' early experience in the operation of this section was described in guarded terms in a study commissioned by the Office of the Deputy Prime Minister (2005). Although 'use of the Well Being power remains limited' (13), and much of its value so far had been as a '"comfort blanket" ... giving reassurance that a proposed action is legal, even when it would have been possible under other statutory or "normal" powers' (61) the researchers found 'some cause for optimism' (14) for better things to come.

Time will tell what will come of general powers such as these. Provisions with similar liberalizing aspirations have been introduced in places like Scotland (McFadden 2004: 49), New Zealand (Bush 2005: 191), several Canadian provinces (Rogers 1971/current: para. 63.11) and all Australian states (Aulich 2005: 201). In the past, however, widely-drawn general powers have not always received wide interpretations. Examples include open-ended powers to regulate for purposes related to health, safety and well-being in Canada (see Rogers 1971/current: para. 63-35) and various 'home rule' provisions in the United States, which, Briffault (2004: 254) tells us, 'continue to roil the courts'. The key point, however, in terms of the art of the locally possible, is that however broadly provisions like these may be interpreted, they are still statutory provisions that need interpretation. They do not give local authorities the inherent capacity for action that the Crown has. Nor do they give them the statutory ability to do whatever they want. S.137 of the *Local Government Act 1972*, for example, existed at the time of the events described in this book, was used actively by the council in other contexts, and will make occasional appearances here. For the most part, though, it was simply not relevant to the kinds of financial decisions that are to be explored. The same would be true of s.2: quite apart from the fact that s.2 cannot be used to 'raise money (whether by precept, borrowing or otherwise)' (see s.3), it is hard to imagine that many of the budget-related decisions described in this book could reasonably be presented as being likely in themselves to lead to the 'promotion or improvement of the economic ... , social ... [or] environmental well-being' of the council's area. Broad powers, in other words, are certainly helpful in expanding the boundaries of the possible, but the art of sustaining it remains much the same whether the powers are narrow or broad.

iv. The 'scope' of statutory powers

Important to all of those powers and duties, and to the range of outputs they can support, is the idea of the 'scope' of statutory powers. This idea has two interrelated aspects, both of which will be seen at work in this book, though the first requires fuller explanation than the second.

The first revolves around the courts' (and therefore government lawyers') approach to the interpretation of statutory powers. Under this approach, every statute – indeed every section – has a scope; it has, as it were, a kind of internal integrity, with the meaning of each part determined by reference to the whole. A classic example is *Chertsey UDC v Mixnam's Properties Ltd* (1964), where the House of Lords held that a local authority's statutory power to impose, in a caravan site licence, 'such conditions as the authority may think it necessary or desirable to impose ... in the interests of persons dwelling thereon in caravans ...' only actually permitted conditions relating to the use of the site. Therefore conditions that protected, among other things, caravan dwellers' security of tenure and their ability to form a tenants' association were beyond the scope of the Act and *ultra vires*.

This kind of scope, derived purely from statutory interpretation, has a significance going far beyond its workaday roots. From a legal point of view, it is no more than a proposition of common sense: that the meaning of a word depends on the context in which it is used. So although opinions may differ in individual cases, such as *Chertsey*, about exactly where to draw the line, there is obviously a line to be drawn somewhere, and identifying it involves reading the words of the Act in context. Thus lawyers in practice, like the lawyers described in this book, simply try to work out in the particular situations they confront what the words of a statute mean, and the scope of each individual statutory power is derived from the legislative context in which it is found.

Less obvious, though, are the wider implications of this approach. When writ large, and applied to local government in general, it leads to the conclusion that there is, legally speaking, a disjointedness between the powers of local authorities, with each statute, each power, having a scope of its own, which may or may not coincide with that of others. This is one of the factors that stands in the way of the arguments that are often made that local authorities should develop for themselves a corporate sense of identity and purpose and a broader understanding of their *governmental* role. The self-contained scopes of their various statutory powers mean that local authorities will often not have the legal wherewithal to realize this broader vision. This can be remedied in part by the enactment of provisions such as the well-being power of s.2 of the *Local Government Act 2000*, but s.2 still has its scope, and other powers still have theirs. The cumulative effect, analysed legally, is not dissimilar to the 'chaos of authorities' from which writers often describe English local government as having emerged in the late nineteenth century. (See, for example, S. and B. Webb 1922: 9–10; Smellie 1949: 30; Byrne 1994: 18–19; Stewart 2000: 37.) Though a modern local authority may look like a multi-purpose agency from the outside, internally, from the point of view of the *ultra vires* rule, it is dissected into a variety of independent statutory purposes and scopes, each created separately and each requiring to be interpreted accordingly.

The second aspect of the notion of the scope of statutory powers is different. Rather than being intrinsic to the statutes, and identified by close textual analysis, it is external to them, an expression by the courts of non-statutory general propositions about what local authorities can or cannot do – unless, of course, legislation clearly says otherwise. Well-established examples are that local authorities cannot enact by-laws that are 'partial and unequal in their operation as between classes' (*Kruse v Johnson*, 1898: 110) or that are 'repugnant to the general law' (*Cross*, 2004: 275). More recently, cases relating to local authorities' anti-apartheid activities have revolved around the idea that local authorities cannot punish people who have done nothing wrong (for example, *Wheeler v Leicester City Council*, 1985; *R v Lewisham LBC, ex parte Shell UK Ltd*, 1987). In Canada, Vancouver City Council's similar attempt to boycott Shell on anti-apartheid grounds failed on the ground that it attempted to affect matters beyond city boundaries without any identifiable benefit to the inhabitants (*Shell Canada Products Ltd v City of Vancouver* 1994). Since the enactment in the United Kingdom of the *Human Rights Act 1998*, these common law limits have been much enhanced by the duty to act in accordance with the European Convention on Human Rights.

Cases like these are infrequent but are of interest from various points of view. No doubt they can be used in studies like McAuslan's (1980) or Griffith's (1997) as representing the 'ideologies' or the 'politics' of the judiciary. They may also serve as ammunition in what Munro (2003: 374), with proper Scottish detachment, describes as the 'lively, if perhaps slightly anglocentric debate' among academic lawyers about the true nature of the principles of judicial review, and about the extent to which these are dependent upon, or independent of, statutory interpretation. They, or cases like them, are especially important in relation to non-statutory governments like the Crown, since the things the Crown does under its inherent capacity to act cannot be limited by reference to the scope of a non-existent enabling statute. In New Zealand, McLean (2006: 138–41) describes external limits like these as having become more significant recently in response to the deliberate adoption of legislative drafting practices that 'discourage ultra vires arguments and aim to encourage flexibility and efficiency'.

From a practical point of view, however, as will be seen in this book, the impact of the cases is more straightforward. They are simply part of the *given law* that local authorities must be aware of, and must apply when relevant, as they go about their daily task of interpreting and applying their statutory powers. One of these rules was, indeed, to play such a persistent and major part in the events to be described here that it deserves to be discussed independently in its own right as an element in the *what* of the *ultra vires* rule. This is the so-called 'fiduciary duty' of local authorities to their local taxpayers.

v. Fiduciary duty

The idea of the fiduciary duty of local authorities, or the trusteeship of the rate fund as it was often called in the days before domestic rates were replaced by the poll tax and subsequently the council tax, is an interesting and controversial feature of the *what* of the *ultra vires* rule. Local authorities, the courts have said, have a responsibility to their ratepayers much as though the rate fund were a trust fund, and the local authority were the trustee of it. To breach that quasi-fiduciary duty is to act *ultra vires*. This principle has stood in the way of local authorities that wanted to act as a model employer when setting employees' wages (*Roberts v Hopwood* 1925), to grant free bus travel to old age pensioners (*Prescott v Birmingham Corpn* 1954) or to subsidize their passenger transport executive to keep the general levels of bus fares down (*Bromley LBC v GLC* 1981). On the other hand, it has not prevented local authorities from charging their tenants less than market rents (*Belcher v Reading* 1949), from subsidizing passenger transport executives after a careful review of the financial implications (*R v Merseyside CC, ex parte Great Universal Stores* 1982), or from reaching a local settlement to the 1978–79 'dirty jobs' strike at wage levels that later turned out to be substantially higher than the national settlement (*Pickwell v Camden LBC* 1982). The recurring themes of the cases are that local authorities should avoid extravagance (or the 'thriftless use of moneys obtained ... from the ratepayers', as Lord Diplock described it in *Bromley LBC v GLC* 1981: 166) and that they should not promote sectional interests with public funds, for to do so is, in effect, 'to make a gift to a particular class of persons ... simply because the local authority concerned are of the opinion that the favoured class of person ought, on benevolent or philanthropic grounds, to be accorded that benefit' (*Prescott v Birmingham Corpn* 1954: 235–6).

The trusteeship principle is a well-established limit on *what* local authorities can do. Equally well known is a critique that sees it as an unfair and logically unnecessary obstacle to the reasonable policies of socialist councils (see Cooper 1998: 75). Fennell (1986) has dubbed it 'the rule against socialism'. Loughlin, though no enthusiast of the fiduciary principle, sees it as having served a useful purpose at one particular time in the mid-nineteenth century (1996: 207) but argues that it 'had virtually no resonance with the modern system that emerged after the 1920s' (1996: 261).

As was mentioned earlier, the trusteeship of the rate fund was to figure prominently throughout this tale of ten budgets. It was repeatedly a key part of the *given law* of the local authority's financial decision-making, not only in the early days, after the House of Lords struck down the GLC's 'Fares Fair' transport subsidy policy in December 1981, but continually thereafter, as the council attempted to bring its policies to fruition in increasingly difficult financial and legislative environments. Writing slightly after the period examined here had ended, Loughlin (1996: 262) argued that as a result of the increasingly regimented system of local government law that had evolved through the late 1980s and early 1990s, the trusteeship principle was dead:

> In this new local government system based on limited powers, specific duties and broad central powers of supervision intended to be actively exercised there is simply no longer any need for a general concept of a fiduciary obligation owed to local taxpayers. The judicially developed concept of fiduciary duty is dead precisely because the entire structure of local government has been reorganized in its image.

More realistic, however, is to think of it as at best dormant in contexts where specific legislation and the fiduciary duty point in the same direction. The fiduciary duty was certainly referred to in passing in *R (Western Riverside Waste Authority) v Wandsworth LBC* (2005), and in general one should anticipate that the more open-ended the language of a particular statutory provision is, the more likely it is that the courts will turn to something like the fiduciary principle as an aid to interpretation. One cannot help thinking that s.2 of the *Local Government Act 2000*, local authorities' broad power to promote the social, economic and environmental well-being of their areas, is exactly the kind of power that will find its parameters influenced by the trusteeship principle.

B. *Why?*

The second 'W' of the *ultra vires* rule relates to motive: to *why* local authorities may act. There are two major principles here, both derived from *APPH v Wednesbury Corporation* (1947: 233–4). One is that a local authority's decision will be *ultra vires* if 'they have taken into account matters which they ought not to take into account, or, conversely, have refused to take into account or neglected to take into account matters which they ought to take into account'. This is commonly referred to as considering the 'relevant considerations'. Second, 'Once that question has been answered in favour of the local authority, it may still be possible to say that, although the local authority has kept within the four corners of the matters which they ought to consider, they have nevertheless come to a conclusion so unreasonable that no reasonable local authority could ever have come to it.' This, since the House of Lords's decision in *CCSU v Minister for the Civil Service* (1984), is often referred to as 'irrationality'.

i. Relevant considerations

Following *APPH v Wednesbury Corporation* (1947), the basic principle of the *why* of the *ultra vires* rule is that local authorities must act on the basis of the relevant considerations and not on the basis of irrelevant ones. Whether a 'consideration' is 'relevant' or 'irrelevant' is a matter of statutory interpretation, often based on inference rather than express statutory language. Situations in which administrative motives are mixed, some being relevant and others irrelevant, constitute 'a legal porcupine which bristles with difficulties as soon as it is touched' (*de Smith* 1999: 206), though the courts will sometimes accept that a decision can be tainted with an element of 'irrelevance' without necessarily being held *ultra vires*. Some considerations, moreover, are not immutably relevant or irrelevant in themselves, and there can sometimes be a 'margin of appreciation within which the decision-maker may decide just what considerations should play a part in his reasoning process' (*R v Somerset CC, ex parte Fewings* 1995: 32). So, for example, the means of council tenants can be a relevant consideration for a council that chooses to adopt a differential rent scheme (*Leeds Corpn v Jenkinson* 1934) but an irrelevant consideration for a council that chooses not to (*Luby v Newcastle-under-Lyne-Corpn* 1963), even though both are acting under exactly the same power. Always, however, statutory interpretation is the key, and numerous cases can be found in which factors that common sense would clearly indicate as being relevant to a particular decision are not relevant in the legal sense, and lead to a decision being *ultra vires*. For example, an education authority which closes its schools in order to prevent a strike by school caretakers from spreading to other services may be acting *ultra vires* because protecting *other* services is not an *educational* consideration (Eveleigh LJ, *Meade v Haringey LBC* 1979: 1027). An authority which closes down a sewage treatment plant prematurely because it wants the site for housing purposes (and will shortly lose the site to a water authority if it remains a sewage treatment plant) is acting *ultra vires* because its housing needs are not relevant to its sewage treatment responsibilities (*A-G v Wellingborough BC* 1974). A local authority which wishes to give preference to its own residents when allocating places at its oversubscribed schools cannot do so unless the legislation permits (*R v Greenwich LBC, ex parte Governors of the John Ball Primary School* 1989).

This aspect of the *why* of the *ultra vires* rule thus reinforces what was said earlier about the scope of local authority powers and the conceptual disjointedness that exists between them. A statute is, in law, a self-contained entity. Any powers it gives are to be used for the purposes for which they are given. Those purposes are pre-determined, being set by the legislation itself. Local authorities may develop policies consistent with the pre-determined statutory purposes, but they cannot invent new purposes for themselves. It is worth bearing this in mind in any discussion of statutory powers as 'resources' that are at local authorities' disposal in their dealings with central government or other bodies. Though statutory powers are indeed resources, and in a situation like the one reviewed in this book they were absolutely critical to the council's reaction to the government's legislation, they are resources with a limited area of utility. They cannot necessarily be deployed for whatever ends local authorities might wish, but only for those that are inherent in the language of the statute itself. For the local authority examined in this book, ensuring that the 'considerations' behind each exercise of statutory power remained 'relevant' was a continuing preoccupation.

ii. Irrationality

Irrationality, the second major aspect of the *why* of the *ultra vires* rule, is a concept that causes confusion because it is used in different senses. In *CCSU v Minister for the Civil Service* (1984) Lord Diplock defined an irrational decision as being 'a decision that is so outrageous in its defiance of logic or of accepted moral standards that no sensible person who had applied his mind to the question to be decided could have arrived at it' (410). In its earlier formulation in *APPH v Wednesbury Corporation* (1947) the same idea had been expressed in terms of coming to 'a conclusion so unreasonable that no reasonable local authority could ever have come to it' (234). This sounds like a boundary that would not be easily crossed.

Inconveniently, though, the courts also use the idea of irrationality (or total unreasonableness) to describe action which is not, in any normal sense of the word, unreasonable, and which only becomes so in a semantic sense once a court has carefully analysed an Act and concluded that a local authority's objectives are not logically supported by the Act as the court understands it. Sharland (2006: 166) gently disapproves this blurring of the 'irrational' with the 'irrelevant'. *Hall & Co Ltd v Shoreham-by-Sea UDC* (1963: 8–9) provides a clear example, with the judge saying on one page that the council's aim in imposing a particular planning condition was 'a perfectly reasonable one', but only a page later that 'Bearing in mind that another and more regular course is open to the defendants, it seems to me that this result would be utterly unreasonable and such as Parliament cannot possibly have intended'.

Leaving aside this purely semantic sense of irrationality, one is still left with a few cases where the courts make substantive pronouncements, largely independent of the wording of particular statutes, about the reasons for which local authorities may, or more usually must not, act. For example, local authorities cannot exercise their powers for party political purposes (*R v GLC, ex parte Bromley LBC* 1984; *Porter v Magill* 2001), nor to take sides in an industrial dispute that has nothing to do with them (*R v Ealing LBC, ex parte Times Newspapers Ltd* 1986). This kind of irrationality is the counterpart, in relation to the *why* of the *ultra vires* rule, of what was said earlier about the courts creating substantive outer limits to the scope of *what* local authorities can do. Just as there are some *things* that, in the absence of clear statutory authority, local authorities cannot do, there are some *reasons* for which, unless clearly authorized, they cannot act.

One would have thought that words like 'irrational' or 'totally unreasonable', used in any normal sense, would be unlikely to be of much practical application in the everyday life of local authorities. They are harsh words, and not the kinds of descriptions that local authorities – or anybody else, for that matter – seem likely to apply to *their own* conduct. A surprising feature, therefore, of the events described in this book is that there were indeed occasions when the council expressly considered whether its actions might be considered so unreasonable that no reasonable authority could do what it was contemplating. It never decided that it failed the test, but the fact that it considered it at all is an indication of just how conscious it was that some of the actions it felt forced to take were close to the edge of what could possibly be justified.

C. *Who?*

The third 'W' of the *ultra vires* rule relates to *who* may lawfully take administrative action. Not surprisingly, the starting point is the statute. When an Act creates a power, it will inevitably confer it on someone. What the courts then do is decide what glosses they will put on this statutory selection of a particular body.

i. Delegation of discretion

First and foremost is the rule against delegation of discretion. As Gordon (1996: 209) puts it: 'It is a public law principle that when statutory power is conferred upon a body, it cannot, without the authority of statute, delegate that power to another body'. A few refinements must be added. First, some powers of some governments are not statutory; these can normally be more freely allocated. Second, the rule prevents not only external delegations to outside agencies, but also internal delegations to employees or committees, unless legislation provides for it. Third, when statutory powers are conferred on Ministers there is a presumption of interpretation, known as the *Carltona* principle, that Parliament did not necessarily intend that the power must be exercised by the Minister in person, and that exercise by an appropriate departmental official is therefore acceptable. The same approach has recently been extended beyond Ministers: *R (Chief Constable of West Midlands Police) v Birmingham JJ* (2002). Fourth, however, even when all these refinements are taken into account, *who* can exercise a power remains an important question. In the realms of the Crown's prerogative power to grant a passport, for example, *Khadr v Canada* (2006) revolves in part around the question of *who*, as between the Canadian Passport Office, the Minister of Foreign Affairs and the Governor-in-Council, can withhold a passport when the reasons for doing so are not listed in an existing non-statutory Order-in-Council on the subject.

In the case of English local government, legislation permits extensive delegations. S.101 of the *Local Government Act 1972* provides a wide power for local authorities to 'arrange for the discharge of their functions' by committees, by sub-committees, by officers or by other local authorities or joint arrangements. Part II of the *Local Government Act 2000* provides a similarly broad power of delegation in relation to the functions that the Act vests in the local authority's executive. Other legislation has permitted various forms of contracting out. In all of these cases, however, whether under s.101 or executive arrangements or the contracting out provisions, whatever allocation of functions takes place will be, as a matter of law, a delegation of functions downwards from the local authority or from its executive to a person or body that Parliament has identified as being an acceptable recipient of the power. Delegations beyond the listed categories remain *ultra vires*, and sub-delegations may occur only to the extent permitted by the statute.

The general effect of the rule against delegation is to ensure that governmental powers can only be exercised by a select few – those few whom Parliament has specifically designated. The *ultra vires* rule then takes the matter one step further, considering a kind of informal delegation to have taken place when a person who, under the terms of a statute, ought to have taken a decision, relies too heavily on the opinion of someone else. *R v Port Talbot BC, ex parte Jones* (1988) provides an example. Here the council had delegated to its Chief Housing Officer the discretion to allocate tenancies, but only in consultation with the Chairman and Vice-Chairman of the Housing Committee. The court held that a tenancy granted by the Chief Housing Officer when feeling he was acting under pressure from the Chairman was *ultra vires*, because the council's authority under s.101 was to delegate to an officer, not to the Chairman, and the dominant role had been played by the Chairman.

The rule against delegation of discretion casts a long shadow over the administrative arrangements of English local government. It affects the political structures, because it is the council or the executive, not the controlling party or group, that must take the council's decisions. Nor, prior to the introduction of the executive arrangements of the *Local Government Act 2000*, could individual leading politicians exercise formal decision-making authority on the council's behalf (*R v Secretary of State for the Environment, ex parte Hillingdon LBC* 1986). The rule against delegation also affects administrative structures, both internal and external. Internally, establishing clearly *who* has the legal authority to take particular decisions is important because the decision will be *ultra vires*, and have no legal effect, if taken by anybody else. Externally, major initiatives such as decentralization and local area agreements (see *Local Government Chronicle* 17 November 2005) can be affected if they give substantial decision-making voice to people whom legislation does not contemplate. Raising the stakes in relation to both internal and external decision-making arrangements is the fact that if the arrangement is not properly structured, *every* decision coming out of it will be *ultra vires*. There are therefore real dangers involved in not taking the *who* of the *ultra vires* rule seriously.

Commentators have sometimes questioned whether the decision-making forms that arise out of the *who* of the *ultra vires* rule actually have much substance. Laffin and Young, for example (1990: 77), have referred to the notion that an officer serves the whole council as being one that 'seems highly unlikely to be used often in practice', and Copus, too, states: 'The reality ... is somewhat different' (2006: 38). However, the events described in this book show that decision-making form does matter, and sometimes it matters enormously. At times, this was a matter of making sure that 'the council', not the party and not the leading members, took the decisions that the council had to take. At other times it was a matter of deciding who, if anyone, had the delegated authority to take decisions that were sometimes pressing and urgent. At all times, however, following proper form in terms of *who* had the legal authority to decide a matter, and sometimes working hard to make sure that the substance followed the form, was one of the major determinants of the way in which events unfolded.

ii. Bias

Complementing the rule against delegation is the rule against bias. The former identifies *who* the eligible decision-makers are; the latter, at least in some situations, disqualifies those who are biased. Bias is, broadly speaking, a lack of impartiality as between the possible outcomes of the decision that is to be made, and the degree of bias that will disqualify a decision-maker is not actual, proven bias, but simply a 'real possibility' of bias, as seen from the perspective of a 'fair-minded and informed observer' (*Porter v Magill* 2001). If a decision is made by a collective body such as a committee, the participation of a single biased individual may be enough to make the decision *ultra vires*. 'That bias is in issue only as to one member of a committee of 4 does nothing to save the committee's decision, at all events when it is not and cannot be proven that an unbiased simple majority voted in favour of planning permission being given' (*Condron v National Assembly for Wales* 2005: para. 69). In English local government law the rule against bias is now supplemented and extended by the Code of Conduct established under the *Local Government Act 2000*, which requires councillors to declare 'personal interests' and to withdraw from decisions when they have 'prejudicial' ones (see Sharland 2006: 14–25). It is also complicated by the requirement under the *Human Rights Act 1998* that people's 'civil rights', which are interpreted broadly, be determined by 'independent and impartial' tribunals (see Sharland 2006: 193).

The rule against bias does not apply equally in all situations. Its most natural application is to tribunals that decide things like disputes and benefit claims, and local authorities do perform some functions of this sort. It has also been applied to licensing and planning decisions (for example, *Bovis New Homes Ltd v New Forest DC* 2002), but with the qualification that when local authorities have clear interests at stake such as a property interest or an established policy position, the council cannot be disqualified from taking the decision that the legislation vests in it, but must, instead, take special care to make sure that its decision is based purely on the merits of the case. (See, for example, *R (Island Farm Development Ltd) v Bridgend CBC* 2006.) As one moves even further along the range from functions with an element of adjudication involved and into the realms of pure government, the less significance the rule against bias has.

A factor that was continually present during most of the ten years of financial decision-making examined in this book, and might in some contexts have raised concerns about potential bias, was the strong commitment of the Labour group to its political objectives. However, in the particular context of the budget-related decisions described here, where the powers that the council was exercising were powers to decide its own actions rather than to control the activities of others, we are just about as far into the realms of pure government, and as far away from adjudication, as it is possible to be. Here the council's strong political commitment raised questions of motive, or *why* decisions were taken, as well as of process, or *how* decisions were taken, but not of bias, or *who* should be disqualified from taking them. The questions of motive, the *why* of the *ultra vires* rule, have already been discussed. The questions of process, the *how*, come next.

D. *How?*

The final 'W' of the *ultra vires* rule is the one that cheats a little with the order of the letters. It relates to *how* local authorities act: to process, in other words.

i. Express duties

The first element is that any procedures laid down by Parliament must be observed. Express duties must be obeyed. Some express duties, as noted previously, may be 'directory' rather than 'mandatory', so that a breach will only make conduct *ultra vires* if it is substantial or causes prejudice, but it was also pointed out that there was never any suggestion during the ten budget-making exercises described here that an express statutory duty might be disregarded as being no more than directory. What emerged more often, indeed, was virtually the opposite: procedural obligations were identified even though legislation did not expressly create them. These duties arose from the basic elements of the *ultra vires* rule, particularly the need to ensure that the right people had considered the right material within the right time-frame, so that the eventual decision would be *intra vires*.

ii. Fairness

The second element of the *how* of the *ultra vires* rule is that administrative procedures must be fair. This is a general principle that has developed over the years as the courts have taken analogies from judicial procedures, and expanded and adapted them, often rationalizing them as being the implied requirements of a legislative scheme. In local government, Sharland writes, 'Implied procedural requirements almost invariably concern the duty to consult' (2006: 177). This duty can arise directly from an Act, but can also be generated by a local authority itself if its actions give rise to a 'legitimate expectation' of consultation. If consultation is required, or even if it is undertaken though not required, it must be 'fair and sufficient' (*R (Capenhurst) v Leicester City Council* 2004). An additional element that has emerged recently (at least in England) is that where an agency's assurances or conduct have given rise to a legitimate expectation that it will act in a particular way, it may be unfair and *ultra vires* for it not to do so (*R (Nadarajah and Abdi) v Secretary of State for the Home Department* 2005).

Cross (2004: 449) writes that the duty of fairness should be seen as applicable to all areas of local government activity, rather than just to functions of a judicial or quasi-judicial nature, but that its specific content always springs from 'the particular circumstances of the case' and that 'In the case of decisions which are "purely" administrative, the content of the duty to act fairly may simply be an obligation to refrain from an *ultra vires* abuse of discretion.' One must view that final statement cautiously, since a duty of fairness may well arise from the 'particular circumstances of the case' however 'administrative' a power may be, depending in part on the authority's own behaviour. Nonetheless it is true that some kinds of decisions are more likely to raise issues of procedural fairness than others, and most of the ones described in this book were not of that kind. Here the council was taking financial and policy decisions that affected the area at large but nobody in particular, and procedural fairness therefore played a comparatively small part in the council's decision-making. When the issue of fairness does appear in this book it is primarily in connection with the council's criticisms of its treatment by the Department of the Environment. The department was also under a duty to act fairly, and there were times when the council seriously considered bringing judicial review proceedings claiming that it was the *victim* of procedurally unfair action. On occasion, indeed, the council's actions were deliberately calculated towards increasing its chances of success if it brought judicial review proceedings on fairness grounds.

iii. The style of administrative decision-making

In addition to the duty to act fairly and in accordance with any express procedural duties, the *how* of the *ultra vires* rule also embodies a variety of elements bearing on the style of the administrative decision-making process.

The first is already familiar: that all relevant considerations must be taken into account and all irrelevant ones disregarded. This was presented above as a statement about motivation, about *why* a power should be exercised, but it is clear that it also relates to *how* decisions are reached: to their factual basis and to the process that is to be followed in reaching them. Under its terms, local authorities must identify and consider the information that the law regards as material to a particular decision, and must not allow anything else to have a substantial influence.

Having thus identified the relevant information, the local authority is expected to exercise its discretion and come to whatever decision it considers appropriate. The phrase 'exercise its discretion' is meant in a very full sense. 'Discretion' implies a power to choose, and the power must be exercised actively. *Lavender v MHLG* (1969) has long served as a classic example. In deciding planning appeals, the Minister of Housing and Local Government had a policy of only releasing agricultural land for mineral workings if the Minister of Agriculture did not object. In Mr Lavender's case, the Minister of Agriculture objected, so the Minister of Housing and Local Government rejected the appeal. The court quashed that decision, saying that although the agricultural objection might be an important factor for the Minister of Housing and Local Government to weigh in the balance with all the others, the Minister had been wrong to treat it as conclusive and had thereby failed to exercise the discretion that was his and his alone.

In the same case, the same flaw was presented in yet another way: as an instance of a public body adopting a general policy and thereby disabling itself from exercising discretion. Under the *ultra vires* rule this is normally referred to as 'fettering discretion'.

'Fettering discretion' can arise under policies or contracts. With policies it operates at two levels. First, at the level of the policy itself, a policy will be an *ultra vires* fetter on the exercise of a statutory power if it is incompatible with the proper exercise of the power as Parliament intended it. Thus Wandsworth LBC's policy of not providing assistance under the *Children and Young Persons Act 1963* to the children of families that had been declared intentionally homeless was held *ultra vires* (*A-G, ex rel. Tilley v Wandsworth LBC* 1981), as was Liverpool CC's decision that it would withdraw grant assistance from any organization that participated in a particular employment training scheme (*R v Liverpool CC, ex parte Secretary of State for Employment* 1988). Second, assuming a policy to be *intra vires*, a local authority 'must "never say never". It must always leave open the possibility of departing from normal policy or reconsidering it in the light of changes or particular circumstances' (Sharland 2006: 161). Sedley (2000: 259) aptly describes the conundrum the case-law presents:

> It has brought us ... to a position in which a discretion unguided by policy risks generating decisions which are vulnerable to challenge as inconsistent and arbitrary, but in which adoption of a policy opens up the possibility of challenges both for following it and for not following it. This, at least, is how the executive must see it.

The position in relation to fettering discretion by contract presents similar difficulties of application. The basic rule is that 'A local authority cannot by agreement divest itself of a power to exercise its discretion. Any clause to this effect in a contract will be invalid' (Sharland 2006: 162). However, 'almost any contract is bound to limit the government's discretion to some extent ... Thus, if strictly applied, the "no-fettering" rule would operate to render most contracts *ultra vires*' (Davies 2006: 104–5). The different ways in which the potential fettering effect of a contract can be analysed is illustrated by the Court of Appeal's 2-1 decision in *R v Hammersmith and Fulham LBC, ex parte Beddowes* (1986). Here Hammersmith LBC had agreed with a development company that, as units came vacant in some housing estates that the council wished to sell, the council would keep the units vacant. The minority view was that the contract was invalid (it had been finalized in haste before a local election at which it was anticipated that party control would change), since keeping the units vacant prevented the authority from discharging its responsibilities as a housing authority. The majority view, however, was that the agreements were a reasonable part of a policy of privatizing council estates, which the outgoing council was perfectly entitled to follow.

There are obvious practical difficulties in determining whether contracts or policies fetter discretion and whether, assuming the contract or policy to be *intra vires* in itself, it may nevertheless have the effect of fettering a discretion when a specific decision is subsequently taken under it. Nonetheless, one can at least state in general terms what the evil is that the rule against fettering discretion is intended to counter. It is the prejudging of cases without reference to their facts. What the courts are asserting, in other words, is the right of the individual case to receive individual attention. In this the rule against fettering discretion is entirely at one with a number of the other elements that bear on the style of administrative decision-making. It links up with the obligation to take all relevant considerations into account and with the strong sense in which the phrase 'to exercise discretion' is intended: a 'fettered discretion' will probably disregard material factors and preclude serious choice. It also connects with the rule against bias: there is clearly much common ground between excluding biased decision-makers and prohibiting the prejudging of cases. There is, in short, a strong element of homogeneity running through all of this. What the *ultra vires* rule requires is, essentially, that when a statutory power is exercised there should be a serious and impartial assessment of the merits of the case by the person in whom the discretion is vested. Apparently simple acts such as having a policy and following it can generate a whole battery of potential legal pitfalls.

This battery of pitfalls continually confronted the local authority studied here. For most of the ten-year period, the council was controlled by a left-leaning Labour group drawn from a left-leaning local party. In law, however, it was *the council* that had to make up its mind on the various issues that it dealt with, whatever the views of the group, or the party, might be. If the council failed to observe this partially artificial distinction, it would be likely to be fettering its discretion, delegating its discretion, failing to take into account relevant considerations, and quite possibly acting out of motives that, though *the party* was free to have them, would render *ultra vires* a decision of *the council*. In an often highly charged political environment, could these multiple legal perils be surmounted? It was to be, at times, an interesting challenge.

E. From law to practice

Writings on local government have offered differing observations on the practical impact of the *ultra vires* rule. The Committee on the Management of Local Government (1967) argued that its effects were 'deleterious' (para. 283), notwithstanding that the Committee's researchers reported that 'The number of members and officers who were not conscious that it exercised any inhibiting effect surprised us' (Vol. 5: 444 and ff). In 1983, Elliot wrote that research had clearly demonstrated that law and legal rules could influence only a small part of local government decision-making (1983: 39). Not long afterwards, though, a different assertion was being made – that local government was becoming 'judicialized' and 'juridified', its decision-making becoming increasingly dominated by legal modes of thought such as 'relevant considerations' and the 'trusteeship of the rate fund' (Loughlin 1986; Bridges *et al.* 1987). As new legislative schemes became more rigid in the 1990s new legal constraints were added: 'limited powers, specific duties and broad central powers of supervision intended to be actively exercised' (Loughlin 1996: 262). On the other hand, studies of the administration of the homelessness legislation at street level present a contradictory and less judicialized picture, asserting that 'the goal of lawful decision-making is not often realised in practice' (Mullen *et al.* 1996: 120; and see Loveland 1995; Halliday 2000, 2004).

As was mentioned in the introduction to this book, it is to be expected that there will be variations in the reported impact of the *ultra vires* rule, both within and between local authorities. Differences of *disposition, information, latitude, autonomy* or *consequences* will naturally produce different outcomes, and different actors will inevitably perceive the law's contribution to any particular chain of events differently.

Commentators, one must add, may also interpret what they see in different ways, some seeing a glass half full where others see a glass half empty. Consider, as a hypothetical example, the case of a local authority officer who follows all proper procedures in performing an everyday statutory task that has been properly delegated, but who takes into account an irrelevant consideration. A breach of the *why* of the *ultra vires* rule has occurred, but the *what*, the *who* and the *how* have all been observed. In assessing the impact of the *ultra vires* rule, does one only look at the breach in relation to *why*, or also at the compliance in relation to the other elements? Assume, next, that the officer honestly believed that the offending 'consideration' was in fact 'relevant'. In terms of the relationship between public law and government practice, does it matter more that the officer attempted to act exactly as the *ultra vires* rule required, or that the attempt was unsuccessful? Consider, even, the situation if the officer actually thought that the consideration was irrelevant and that he or she was, as it was put in interviews conducted in the late 1970s (Rattenbury 1984: ch. X), 'bending the law' in the interests of a greater good. (Note that interviewees always carefully differentiated 'bending the law', which several agreed they sometimes did, from 'breaking the law' or 'acting *ultra vires*', which all of them said they never would.) At first sight, consciously bending the law seems unlikely to produce a *bona fide* exercise of statutory power. Yet bending the law comes in many forms. It may amount to no more than adapting old law to new circumstances with an awareness that there is doubt about whether the law applies. It may in fact produce a proper application of the law though the officer does not know it. Always, moreover, it is 'the law' that is being bent. This means that there must still at least be *some* logical relationship between the action taken and the law that is relied on to sustain it.

There can also be a relationship when the *ultra vires* rule is barely noticed, for its impact is often buried deep. The statute-based model of English local government makes *law* one of the key determinants of the roles that individuals, professions, departments and local authorities accept as their own. For example, it plays a large part in the establishment of the administrative frameworks through which local authority activities occur. When new statutory powers are put in place (and all statutory powers are new at some time), lawyers will generally be involved, assisting and advising the departments affected, and will quietly inject the four 'W's of the *ultra vires* rule into whatever operational arrangements result. The same will often occur when there are major changes of policies or practices, and even when such apparently mundane tasks are undertaken as developing standard form documents or checklists to be used by non-legal officers. All aspects of the *ultra vires* rule will be fed into the process, and the resulting policies, practices and documents will convert *law* into procedure in such a way that, if the procedures are followed, the *law* will probably have been observed.

Various terms have been used to describe this process of internalization of external norms so that they become virtually invisible. Lukes (1974: 24), whose subject is the analysis of power relationships, describes it as an extremely important 'third dimension' of power:

> is it not the supreme and most insidious exercise of power to prevent people, to whatever degree, from having grievances by shaping their perceptions, cognitions and preferences in such a way that they accept their role in the existing order of things, either because they can see or imagine no alternative to it, or because they value it as divinely ordained and beneficial?

Cooper (1998: 12), focusing specifically on government, describes the same phenomenon as 'governance at a distance', a process of 'guiding the actions of subjects through the production of expertise and normative inculcation so that they guide themselves. ... Subjects ... internalise these rules in the sense that they "know" their powers, duties, functions, responsibilities and what is appropriate or inappropriate behaviour'. However one describes it, the process is real, and through it the *what*, the *why*, the *who*, and the *how* of the *ultra vires* rule become operationalized in the working routines of local authorities even though the people performing those routines are sometimes unaware that *law* is involved at all.

A similar unobtrusiveness can continue even when *law* is fed directly into decision-making. This is often seen when legal advice is requested on particular matters or when decisions are processed through interdepartmental or corporate structures which provide for legal input. With lawyers thus *organized in*, the four 'W's become one of the screens through which items must pass before a decision is reached. The process may be unremarked and unremarkable; legal advice is not always unwelcome or problematic, and if everything is in order, the lawyers may say nothing. They may even say nothing if things are not entirely in order but the particular legal deficiency seems harmless in the circumstances; lawyers, like everybody else, will sometimes hold their tongues even though there is something that could be said. Silence, though, should not be mistaken as an indication that the *ultra vires* rule was not an element in the decision-making process. All that it means is that nothing stood out as requiring comment from a legal point of view.

Ultra vires actions do, of course, occur despite all of this. Some are accidental. Others, Loveland (1995), Mullen *et al.* (1996) and Halliday (2000) suggest in their various studies of front-line administration of the homelessness legislation, are less so. Their comments are a reminder that even when outputs *can* be legal, there is no guarantee that they *will* be. When this occurs, however, it is not for lack of a system that is designed, intended, and (usually) believed to produce *intra vires* decision-making. The weak links are likely to revolve around either a lack of *information* or the combined existence of both the *disposition* and the *autonomy* that make it possible to 'bend the law' in service of some higher goal or in response to a perceived operational necessity.

These factors apply differently, however, in the contexts described in this book, which are at the top end, rather than the bottom, of the administrative pyramid. The decisions to be considered here are financial decisions taken at the highest level, often involving formal committee or council decisions and always involving the council's senior financial and legal officials – who will be referred to both in the text and in quotations from council documents as the Treasurer (the chief financial officer), the Solicitor (the chief legal officer) and the Deputy Solicitor (who was the council's main legal advisor on capital transactions). At this level of decision-making, there can be no danger that conduct will diverge from *law* because of a failure of *information* to filter down to the people who need it. The Treasurer, the Solicitor, and the Deputy Solicitor were not only the principal actors but also the principal repositories of the council's *information* about its financial *vires*. Nor was there much individual *autonomy* available. Many of the relevant decisions – on rents and rates, for example – could only be taken by the council, and though the Treasurer had, technically speaking, the *autonomy* to enter financial transactions on the council's behalf by virtue of a delegation under s.101 of the *Local Government Act 1972*, the reality was that large-scale transactions of the kind examined here would normally need to be approved by the council or the relevant committee. In short, there was no hiding place from the *ultra vires* rule. To one degree or another, it was going to be in the minds of the principal actors, especially the lawyers, whose task and professional mindset it was to filter other people's visions of the politically desirable through the prism of public law.

The mission of the following chapters, therefore, will be to describe and explain the wealth of possibilities encompassed by that simple phrase 'to one degree or another'. The main features of the analysis have already been introduced. The overall focus is on the interaction between *law* and *policy* in the contexts set by *organization*. The key variables are *disposition*, *information*, *latitude*, *autonomy*, and *consequences*. Within those frameworks there are two sets of operational distinctions to be observed: one is of the *ultra vires* rule operating as a *subliminal*, *peripheral*, *explicit*, *determinative*, or *contested* factor in decision-making at different times; the other is of its being applied in differing situations in an *intuitive*, a *reasoned*, or a *meticulous* manner. What remains to be done is to add the facts. They demonstrate that, rich and varied though the workings of public law within government are, they have an underlying logic that sustained the flow of events in the particular story that is to be set out here, and that seems equally impossible to avoid in other governmental settings.

3
Out With the Old: The 1980 Budget

Our story begins with the election in May 1979 of a new Conservative government under Margaret Thatcher. Though local authority finance under the outgoing Labour government had been difficult for several years (see for example Rhodes 1992: 53), the election result was a sure sign of worse to come. The new government was committed to containing public expenditure, and legislation on local authority finance was one of its chosen tools. The government moved swiftly, and by December 1979 its *Local Government, Planning and Land Bill* was ready for introduction in Parliament. However, the Bill would not be passed and in force before the start of the council's new financial year in April 1980, which meant that the council's 1980 budget, the first of the ten to be examined here, would be prepared in a new political environment, but under old *law*.

Here, then, were the beginnings of the life-cycle of the *Local Government, Planning and Land Act 1980*. New *law* was on the way in but still in gestation. Old *law* was on the way out but still in force. From the council's point of view the 1980 budget provides a baseline measurement of existing law and practice in the period immediately before new legislation was added. From a more general perspective of public administration and public law it presents a scenario of government decision-making in a familiar and stable legal context. It might be tempting to regard this as normality, but would be mistaken. Legal change in government is at least as normal as legal stability, and internally generated change in a government that has legislative capacity can be every bit as disruptive as externally imposed change in a government that does not. Nonetheless, legal stability does exist in some areas of activity for many governments at some times, and the scenario described in this chapter exemplifies one of them.

A. Setting the scene

In May 1979 all was not well with our council. The financial situation was difficult; the area's problems were severe; and compounding these external challenges was the internal fractiousness of the ruling Labour group. Relatively evenly balanced between Left and Right, the group enjoyed an overwhelming numerical advantage, yet the 1979 budget, adopted in mid-March, had still only passed by one vote. In mid-May, only a week after the general election that brought Margaret Thatcher's Conservatives to power nationally, local power also shifted in what the local newspaper trumpeted as a 'Night of the long knives for Labour's left wing. Leftists dumped in town hall coup'. This change of leadership, however, did not alter the political arithmetic or the internal dynamics. The same individuals were still councillors; Left and Right were still at odds; and the members who were not clearly in either camp, though some of them held important leadership positions, were too few in number to marginalize the strife. The council was, for all practical purposes, hung. Leach and Stewart (1992: 144) point out that 'hungness', as they call it, comes in many forms, and that the features often associated with it – 'inconsistency, fragmentation, avoidance of the "difficult" decision' – are not necessary characteristics of 'hungness' nor are they necessarily absent in councils that are not hung. At the time this story begins, our council was mired in its own special form of hungness. Numerically it was close to a one-party state. Politically, it was close to deadlocked. 'Internecine hungness' seems an apt description of this uncomfortable condition, which was to persist for another three years.

From the point of view of public law, two related themes were key to the preparation of the 1980 budget. The first was that the budgetary process was very familiar; everyone knew how it worked. The underlying *law* been absorbed into the administrative process long ago, and tended now to operate in the range between the *subliminal* and the *peripheral*, to use the expressions presented in Chapter 1, rather than at the more conscious levels of the *explicit*, the *determinative* or the *contested*. The council's financial officers made most of the running, with little input from the lawyers, and this was to continue even as the new *given law* that was to govern future budgets, the *Local Government, Planning and Land Act 1980*, emerged throughout the year. The accumulated weight of past experience simply absorbed the new *law* into well-established procedures, and rolled on much as before. 'Looking back,' wrote the Solicitor when commenting on a draft of this chapter, 'some might think it surprising that there was so little involvement of [the] Legal [Department] in the budget setting process around 1980. However, it was so.'

The second, and related, theme, was that of the council's *policy*. Despite all the tribulations of its internecine hungness, and sometimes by very small majorities, the council managed to maintain a *policy* which steered it away from areas in which *law* might have become problematic. Thus it remained possible for the budgetary process to play itself out once more in 'business as usual' fashion.

B. Strategies of restraint

Both the newly elected government and the newly controlled council set to work quickly on their respective post-election and post-'coup' agendas for reducing spending, with the government's, of course (see Gibson 1982), compounding the difficulties of the council's. Shortly after the election the government called for reductions in local authority spending. In June the council's own agenda began to bite, with the local newspaper reporting 'savage cuts in council spending' coming out of a 'bitter night of rows, abuse, demonstrations and backstabbing ... eight hours of spiteful wrangling ...' at a meeting that was not even completed; it was resumed and concluded the following week. At much the same time the government also made clear its intentions for the coming financial year, seeking to consult local authorities about potential reductions in rate support grant of 2.5%, 5% or 7.5%.

The *policy* that the council adopted in response, in July 1979, was one of grudging acquiescence. Though the Labour group united in recording its 'outright opposition' to the threatened cut in grant and to the likelihood that the reduced amount would be distributed unfavourably to inner city areas like the council, it split before accepting, by a majority, the Leader's recommendation that the council should nevertheless consider major cuts in services. Rejected along the way was an amendment from the Left that would have deleted any reference to cuts and merely required the council to 'examine in depth the needs of the borough and report by November on the levels of service which are essential to meet those needs, with their full financial implications'. This rejection is of interest from a legal point of view, because in later years, when the Left had gained control and was attempting to defend its increased spending against the government's desire for cuts, the argument that the council's assessment of its service needs must be the first step in determining spending levels became part of the council's legal armoury. Technically, moreover, that is a strong argument. Examining first and foremost the council's service requirements is a more *meticulous* way to develop an *intra vires* budget than the broad sweep that the Leadership proposed in July 1979. At the time, however, this was not in any sense a discussion of *law*. The debate was purely one of *policy*. By a vote of 29-14, the Left were defeated.

C. The shape of things to come

The new legal framework in which the government intended to recast its financial involvement with local government was revealed in December 1979, when the contents of the proposed *Local Government, Planning and Land Bill* were published. The government initially planned to introduce the Bill in the House of Lords, but following political uproar at the idea that such important legislation might be dealt with in the Lords before the Commons, it abandoned the Bill, replacing it with a *(No.2)* Bill that was introduced in the Commons in January 1980. The government, 'surprised at the vehemence of the opposition to the Bill' (*The Times*, 22 December 1979), had made some 'concessions' (*The Times*, 23 January 1980) in the *(No.2)* Bill, but the broad outlines of the financial provisions were the same.

Both revenue and capital were to be affected. On the revenue side, the calculation of rate support grant was to change, so as to be driven by the government's assessment of local spending needs, with grant aid tapering as a local authority's spending exceeded the government's assessment. 'Unitary grants, block grants, rate support grants – call them what you will; whatever the name the new concept excited the indignation of all with a genuine concern for local government' (Cheetham 1981: 39; for further background and details see Travers 1982; Rhodes 1984; Audit Commission 1984; Grant 1986: ch. 3; Loughlin 1986: ch. 2). On the capital expenditure side, where the proposals were 'Rather less unpopular, rather less noticed, but still far from welcome' (Cheetham 1981: 39), central control through loan sanction was to be replaced by a system that allowed each local authority to incur a certain amount of capital spending each year. Its main components were an 'allocation' of a certain amount by the government, a 10% 'tolerance' allowing local authorities to move a portion of their capital spending authority between years, and an ability to spend a proportion of the authority's 'capital receipts'. (See Audit Commission 1985 for further details.) Technically, one should note, the term used in the body of the Bill to describe what this amount could be spent on was 'prescribed expenditure' rather than 'capital expenditure'. In later years, when control of the council shifted back to the Left and the council's financial *policies* became more assertive, there were to be times when careful distinctions would be drawn between these two terms, and the council treated some items as 'capital' even though they were not 'prescribed'. In early 1980, however, in the context of the council's *policy* of financial self-restraint, this particular point of wording did not seem significant: 'prescribing' was merely seen as the mechanism by which the government would define the items that counted as 'capital' expenditure.

This new statutory framework would first apply to the 1981/82 financial year rather than to the 1980/81 budget that the council was preparing in December 1979, but the Bill contained a sting in the tail for 1980/81 as well. Impatient to start putting its new financial order in place, the government had included in the Bill some 'transitional arrangements' under which, as soon as the Act was in force, the Secretary of State for the Environment could reduce the rate support grant payable to any local authority whose 'uniform rate' exceeded the 'notional uniform rate' for local authorities across the country. These transitional arrangements, the government's first direct attack on so-called overspenders, seemed very likely to catch our council.

D. Rents and rates, the old way

Against this disconcerting background the Leader presented his proposed financial strategy for 1980/81 to the policy committee and to council in January 1980. The package was for a net cut in spending of 5.3%, a 15% rise in rents and a 41% rise in rates (which one should add was not an exorbitant increase by the standards of the day). The three items were closely connected, since council house rents were partially subsidized through the rates in those days, so at any given level of overall spending, the higher the rents were, the lower the rates could be, and *vice versa*. The Leader's paper rapidly dismissed the alternative of not making cuts, which would require even greater increases in rents or rates or both. It did not even refer to a third possibility that he had publicly mentioned but discounted at a borough conference in November 1979: not making cuts but not raising rents or rates either. He had dismissed this then as being a recipe for an unbalanced, and therefore illegal, budget – a rare reminder in the context of the 1980 budget that the *ultra vires* rule did in fact provide a *peripheral* context of *law* within which *policy* decisions were to be taken.

The Leader's proposals were adopted by the policy committee but were hotly debated through much of a five-hour council meeting two weeks later, which eventually adjourned with the matter unresolved, and through much of the 3½ hour conclusion of that meeting on 1 February. A Conservative motion to raise the rent increase to 20% failed, as did a move by the Labour Left to restrict the increase to 10%. The Left came closer with an attempt to establish a general policy that 'savings be implemented only when there are no cuts in direct services to the general public or which do not result in compulsory redundancies'. This one they only lost by the tantalizingly narrow margin of 22 votes to 26. Ultimately, though, the Leader's proposed strategy was approved, and the package of 5.3% cuts, a 15% rent rise and a 41% rate rise was formally adopted.

A point to note in terms of *law*, however, and of the different ways in which it sustains the political process, is that there was actually a statutory power exercised on 1 February 1980. This was the approval of the 15% rent increase, which had to be confirmed then in order to take effect on 1 April as intended. By contrast, much of the substantial discussion, at least as formally minuted, was of the council's overall budgetary policy. In later years there were to be times when the council's lawyers, more exercised than they were in 1980 to ensure that decisions remained *intra vires*, would make major efforts to ensure that this natural intermingling of closely related matters did not occur: that rent decisions were based only on considerations that were specifically identified as being 'relevant' to a decision on rent levels. In 1980, however, the climate in which the council conducted its business – partly the legal climate, but just as importantly the internal administrative one – had not yet changed to make that necessary. The budgetary process was familiar from earlier years; the council was simply taking financial decisions in the way it had always done, and without detailed reflection upon the strict legalities of the process. On the spectrum of possibilities leading from *intuitive* through *reasoned* to legally *meticulous* decision-making, this was emphatically at the *intuitive* end. The council's *policy*, moreover, was steering the council in a direction that seemed legally uncontroversial. In a situation like this, with a council operating well within the margins of what may be termed its legal 'comfort zone', the undoubted technical distinctions between the rents decision and the rate decision did not receive the deliberate attention that, in other factual or *policy* environments, they might.

In March 1980 came the time for making the rate. The government had not yet announced its detailed intentions in relation to penalties under the transitional arrangements, but the little that was known clearly spelled trouble. Selection for penalty was to be determined by the excess of a local authority's 'actual uniform rate' over a nationwide 'notional uniform rate', and for our council the excess was a very large 100% when the precepts it collected for the metropolitan authority were included, and a massive 300% if they were excluded so that the figures only reflected the council's expenditure on its own services. The council was undeniably at risk of penalty. The only way out seemed to be through the government's concession that penalty would be waived for authorities that could show a 2.5% reduction in spending, in real terms, in the three financial years 1978/79 to 1980/81. Even here, though, the prospects did not look good. None of the calculations so far brought the council within the government's guideline.

An additional problem was that the government had now announced several subsidies the council would receive, and these were £1.25m less than the council had estimated. (All monetary amounts in this book are rounded.) The policy committee, extremely reluctant to raise rates beyond the 41% previously agreed, decided to make additional cuts, and recommended these to council at its rate-making meeting on 18 March 1980.

There, though, internecine hungness struck. A motion from the Labour Left to reject these additional cuts was rejected by a slim majority of only four votes. A motion from the Conservatives to limit the rate rise to 32%, only slightly above the 28% that was the average of neighbouring Conservative-controlled authorities, was defeated heavily. Then, though, the tables were turned as the Leader's substantive motion was put ... and also defeated. The meeting ended in 'chaos and farce', said the local newspaper, as the Conservatives joined the Left in an 'unholy alliance' opposing the motion, which failed by a margin of one vote. The meeting was adjourned, to resume a week later, on 25 March.

The Leadership scrambled to produce a revised budget which still made the cuts that supported the 41% rate increase, but which included provision for the possible (though not certain) expenditure of a further £500,000. This was balanced off by, among other things, revised estimates of receipts from the government, and a revised funding method for the £375,000 acquisition cost of a major development site. Approved by the policy committee on 21 March 1980, this package was altered once more when the Leader proposed directly to council on 25 March a further increase in the estimate of receipts from the government as well as a different funding proposal for the development site involving the acceptance and use of a gift of £250,000.

If the revised budget was, as a Conservative member contended at the council meeting, 'cosmetic accounting designed to achieve a consensus decision on the rates', it was not noticeably successful. ('Fists fly as 41% rate fixed', said the local newspaper.) The meeting lasted until after midnight, with considerable debate, and again the Conservatives voted with the Left in opposing the motion. This time, however, the Leadership had the numbers, just, to support the budget. Two Labour councillors had been persuaded to switch their votes to support the Leadership, and the budget passed by a vote of 26-24. The 1980/81 rate was therefore made on the same policy base of a 41% rate rise that had been agreed in February.

Given, though, that the February decision, persevered with in March, for a 41% rate increase was purely one of *policy*, it is particularly interesting to see the allegation of 'cosmetic accounting' raising its head, just as it would in later years when there were specific issues of *law* that the accounting was designed to negotiate. There can be no doubt that some of the last-minute adjustments, small though they were by the standards of later years, had something of the cosmetic about them. The council's estimate of its rate support grant was revised and re-revised in a matter of days; the funding arrangements for the £375,000 development site were adjusted and readjusted. Note, though that these various manoeuvrings were not the result of any legal obligation to keep the rate increase down to 41%. The council's desire to do so was purely internally generated, a matter of *policy*, not *law*. Its effect in relation to the political process, however, was every bit as binding as a rate-cap.

E. Confronting penalties

The 1980 budget did not end with the rate-making in March. Still to be confronted was the prospect of penalties under the transitional arrangements. Here too, and perhaps surprisingly given the controversial nature of the penalty scheme, *policy* rather than *law* continued to be the dominant factor as the story unfolded over the remaining months of 1980.

In June the Secretary of State for the Environment announced that local authorities' budgets were above the government's guideline figure for the financial year. He asked that they review their budgets to eliminate the overspend. In September, the government announced that this review had reduced the overspend, but had not eliminated it. (Our council had submitted a revised budget that made £2m in savings, compared to the £7m that would have been required to reach the government's target.) The government therefore announced three steps, all of which affected our council: rate support grant was to be withheld temporarily for all local authorities; penalties under the transitional provisions of the *Local Government, Planning and Land Act 1980* were to be applied against the highest overspenders; and any Partnership funding (which reimbursed certain local authorities for 75% of their spending on agreed projects in deprived areas) for overspenders was to be restricted. Under the first and second of these combined, the council stood to lose £3.5m, a large amount to adjust for so late in the financial year. The effect of the third was also substantial but less easy to calculate.

There was, however, the possibility that penalties would be waived for authorities which had made exceptional efforts to reduce expenditure or to achieve the target requested by the government. (*R v Secretary of State for the Environment, ex parte Brent LBC* 1982, provides a good account of these events.) The target now requested was a 2% reduction in expenditure in real terms between the 1978/79 out-turn figures and the 1980/81 budget, but the council was still above it. The Treasurer noted, however, that the government had said that it would consider Partnership spending in waiver applications, and that if the relevant figure here was the council's net, rather than gross, spending, the council would be within target. The Treasurer also noted that the second review of income and expenditure for 1980/81 indicated that at the end of the year the council's expenditure would be within the target range, even though its budget figures had exceeded it. The Treasurer set out in absolutely uncomplicated terms, and without additional comment from the Solicitor, the council's options:

(1) To apply for a waiver and consider further action if a waiver is not allowed.
(2) To apply for a waiver but levy a supplementary rate in order to ensure that the council's finances are kept in balance.
(3) To apply for a waiver but consider reductions in expenditure in order to make up some or all of the possible loss of grant.

It should be noted that levying a supplementary rate, an additional rate demanded during the financial year (legislation permitted this at the time but was repealed later), would have been a new departure for this council. Though the idea had received a little attention in 1977/78 it had not been pursued. This was therefore the kind of unfamiliar exercise of statutory power that might have been expected to receive at least the *reasoned* attention of the Legal Department, which would be reflected in written 'legal observations' in the Treasurer's report. This, though, did not occur, which demonstrates again that the low profile of *law* in the council's financial decision-making at this time was not restricted to the well-worn and the familiar. Even in this unusual situation, *law* was, at best, *peripheral*, and as between the Legal Department and the Treasurer's Department, the situation was one in which the Treasurer took the lead and the Solicitor saw little need to become involved.

Under each of the three potential *policies* that the Treasurer suggested in September 1980 the first step was to apply for a waiver of the government's penalties. This was done. As things then turned out, the choice among the three alternative second steps never had to be taken. After a meeting with the Under-Secretary of State for the Environment, the council received its waiver. The key to this was the council's projection of its out-turn figures for 1980/81, but the precise basis for the decision seems to have been left a little obscure. The government did not accept the council's arguments about the treatment of Partnership money, though the council had apparently seen this as the more promising of its two claims. The council seems to have had less confidence in its projected out-turn figures, though the government, while allowing the waiver because of them, reserved the power to re-impose the penalties if events did not bear out the council's projections. Nonetheless, with the government and the council having reached an accommodation, the strict legalities of the situation never received a thorough examination. On the particularly important question for the council of how the government's 75% contribution to Partnership expenditure should be treated, the Solicitor expressed the view in an internal memorandum that 'Whilst it is a matter we could pursue, my initial reaction is that it is most unlikely that the Court could be persuaded to interfere with the Secretary of State's decision if he chose to use a 100% (as opposed to a 25%) basis of assessment'. However, with the question of penalties in 1980/81 no longer being one that had to be resolved along strictly legal lines, the need for a searching legal analysis fell by the wayside. *Policy*, and the successful outcome to which it had led, made *law* immaterial. The council was therefore not involved as the councils that had in fact been penalized pursued their legal complaints to initial success in *R v Secretary of State for the Environment, ex parte Brent LBC* (1981), but ultimately to failure, since their initial success was based on the Secretary of State's failure to consult with them, and this enabled him to consult later but still end up taking the same decision (*R v Secretary of State for the Environment, ex parte Hackney LBC* 1983).

Loughlin (1986: 37–8) has said of the *Brent* decision that it 'marks most clearly the commencement of a new era in legal relations between central departments and local authorities ... disputes between central authorities and local authorities will not merely be dealt with administratively through the traditional channels, but the nature and limits of powers will also be tested in the courts'. Our council's brush with it, however, highlights a different point: that the *policies* and attitudes, both of local and of central government, will determine the part that the *law* plays in their relationship. In the council examined here, the dominant *policy* through the 1980 budget was, essentially, to 'grumble and get on with it'. Potential legal questions as to exactly what was or was not within the council's powers – or, indeed, the government's – were not clearly confronted because they did not have to be. One has the impression, indeed, of an almost deliberate lack of legal precision in the dealings between the Department of the Environment and the council in the final stages. The strict legalities of the situation were of little practical significance given that the Department was prepared to accept the council's presentation of its figures. The underlying reality was that the council's budgetary *policy*, which was broadly consistent with the government's wishes, steered it away from the legal clash which might otherwise have occurred. This meant that within the council, too, and despite the legal novelty of the situation that the prospect of penalties presented, there was nothing to disturb the established administrative dynamic in which both the Legal Department and the Treasurer's Department expected that the Treasurer's Department would make the running on matters of this sort. In subsequent years this was to change. When, with an intake of new members in the 1982 local elections, the council's centre of political gravity moved to the Left and its political disposition changed from 'grumble' to 'resist', precision on legal matters was to become extremely important. Once the council decided to stand its ground, it had to choose its ground carefully and know it well. That, however, was a matter for the future.

4
In With the New: The 1981 Budget

The 1981 budget was the first to be drawn up under the *Local Government, Planning and Land Act 1980*. The Act received Royal Assent in November 1980, when planning for the 1981 budget was still in a relatively early stage. The council's preparations for the new legal framework, however, had been going on ever since the content of the Bill became known a year earlier. Things began normally enough, as an ordinary exercise in the implementation of new legislation, but as the year wore on events veered towards the chaotic. The new *given law* of the Act (anticipated) combined with further new *given law* from the courts (unanticipated) and with the ever-increasing turbulence of the council's 'internecine hungness' to cast a variety of new lights on the council's financial *vires*.

This chapter therefore combines both typical and atypical elements of a government identifying, under a new piece of legislation, the boundaries of the possible. The typical part involves understanding the *given law*, and converting it into *operative law*, as far as necessary for the purposes of one's own particular activities. The atypical part is that in this particular case, as a result of both internal and external stimuli, the boundaries were shifting from almost the very first minute.

A. New *law*: the first encounters

Chapter 2 has summarized the normal process for examining and implementing new legislation in local government. Lawyers examine Bills with the departments affected and together they work out appropriate measures for putting the legislation in place in accordance with the *what*, the *why*, the *who* and the *how* of the *ultra vires* rule. That was the process followed in our council with most of the *Local Government, Planning and Land Bill*; the different Parts, which included subject-matter as diverse as direct labour organizations, urban development corporations, councillors' allowances and the relaxation of miscellaneous central controls, were assigned to different solicitors for review, and their contributions were finally combined by the Solicitor into a report to the policy committee in March 1980.

The major financial provisions, however, received different treatment. Here the Treasurer took the lead, commissioning a report by Coopers and Lybrand into their implications. The Legal Department's role as a spectator rather than a principal actor when important new *law* was being built into the council's administrative framework was unusual, and underscores the observation in the previous chapter that the council's financial officers took the lead in this area at this time, and that the lawyers, to the extent they thought about the law, were content with the financial officers' understanding of it. In a memorandum written two years later, when things began to change, the Solicitor was to describe the involvement of his department in these and earlier days as being little more than polishing up the wording of the annual rate resolution. This largely disengaged role can be expressed in terms of the *organization* of the council in early 1980. At that time the council's lawyers, although not, strictly speaking, *organized out* of the major financial decisions, were far from being actively *organized in*. Still, the Solicitor's report to committee in March 1980 on the non-financial aspects of the Bill did include an indication of the Treasurer's thinking on the financial ones. The capital expenditure provisions, based on annual allocations by the government, were 'likely to give additional freedom to local authorities in some directions' but were going to impose significant controls in others. The rate support grant provisions, with amounts and tapering provisions revolving around the government's view of the council's spending need, had 'substantial and disturbing implications'. ('We understated!' exclaimed the Solicitor in a comment on a draft of this chapter.)

The Bill was only a Bill, however. Before it became law, local authorities had the opportunity to attempt to influence the substance of the *given law* it would create. On rate support grant their attempts were largely unsuccessful. Though at times it seemed the government might be willing, or might be forced, to contemplate alternatives to the proposed new block grant (see Rhodes 1986b: 141–2), ultimately the block grant was implemented. As for the capital expenditure provisions, the government did eventually accept several of the modifications that local authorities suggested. Some of these are worth mentioning because they created areas of *latitude* that were to play noteworthy parts in the events of the following ten years.

One that the local authority associations were eager to see was an alteration in the legal consequences of a capital overspend. Under the original form of the Bill it would have been *ultra vires*. In response to local authority representations, however, this was changed so that excess expenditure was only unlawful if the Secretary of State, believing that an authority either had exceeded or would exceed its permitted amount, issued a direction and the authority contravened it (see ss.78 and 79). In the absence of a direction, the over-expenditure would not be unlawful, but would have to be made up out of the subsequent year's expenditure. This concession was an important adjustment to the legal *consequences* of overspending. Its effect was to enable the council, in later years, to grapple with the limits on its capital spending with far more equanimity than would otherwise have been the case. (There were also times, though, when the prospect of having the Secretary of State give a binding direction on the council's capital spending was a far more worrying *consequence* than a risk of acting *ultra vires* would probably have been.) An interesting side-note on this particular issue is that although the distinction between overspending being *ultra vires*, or being *intra vires* but subject to possible restraint by the Secretary of State, was obviously seen as a major distinction at the time, future years were to reveal a consistent lack of clarity as to the exact legal status of capital overspending. We will meet this issue again.

Leasing was another area in which the prospective *given law* of the Bill evolved in significant ways. The Bill's general approach, subject to exceptions created partly by the Bill and partly by Regulation, was to value a lease of land or of goods in the same way as an outright sale or purchase (depending on whether the local authority was the lessor or the lessee). This, of course, did not match the actual flow of cash, and the local authority associations persuaded the government to apply this financially unrealistic structure to fewer leases than had originally been planned. Leases of land, for example, were ultimately treated as not involving 'prescribed expenditure' if they were for 20 years or less. (Remember that number.) Leases of vehicles, plant and machinery were also eventually excluded unless the lease provided for the local authority to eventually own the property. (Remember that exclusion.) In the light of the *latitude* that local authorities were in due course to identify in the leasing provisions of the Act, one comment particularly stands out in a letter from the Association of Metropolitan Authorities to its members in April 1980. Written shortly before the Bill's Report stage in the House of Commons, it commented that the Association was expecting to see a 'relaxation on the treatment of lease and leaseback arrangements – the Minister stressed that the Government wants to encourage this sort of operation.'

At the same time that the *given law* of the *Local Government, Planning and Land Act 1980* was developing through the legislative and regulatory process, the *operative law* of what it meant in real life situations for the council was also being considered. In November 1980, for example, there was discussion of the £375,000 development site that was to be partly financed by the £250,000 gift that emerged in the closing days of the 1980 budget. Would this particular gift generate a 'capital receipt'? The answer would determine whether some, all or none of the money was available to fund the acquisition, and possibly whether different portions of it might be available in different financial years. The site, furthermore, was to be acquired by a general vesting declaration under compulsory purchase legislation, a means of acquiring title before the compensation was determined. Was it the general vesting declaration, or was it the eventual payment of the compensation money, that constituted the 'prescribed expenditure' for the purposes of the legislation? This would determine the year or years of the council's capital allocations against which the cost had to be charged, and this, in turn would affect key parts of the council's financial plans.

Commonplace transactions, too, needed to be analysed in terms of their capital budget implications. The analysis was not always easy. One example that surfaced periodically throughout the ten years under review and was never conclusively resolved was whether business leases for less than 20 years (remember that number?) needed to be treated as capital items. On the face of things one would think not. However, the *Landlord and Tenant Act 1954* contains security of tenure provisions under which even short business leases may last for more than 20 years, and this might arguably bring them within the definition of a capital item. Counsel's advice was taken, and the council proceeded thereafter on the basis that short business leases were not capital items. The council had a large stock of business premises, and much depended, in practical terms, on this interpretation.

Decisions on issues like these simply cannot be avoided as the *operative law* of new statutory powers falls into place and the outlines of the locally possible form. In some cases, such as the £250,000 gift, the circumstances may be unique to a particular authority. In others, such as the business lettings, the same legal issue may affect many local authorities, and there may well be a national consensus that develops, though individual solicitors in individual authorities may have their reservations, strong or weak, about whether the national consensus is correct.

Either way, all one can do is reach a conclusion and act on it, though possibly with an awareness that, in the fullness of time, one's interpretation may turn out to be wrong.

A particularly significant project that was in the pipeline for our council at the time was a lease/leaseback arrangement for the construction of new municipal offices. The original plan was for the council to lease the site to the developer and then take the leaseback of the new offices once they were completed. The danger now, though, was that the leaseback of the completed offices would have to be accounted for as though it were a purchase of the freehold, thus using up several million pounds of the council's capital allocation for that year. To counter this the Legal Department suggested that the arrangement should be restructured: the formal lease and leaseback should both be completed before the new capital controls took effect, but the leaseback should be at a nominal rent until the building was completed. The department reviewed its advice periodically as time passed and the transaction had still not been completed.

Obviously, these early attempts to convert the *given law* of the *Local Government, Planning and Land Act 1980* into the *operative law* that informs administrative action contain the seeds of what was later often known as 'creative accounting' or 'creative financing'. At base, however, nothing even remotely 'creative' was involved. The simple fact was that the legislation forced lawyers and accountants to engage in this kind of analysis. It was essential, in relation to any actual or potential capital transaction, to be aware of the implications of the legal arrangements in terms of the council's annual capital allocations and to act accordingly. The attempt to restructure the legal arrangements for the construction of the new municipal offices, for example, was not 'creativity' but simply an exercise in common sense. Given that the council had not yet entered a legal commitment, why should it proceed with a disadvantageous arrangement if a better one was possible? The Solicitor, one may add, when commenting on a draft of this chapter, vigorously rejected the idea that the word 'creative' could in any way be applied to the proposed lease/leaseback transaction as it was contemplated in early 1980. The Audit Commission apparently felt differently, describing lease/leaseback schemes in the years immediately preceding the *Local Government, Planning and Land Act 1980* (along with deferrred purchase schemes and leasing of plant and equipment) as 'innovative ways of financing capital expenditure' that were 'largely designed to circumvent the borrowing regulations, or to secure for local authorities advantages which they were not entitled to in their own right' (Audit

Commission 1985: 56–7). This, though, seems to be flatly contradicted by the government's preparedness to alter its legislative scheme in order to accommodate lease/leaseback arrangements – even to 'encourage' them, according to the Association of Metropolitan Authorities's letter of April 1980 that was quoted earlier in this chapter.

Three points, then, are to be made about the implications of the new capital controls in terms of the relationship between public law and government practice. First, what made 'creative financing' possible, an ability to analyse potential legal transactions in terms of their legal and financial impact, was an essential skill for anyone who wished to function under the new legislation. Second, once one had that skill, one had to use it. Failure to do so would be a breach of the duty to serve one's council to the best of one's ability. Third, with specific reference to the council under review here, when the *Local Government, Planning and Land Act 1980* came into force, the council was already committed to a major project that was to be funded by what some people (though emphatically not the Solicitor) might consider 'creative' means, and without the slightest qualms about it. Given the fact that, as this book will demonstrate, local authorities' internal decisions on their *vires* tend to proceed by once-for-all decisions, the *operative law* building up one step at a time, a decision of this sort, taken so easily and so early in the new régime, was a significant beginning. Both in terms of *law* and in terms of attitude, innovative financing methods were something that the council was already beginning to take on board.

B. Rents and rates: the well-worn path

In relation to the key budgetary decisions on rents and rates, by contrast, no new legal skills were yet needed. In retrospect, indeed, the 1981 budget was notable for its lack of legal input. In this it was the last of the old-fashioned budgets. Neither the rent-setting nor the rate-making process was expressly altered by the *Local Government, Planning and Land Act 1980*, and that new *given law*, though hugely important to the council's financial calculations, was simply absorbed into the non-legalistic pattern of budget-making described in the previous chapter. It was still a matter of finance and of *policy* rather than of *law*. The budget did not lack political excitement, however, as various factors – the government's public expenditure plans, its redistribution of rate support grant away from the metropolitan areas, and the ever-growing threat of penalties – combined to face the council with difficult financial decisions. The council's 'internecine hungness', moreover, got worse as the year wore on.

The council's general *policy* for the 1981 budget was established as early as June and July 1980, several months before the *Local Government, Planning and Land Act 1980* had completed its passage through Parliament. That month, the Leader proposed, and the council adopted, over the vigorous opposition of the Left, a policy guideline of a 3% cut.

Serious discussion of rents began in November 1980, shortly after the flurry in which the council had briefly been targeted for penalties under the transitional arrangements of the *Local Government, Planning and Land Act 1980*. In November the expectation was that the council would suffer a grant reduction for 1981/82 in the range of £3.5m to £6m. The Treasurer's Department produced a report that compared rent rises since 1974 (60%) with a variety of other factors and concluded that there had been a 25% to 35% decline in rents in real terms over that period. This report, like those of the past but not of the future, contained no specific legal observations nor any reference to the application of the *ultra vires* doctrine to the rent decision. It recommended a rent increase of 15% or 20%. It mentioned, but only in passing, the fact that the government's rate support grant calculation was expected to assume a rent increase of about £3, or roughly 33%, in this authority.

When the announcement on rate support grant came, in December, it was worse than expected. The anticipated reduction of up to £6m had almost tripled to £16m. The Leader's working group considered that the council should follow a policy of maximizing grant income, and proposed a 33% rent increase, equal to the government's guideline. This was put to council on 27 January 1981.

Once more, the Treasurer's report spoke purely in monetary terms, without reference to *law*. It did not argue for any particular level of increase, but spent some time describing the combined effect of rent rises, rent rebates (which the council provided but the Government substantially funded) and block grant. A 33% rent increase would produce over £7m to the council, with more than £4m of this coming from the government either for rent rebates (£1.5m) or in additional grant (£2.5m). The 'low option' of a 15% rent increase would only produce £3m, with only £1.5m of this coming from the government. Against the Left's opposition, the 33% rent increase was adopted.

With the rent decision taken, the final piece of the puzzle for the 1981 budget was the making of the rate itself. The decision was taken on 21 March, and was for a 21.9% increase – low by the standards of surrounding authorities. Legal advice was not felt to be called for – and in retrospect once more it is interesting to note the absence of legal comment on the penalty implications of the decision. The council rejected trying to set its budget at the government's Grant Related Expenditure level (the government's assessment of the council's spending need for rate support grant purposes); the gap was so large as to be unbridgeable. In relation to the government's expenditure guidelines, the policy committee noted that the government wanted a 3.6% reduction in real terms for 1981/82 over 1980/81, but stated very matter-of-factly and without legal angst that the budget was £2m over that target, and that although the final result would probably be lower, the overspend was unlikely to be eliminated unless the government ignored Partnership spending, which it had previously refused to do. Potentially, then, there were legal issues to be raised here, the effect of grant loss and the treatment of Partnership money being among them. The fact that legal comment was not added was largely a reflection of the council's political *disposition*. The council was still moving generally in the direction the government wanted and had survived the previous year without proceeding legalistically. *Policy* was still steering the council in directions in which *law*, as it was understood at the time, was no more than *peripheral* to its decisions.

C. A parallel universe

Other councils, however, were of a different *disposition*, and had to consider issues of *vires* directly. In some cases, as Jacobs (1984: 80) has observed, this was not because of anything they decided to do, but merely because the new legislation, when applied to existing financial commitments and policies, placed authorities 'in precarious legal difficulties at a very early stage'. In early 1981, therefore, the Solicitor had the luxury of watching from the sidelines as other local authorities explored the *operative law* of budgets that would incur significant grant loss. From one of them the Solicitor received a copy of a Counsel's opinion that provided interesting information on issues which he saw no need at the time to broach within his own council, though this was soon to change.

Counsel answered four questions. The first was whether a budget that was above 'Grant Related Expenditure' (the government's assessment of the council's spending need) and 'threshold' (the point at which grant penalties kicked in) was contrary to law. The answer was no, provided that the council, in setting its budget, had acted on the 'relevant considerations' and disregarded all 'irrelevant' ones. The second question was whether, if the budget was so high as to result in a withholding of grant, there would be any risk of a finding that councillors or officers were guilty of 'wilful misconduct' – a key phrase, because if loss was caused to a local authority by wilful misconduct, the district auditor could at the time recover the sums involved from the people responsible by a process generally referred to as a 'surcharge', and those sums could be very large. Again the answer was no, as long as all 'relevant considerations' were taken into account, but Counsel added that there was nevertheless a real risk that some part of the budget in question might be so high as to be 'contrary to law'. This was another key phrase, since it too might lead to a surcharge, though by a different procedural route, and only where the person responsible failed to act 'reasonably or in the belief that the expenditure was authorized by law' (s.161, *Local Government Act 1972*). The third question sought advice about who would be liable to surcharge if wilful misconduct were identified. The answer was that it was those who were responsible for the action in question, with some elaboration of what being 'responsible' meant. The fourth question related to the legal position of officers in such a situation. The answer is worth quoting, for it set out some of the major bureaucratic groundrules, no doubt in many councils beyond our own, for the engagement in this particular scenario of public law rules with the art of the locally possible.

> To avoid any justifiable charge of liability for unlawful expenditure or loss or deficiency under section 161(1) and 161(4) respectively an officer of a local authority must, in my view, bring to the attention of his council any factor which is material to its consideration of whether its action or decision is unlawful in any field for which he is responsible. The responsibility of the Chief Executive, the Treasurer and the council's principal solicitor range, of course, over the whole spectrum of the council's expenditure. They must warn the council of the possible consequences in law of any decision which the council might to their knowledge take, and present the council with possible courses of action which would or might avoid those consequences.

When received, this opinion was of no immediate practical concern to the Solicitor. The council was not trying to probe the limits of the legislation, so the question of exactly how far it could go, and with what *consequences*, was immaterial. Less than a month after the council's budget-making in March 1981, however, all this changed. Caught up in the continuing turmoil of Labour Party politics, both locally and nationally (these were the days of the painful birth-pangs of the Social

Democratic Alliance), the balance of the council's 'hungness' tilted a little, and the Left gained sufficient control of the Labour group to claim the leadership of the council. Within a matter of days the Solicitor had written to the Chief Executive, the Treasurer and the chief officer of the council's policy unit setting out the ground rules for the period of tension between *policy* and *law* that was now to be anticipated:

> <u>The Role of officers</u>
> 9. The officers concerned in advising an authority on budgetary matters must bring to the attention of the authority any factors which they believe to be material and ought to be considered. That may well include factors which are politically unpalatable. The Treasurer in particular stands 'in a fiduciary relation' to the ratepayers and owes a duty by reason of that relationship (Attorney-General v De Winton).
>
> <u>Surcharge</u>
> 10. It is clear as the law currently stands that, in themselves, financial decisions which result in reductions in the rate or total of rate support grant, are not unlawful. But if such decisions are taken unreasonably – for example, without considering material, relevant factors, by giving weight to irrelevant factors or without proper consideration of the balance between the different parts of the community – then the Court, on application from the District Auditor, might well declare items of account to be 'contrary to law'. The risk of this would be likely to increase as the levels of expenditure above threshold, or the loss of rate support grant, increased.
> 11. The present state of the law does not enable any lawyer to draw a clean, helpful line. What I would simply say is that there would be some risk of surcharge – both to members (if they took an unreasonable – unlawful – decision on levels of expenditure or rents) or to officers (if comprehensive and objective advice were not given to members).

As it turned out, the change of political control might not by itself have led the council into more legally contentious territory. It soon became clear that the Left's hold was far from secure, and at the council meeting of 28 April 1980, the first one after the change of control, the council as a collective entity shackled the new leadership with a resolution confirming the existing budget and rate strategy and instructing 'that no action be taken which could lead to levying a supplementary rate for Borough use.'

By the time of the next council meeting another important political event had occurred. County elections in May 1981 had produced Labour gains. Transportation subsidies had been an election issue, and talk of supplementary precepts was in the air in various parts of the country. (See Bridges *et al.* 1987: chs 3, 4 and 5.) If the metropolitan authority imposed a supplementary precept, which the council was going to have to pay in full, the council was going to have to consider whether to impose a supplementary rate in order to recover the cost.

Then in June came a third major event. The government announced its proposals for penalizing authorities that it considered to be overspending. (See Gibson 1982: 15.) The government was seeking further reductions to be submitted by 31 July, but initial indications (later revised downwards when the government provided further details) were that the council was liable to a penalty of more than £3m. It was time, once more, for a decision of *policy*.

The first step, taken on 16 June 1981, was to reject the government's request to submit a reduced budget. (Smith and Stewart 1985 provide an interesting survey of local authority responses to the different grant and penalty regimes from 1981/82 to 1985/6.) Many other councils also submitted no change to their original budgets (*The Times*, 4 August 1981). The policy committee's decision again noted that if Partnership money were treated in the way the council had consistently urged, as being local expenditure only to the extent of the 25% that actually came from the council's own resources, penalties would not apply.

This first step then led into substantial decisions at the council meeting on 28 July 1981. By now the amount of the metropolitan authority's supplementary precept was known, as was the likely penalty from the government's recalculation of the rate support grant. The policy committee voted in favour of levying a supplementary rate to cover both of these new items, its minute carefully observing that

> In arriving at these decisions we are reminded that the law places on local authorities a duty to ensure that in each financial year its estimated income adequately reflects its estimated expenditure, and that if it becomes apparent that a council is likely to incur a substantial deficit, it is obliged to reduce net expenditure or levy a supplementary rate or carry out a combination of these measures.

With the change in political control, the council was moving into the area where financial matters became legal matters. Those who were preparing its minutes, moreover, were already showing an understanding of the potential value of *law* as a means of bolstering *policy* positions. The Solicitor (at interview) has referred to this example as the start of a practice of 'judge-proofing' major council decisions. 'Judge-proofing' is a loose and slightly misleading expression, but what it signifies here is that in this particular authority at this particular time lawyers were becoming sensitive to the fact that inattention to detail, or to the documentation of detail, can sometimes undermine a perfectly valid decision, and that good solid paperwork may sometimes shore up the *vires* of a decision that might be vulnerable without it. This is, of course, the starting point of juridification, 'a process by which relations hitherto governed by other values and expectations come to be subjected to legal values and rules' (Scott 1998: 19), and it is interesting to note this process emerging in our council several months before the two court decisions that tend to be thought of as the main triggers to the juridification of local government in the early 1980s, namely *R v Secretary of State for the Environment, ex parte Brent LBC* (1981), dealing with penalties under the 'transitional arrangements' of the *Local Government, Planning and Land Act 1980*, and *Bromley LBC v GLC* (1981), the 'Fares Fair' case in which the House of Lords struck down the Greater London council's transport subsidy policy.

The council votes on the supplementary rate were close once more. By a consistent margin of 24-22, however, the Left first turned back two amendments – one to press for a reduction in the supplementary precepts, the other for the council to absorb its own penalty without additional rating – and then adopted the policy committee's resolution. The supplementary rate was therefore approved.

D. Capital: the 'happy accident'

At the same meeting in July 1981 there were also some important developments on the capital front. The new controls were already causing difficulties, and there was heated debate about what kinds of property, if any, the council might be willing to sell in order to generate capital receipts to help fund its housing rehabilitation programme. A separate agenda item from the Treasurer made the point more than once that 'expenditure in excess of resources will be illegal under the new capital expenditure controls', which was not, of course, technically accurate. It also pointed out that the new legislation was unforgiving: 'The council has only two possible sources of money for its housing programmes. The major one is the government allocation of housing investment monies and the second source is capital receipts from the sale of land and property. Beyond this there is little room for manoeuvre.'

On the same agenda, however, was another item that was to begin the swift erosion of the idea that the new capital controls left so little *latitude*. The new municipal offices were to be discussed once more, with a revised proposal for the financial arrangements. Initially envisaged as a lease/leaseback transaction, this had subsequently been revised into a sale/leaseback format. By July 1981, the plan had changed once more. The legal details of the revised plan deserve brief examination, for these were the kind of finely nuanced legal intricacies upon which the art of the locally possible was to depend heavily in our council in the years to come.

The background to the Treasurer's new report was that the company with which the council had been previously dealing – let us call it Company A – had been let down by its funding source and had been unable to find another. Subsequent discussions had produced a proposal from another company – Company B – which involved a careful negotiation of the fine print of the *Local Government Planning and Land Act 1980* and regulations and would, the Treasurer reported, 'provide the finance for the development in such a way as to avoid completely any charge against the council's capital expenditure allocations'.

The Company B proposal involved splitting the financing of the council's new offices into two parts: the 'fixed equipment' costs, which were the building's central heating system and lifts, and the cost of the building itself. The former would be financed 'by a straightforward leasing agreement and would provide that the equipment would never pass into the council's ownership'. The latter would be financed by 'the use of a covenant scheme involving a merchant bank.'

The leasing part of this took advantage of the *latitude* that the government had knowingly built into the new capital controls through its concession that leasing of 'any vehicle, vessel or item of plant, machinery or apparatus' would not count as prescribed expenditure 'where the agreement ... does not entitle the authority to the immediate or future property in such an item' *(Local Government (Prescribed Expenditure) Regulations 1981, Sch.3)*. Leasing also had tax, and therefore cost, advantages, attracting capital allowances under Section 64/11 of the *Finance Act 1980*. (See Audit Commission 1985: 57.)

The covenant scheme with the merchant bank also had some novel features. Here, instead of simply entering into a construction contract with a builder, the council would set the specifications for the building and select the builders, but it would be the bank that hired and paid them, while the council undertook ('covenanted') to make payments to the bank after the building was completed. The amount to be paid by the council was based on the cost of the building plus the amount that would have been payable in interest if the money had been borrowed.

One key interpretation here was that a payment by the bank to the builder, followed by a payment by the council to the bank, did not involve 'borrowing'. Another was that the council's eventual payments to the bank did not come within the definition of 'prescribed expenditure' under the *Local Government, Planning and Land Act 1980*. This was because, by virtue of general land law principles, when the builder built on the council's land, the building automatically became part of the land and belonged to the council. Whatever else the council might be doing when it paid the bank, therefore, one thing that it was not doing was acquiring any interest in land within the meaning of the capital expenditure controls.

In years to come it was not uncommon for people to say that under arrangements like these money was being borrowed in fact although it did not count as borrowing in law. Those involved in this council in July 1981, however, would not have seen it that way at that time, nor would they have done so subsequently. From their point of view this was simply an *intra vires* transaction that, when analysed technically in the way the *Local Government, Planning and Land Act 1980* required, produced a particular, and no doubt highly palatable, legal and financial result. Initially the Deputy Solicitor, who took the lead on capital finance issues, had considerable doubts about this, but advice obtained from Leading Counsel confirmed the interpretations upon which Company B had based its scheme. The Treasurer's report commented that 'officers could not be certain that the law itself would not be changed, perhaps with retroactive effect on this type of agreement'. What prompted this comment was that it seemed hard to believe that anything so simple could really so comprehensively outflank the government's annual capital expenditure limits, or, if it could, that the government would not plug the gap immediately. In the event, however, it was to be another five years before the government took that step, and then only prospectively. By then covenant schemes had gone through several stages of refinement beyond the rather rudimentary one under which the council's new offices were constructed.

The Treasurer (at interview) has described the Company B scheme as a 'happy accident' that simply fell into the council's lap at a time when the Company A arrangements were breaking down. The Solicitor accepts that the Company B arrangements, unlike those with Company A, can fairly be described as 'creative'. Yet in terms of the functioning of public law within government it is worth noting that what had occurred by this stage does not match familiar descriptions of 'creative compliance' either in general or in its particular application in 1980s local government. Black (1997: 13), drawing on work by McBarnet and Whelan, describes creative compliance as 'the deliberate and tactical use of an alternative interpretive strategy, one of literalism and formalism, to circumvent the purpose of the rule'. In our council at this point, though, there was no deliberate and tactical interpretation by the council of the new capital controls; there was simply an analysis of the scheme that Company B presented, and a confirmation by Leading Counsel that it did in fact produce the legal effects that Company B suggested. Similarly, the Company B arrangements for the municipal offices fall slightly beyond both Loughlin's explanation that local government creative accounting developed in the 1980s as a legalistic response when the central government's unilateral attempts to impose its financial will destroyed the conventional understandings of the central-local financial relationship (Loughlin 1996: 325) and his description of 'the manner in which the [municipal socialist] movement undertook a systematic examination of the organizational arrangements, the statutory powers and the general institutional power of local government with a view to determining how the local authority might be adapted to the pursuit of socialist objectives' (Loughlin 1996: 135). Whatever may have come later, at this particular time in mid-1981 the council was not municipal socialist (the Left's position was not yet strong enough), it was not systematically examining its potential as an agent of change, and it was not responding to any breakdown of conventional understandings. All that had broken down were the Company A arrangements, and the Company B scheme simply happened to be in the right place at the right time – and, importantly, at the right price – to fill the void.

There was also a preexisting framework of behaviour out of which these kinds of arrangements emerged. Davies (1987: 26) mentions that when, in the 1970s, the Wilson and Callaghan governments started to restrain local authority borrowing approvals:

> The result was that authorities turned to the financial institutions to create instruments which were not legally classed as borrowing and which allowed capital schemes to be carried out. By the end of the decade there had been a rapid growth in leasing, lease/leaseback and sale and leaseback techniques and, to a lesser extent, credit sales, the forerunner of the deferred purchase technique.

Similarly Sbragia (1986) writes of 'the local borrowing "game" as carried on during the 1960s and 1970s' (314) in terms that are strikingly similar to those that are often considered a defining characteristic of the 1980s: 'the authorities manoeuvre, the Treasury becomes concerned and bargains with them on new regulations, authorities manoeuvre around those regulations, new regulations are agreed, and so on' (324). Nor is this purely an English phenomenon. McCarthy and Reynolds's description of American municipalities' responses to constitutional and statutory debt limitation provisions (2003: 418–25), mentioning both 'ingenuity' on the one hand and 'subterfuge' on the other (425), has a very familiar ring, and Valente *et al.* (2001: vii) expand on the theme:

> Voter initiatives and other state constitutional limitations have imposed new legal restrictions on state and local taxation and debt. The ever-rising demand for state and local services, however, has sparked the creation of a host of revenue-raising and borrowing devices, and expanded the role of special districts and public authorities in order to avoid these constraints. This point-counterpoint of restriction and evasion has generated an extensive body of challenging case law, and has proved to be of vital importance to the financing of state and local governments.

Against this background, a note of caution must be added about the word 'creative', as used both by this book and in many of the quotations it contains. Expressions like 'creative accountancy' and 'creative compliance' have a pejorative ring, but they involve a blend of both the acceptable and the unacceptable that is hard to disentangle. This shows up well in McBarnet's brief overview (2004: *xvii*): 'By "creative compliance" I mean using the law itself, often in novel, unanticipated ways [so far, so good], to construct legal forms for business deals, or other transactions, which can claim compliance with the letter of the law [nothing wrong with that ... but the sting is in the tail], while totally undermining its spirit.' McBarnet notes, though, that some of the self-interested products of creative legal work 'may ultimately be endorsed by judges or legislators (who may indeed be ascribed credit for their invention)'. Witness, perhaps, the Private Finance Initiative.

This book will not attempt the difficult task of establishing exactly when acceptable creativity crosses the line into its unacceptable form. The task may be especially challenging in an intergovernmental context like the one in this book, where both the council and the government would claim to be acting in the public interest at all times, and where any claim that the council was 'undermining the purpose of the law' could be met with the answer: 'Which law? We are acting under this one and simply doing our best to discharge our statutory responsibilities.' The result is that the word 'creative' is used non-judgmentally in this book. It will certainly be associated with 'using the law ... in novel, unanticipated ways', and these may well involve heavy reliance on 'the letter of the law', but no comment is implied about the state of the law's 'spirit'. The spirit *of the law* must, in any event, always be carefully distinguished from the policy objectives that inspired it, or 'what the government wanted but did not necessarily make the Act say'. For the council, as an *autonomous* statutory body, there was no reason at all why it should do what the government wanted unless *the law* effectively embodied the government's wishes.

A vital area in which the council lacked *autonomy*, however, must also be highlighted immediately. Whatever the council's *vires* in relation to creative arrangements such as the new municipal offices and others to come, it could never act alone. Its own interpretations of its statutory powers could accomplish nothing unless it had a willing financial partner who took the same view. Indeed, even that was not enough. A potential financial partner might well share the council's view of the *law*, but still decide that it simply did not want to do the deal. Luckily for the council, circumstances in the early 1980s were propitious. Company B, in particular, was recently formed and had a specific (and profitable) focus on identifying the *latitude* that was available to local authorities under the *Local Government, Planning and Land Act 1980*. Company B also had willing financiers available, partly, the Treasurer advises (at interview), because foreign banks were looking for openings in the English market at the time, and non-traditional arrangements offered some opportunities. Lansley, Goss and Wolmar (1989: 42) have spoken of the banks and the City as the 'bizarre bedfellows' of left-wing councils in the 1980s, devising 'an increasingly exotic range of creative accounting measures'. Loughlin (1996: 326) writes that 'During the 1980s a major industry, with local authority treasurers and lawyers working hand in hand with financial institutions, has evolved.' Sbragia (1986: 330–1) indicates, however, that these 'important – and very sophisticated – allies' in the financial sector were already hard at work under the previous financial régime, and quotes one local authority officer saying:

> Under the new Government bill [the *Local Government, Planning and Land Bill*], it seems as if we'll be able to use capital receipts without penalty but not revenue for capital. We spend about £9 million a year on capital from revenue. It won't take a merchant banker six

> months to figure out a way to transform revenue into capital receipts and then we'll be able to spend it on capital without penalty.

Six months was, in fact, roughly how long the *Local Government, Planning and Land Act 1980* had been in force when the council entered the Company B arrangements. They were to be the harbinger of more to come. The 'local borrowing game as carried on in the 1960s and 1970s', which Sbragia seems to have thought the government might have finally 'won' through its resort to legislation (325–6), was actually far from over.

E. The final shambles

Meanwhile on the revenue side the story of the 1981 budget was becoming increasingly convoluted. In September came a surprise. Though the government announced, as expected, that local authorities overall had not reduced their revised budgets sufficiently, and that rate support grant was therefore to be withheld, it also announced that Partnership expenditure was to be disregarded for penalty purposes. This change of tack was part of its inner-city initiatives in response to riots in Southall and Toxteth. For the council, the result was that it was now clear of penalty for the 1981/82 financial year, and penalty had been one of the two *raisons d'être* for the supplementary rate that had been agreed in July, though not yet actually levied. The Right moved quickly, convening an extraordinary (in the technical sense of 'not scheduled') council meeting to deduct the corresponding 3.5p from the supplementary rate. The mayor, evidently primed beforehand as to the *law* relating to the issues of *policy* that some members were known to be planning to raise, is reported in the council's minutes to have opened the meeting by stating:

> that she wanted to indicate before the debate started, that if any amendment was moved that the supplementary rate should be reduced by more that 3.5p (the amount known by everyone to have been included in the supplementary rate resolution of 28th July 1981 to meet the then expected RSG penalty and which was now unlikely to be imposed) then it would be necessary for the council to resolve to refer that issue to the policy committee for consideration and report pursuant to SO[Standing Order]12(4). In her opinion this was the correct way of dealing with the matter because the

> council had no detailed financial implications on such a proposal from the Treasurer and all members needed to be aware of what these were.

With the political balance on the council tenuous, the legal rules of the game were of growing importance, and could give political advantage to one side or the other. In this case, a particular discussion that the Leadership did not wish to have could be avoided because of the *why* of the *ultra vires* rule, the absence of 'relevant considerations' on which to base a decision. In the event, a motion was indeed put for a greater reduction in the supplementary rate, but it was withdrawn when the mayor stood by her earlier ruling. The 3.5p reduction was approved.

Then came Bromley LBC's challenge of the supplementary precept levied in London by the GLC. Launched in September, it was unsuccessful in the Divisional Court, which, on 3 November, upheld the GLC's action. Only eight days later, however, the Court of Appeal allowed the appeal, and in December the House of Lords gave the final ruling: the supplementary precept was invalid. Bridges *et al.* (1987: especially chs 3, 4 and 5) have described the immediate consequences of this decision in the precepting authorities: there was confusion not only in London but also elsewhere, and not only in relation to the recent supplementary precepts, but also as to the effect of *Bromley LBC v GLC* on earlier transportation subsidy policies. In rating authorities within those areas, like our council, the range of questions was different, but no less complicated. Were supplementary rates *ultra vires* if made in order to accommodate an *ultra vires* supplementary precept? If they were not *ultra vires*, should they nonetheless be revoked? Could they even be revoked? Legal opinions on these issues differed and changed over the course of time.

Meanwhile the political complexion of the council had also changed once more. For some time the Left had been struggling to retain its control, as was attested to by such formalistic legal moves as, in mid-October, a vote to suspend the standing order that entitled the mayor to *ex officio* membership on all committees. Their political balance was now so uncertain that one vote could make a difference, and the Left could no longer count on the mayor's vote. In December the old guard reasserted itself. It convened another extraordinary council meeting at which, no less adept than the Left at playing by the legal rules of the political game, and recognizing that its first and fundamental step in taking control of the council's decision-making must be to alter *who* had the legal authority to take decisions on the council's behalf, it revoked all appointments to committees (with a couple of minor exceptions where, for particular reasons, continuing membership was required), established a new six-person committee called the co-ordinating committee (dominated, naturally, by the new Leadership) and vested in the co-ordinating committee virtually all of the functions of the council. A further extraordinary council meeting was called for 17 December, in order to reconstitute the ordinary committees and terminate the co-ordinating committee. (The mayor's *ex officio* membership of all committees was also restored – surprise! – thus gaining one more precious vote for the new majority.)

As it turned out, 17 December was also the day on which the House of Lords announced its decision in the GLC case. The council's minutes record that the new Leader made a statement to the meeting, describing the 'real financial and administrative headache' that this would cause. 'Members should appreciate that we are in a unique and complex legal and financial situation, which will take a lot of unscrambling. More detailed reports will be presented to Finance Sub and Policy Committees in January. In the meantime, a copy of the House of Lords judgements has been put in the Members' Room. But be warned, they are very technical'.

It was therefore not until February 1982, only eight weeks before the end of the 1981/82 financial year, that the council took the last of its decisions on its 1981 budget. For the members now back in control, anxious to re-establish the policy orientation that had led to the comparatively moderate rate increases of the past few years, and very conscious that local elections that might confirm or displace its control of the council were due in less than three months, the issue now was not merely whether the supplementary rate could or should be rescinded (the council's *disposition* was to do so, and to avoid, if possible, replacing it with anything else), but also whether refunds could be paid, and if so, whether interest could be paid on the refunds. (Counsel said yes under certain conditions; the Department of the Environment said no, and had written to say local authorities would be 'extremely ill advised' to do so.)

The council met on 2 February 1982, and took the expected decision to revoke the supplementary rate. The legal dimensions of the decision featured prominently in the policy committee's report to council:

> We noted that before deciding whether to levy a supplementary rate, a rating authority is required to consider its estimated income from other sources. An authority is permitted to budget for a reasonable working balance, but if an unreasonably high level of balances is

> included in the rate, it may be challenged by a ratepayer under the General Rate Act 1967. The Treasurer considers that the balances currently forecast are sufficient to maintain a reasonable working balance ... and in these circumstances both he and the Solicitor feel that a decision to impose a new supplementary rate would face the real risk of successful legal challenge. That view is shared by counsel whose advice has been taken.

This minute offers an interesting comparison with the one in July in which the council, led then from the Left, had explained why it was 'obliged' to levy a supplementary rate. Now, after the decision in *Bromley LBC v GLC* and the shift in political control, the council had apparently become equally obliged to revoke it and put nothing in its place. Both decisions are notable for the way in which a financial decision becomes framed in terms of legal duty. There is no legal reason why the decision that the council thought financially appropriate had to be expressed in that way. However, the marginal political control at both times placed a premium on being able to say, in support of whichever decision, 'We are legally obliged to do this'. Thus the *ultra vires* rule can figure in internal debates as a means of bolstering political positions. The Solicitor has commented (at interview) that it was coming to do so rather more in our council as Left battled Right through 1981/82.

Also illustrated here is that the distinction between a local authority's discretions and its duties is not always clear cut. Under the *why* of the *ultra vires* rule a local authority must take all 'relevant considerations' into account when exercising its statutory powers, but when, having done so, its course of action is clear, it is legally accurate to say that it *may* follow that course, but equally accurate to say that it *must*, for to act otherwise would be 'irrational' – inconsistent with its own assessment of the facts – in the circumstances. The difference between the two formulations, as discretion or as duty, may sometimes be an accident of word choice and sometimes a matter of deliberate rhetoric, but it is important to recognize that public law duties may be of different kinds. Some are absolute, while others are contingent, dependent on an authority's own opinions and beliefs, and contingent duties are unstable. In a council like ours, for example, where political control is on a knife-edge, all it takes is for two or three members to change their minds about a particular issue and the council's collective obligation, as a matter of *operative law*, to do one thing can become an obligation to do the opposite.

From this one final observation emerges about the relationship between *policy* and *law* under the *ultra vires* rule. The relationship goes two ways. *Policy* must of course always be consistent with *law*, but there are many situations in which *policy* will actually be one of the determinants of what the *law* is, specifically the *operative law* of what a particular local authority can or cannot do in a particular situation. A local authority that considers its resources inadequate may have an obligation to levy a supplementary rate. Yet the moment it changes its mind about the adequacy of its resources, levying that supplementary rate becomes *ultra vires*. The *operative law* has reversed itself, but all that has changed in reality is the council's own assessment of its financial situation.

This interaction between *policy* and *law*, with *policy* partly shaping the contours of the *operative law*, will be observed on several occasions in the course of this book. It is especially evident when *policy* changes, and a course of conduct that had been considered *ultra vires* one week becomes *intra vires* the next. Outside observers may be bemused by this phenomenon. A natural reaction would be scepticism, a belief that *law* must be more absolute than this, and that if legal advice can change so readily, all that it really shows is that local authority lawyers can easily be prevailed upon to give their councils whatever advice the councils want to hear, with the *law* no more than window-dressing.

That sceptical account should not be accepted too readily. Whether it has the ring of truth in particular cases would no doubt be disputed as between the critics of a decision and the people involved in taking it, but more important for present purposes is to make the point that apparently abrupt changes and reversals in the *operative law* of a local authority's powers and duties are not, in themselves, cause for scepticism. This is simply the way the *ultra vires* rule works. As a matter of legal analysis, a change in a council's *policies* will in some contexts genuinely alter its legal options. What is 'rational' for council A, holding the particular and legitimate beliefs that it does, may be 'irrational' for council B, with a different set of beliefs – and council B may sometimes be none other than council A after a small but significant shift in political loyalties. Counter-intuitive though it may seem, *policy* can be one of the determinants of *law*. What a council *can* do, or sometimes *must* do, as a matter of *law*, is often partially the product of what it believes it *ought* to be doing, as a matter of *policy*.

5
A Heightened Awareness: The 1982 Budget

17 December 1981 had been a pivotal day for our council in the evolving encounter of *law* with *policy* under the *Local Government, Planning and Land Act 1980*. On that day new and challenging *given law* had been added to the mix by the House of Lords's decision in *Bromley LBC v GLC* (1981), and new and uncertain *policy* had been set in motion by the formal ousting of the Labour Left as the controlling faction on the council. How would these two new forces intermesh in the few short months remaining for the preparation of the council's 1982 budget? The key statutory decisions on rents and rates were imminent and were, in themselves, familiar. They would play themselves out differently, though, in this unsettled new environment of *law* and *policy*.

'Juridification' and 'dejuridification' of the political process are the two key themes of this chapter. Juridification is Scott's 'process by which relations hitherto governed by other values and expectations come to be subjected to legal values and rules' (1998: 19). Dejuridification, which is less remarked upon in the literature, is its opposite. This chapter not only explores both processes but also shows them going on at virtually the same time and on virtually the same subject-matter within a single government. It demonstrates, therefore, how the contribution of public law to the political process can ebb and flow in response to both subjective and objective forces.

A. Absorbing *Bromley*

The *Bromley* decision (discussed in Loughlin 1983 ch. 3 and Bridges *et al.* 1987) was one of those strange cases that change everything and nothing. In terms of pure legal analysis, the Solicitor's 'first thoughts', conveyed by a memorandum of 23 December 1981 to the newly installed leadership and to senior officers, were that the case was nothing new. Recirculating a copy of the memorandum he had prepared after the Left took control in April 1981, he stated that the legal position on rate support grant penalties was still that the council could decide to adopt a budget that incurred penalties, but that

> ... before doing so, it must think long and hard about the right balance between the interests of the ratepayers who would have to pay up and the various parts of the community who would benefit from the policies.
>
> This is an aspect the reports leading up to the budget-making will need to explore in detail.

On the other hand, the very urgency with which the Solicitor pointed out, mere days after the *Bromley* decision, that the case was nothing special was itself an indication that the case was indeed special. At the time 'a wide body of legal opinion concluded that spending above target might be illegal' under the fiduciary duty doctrine (*The Times*, 19 January 1982), though the Solicitor did not subscribe to it. *Bromley*'s significance was increased by the tighter régime of penalties that was then being introduced by the highly controversial Bill that was to become the *Local Government Finance Act 1982*.

The government also stepped into the confusing swirl of opinions. In February 1982, it took the exceptional step of circulating some internal legal opinions indicating that local authorities were less constrained by the *Bromley* decision than some of them apparently thought. In one the government's Law Officers advised the Secretary of State for Transport that Counsel for the GLC were wrong in thinking that the revised budget that the London Transport Executive drew up in response to *Bromley* depended on the GLC providing a level of subsidy that would be *ultra vires* (see Loughlin 1996: 243). In another, the Department of the Environment set out its own lawyers' views on rate-making in the wake of *Bromley*. Some key passages are worth quoting:

> When a local authority considers its expenditure plans, it should address itself to its functions (some of which are, of course duties) under all relevant legislation: its assessment of the needs and resources of its area; any relevant information about spending plans provided by central government, including potential block grant entitlements having regard to Grant-related Expenditure (GRE) targets and the rate poundage schedules; and the effects on ratepayers. Expenditure

> by a local authority above its GRE or target is certainly not made unlawful by that fact alone; the spending level adopted must be a matter of judgment having regard to all relevant considerations. (This is the case whether or not an authority is proposing to spend above target or above the threshold over GRE, at which points an authority will begin to receive proportionately less grant for each increment of expenditure.) Moreover, the fact that an authority is on negative marginal rates of grant does not of itself demonstrate that the authority is in breach of its fiduciary duty since such an authority could be spending at or below its GRE or target.
>
> It is however probable that if an authority is challenged in court on the level of its expenditure or on a specific item of expenditure, the Court would expect to see that the authority had considered very carefully the full possibilities and implications of alternative lower levels of different items of expenditure in relation to the different costs to the ratepayers and that the further the authority spends above its GRE or target, the heavier will be the onus of justification.

In terms of *law*, this was substantially a confirmation of the position that the Solicitor had already taken. In terms of the relationship between public law and government practice, however, this view of the law had important implications. Budget-making was now very clearly reaching the point at which *law* might be expected to become more than a *subliminal* or a *peripheral* factor, moving at least into the realms of the *explicit*. It was thus changing from an almost exclusively financial exercise into one in which lawyers, seeking to avoid trouble with the *ultra vires* doctrine, would feel compelled to comment on both the substance and the process of the annual budget. Abruptly heralded into the council's budgetary procedures, therefore, were both judicialization, 'the process of the courts and lawyers increasingly being drawn into administrative and political decision-making' (Bridges *et al.* 1987: 3), and juridification. Different authors use these terms differently, and sometimes interchangeably, but the usage here will be that 'judicialization' has to do with *who* is involved in decision-making, whereas 'juridification' has to do with *how* they act. Thus 'judicialization' relates to whether and to what extent lawyers are *organized into* decision-making, while 'juridification' deals with how *meticulously*, once *organized in*, they perform their roles, and with what impact on the conduct of others. Using the terms in this way, it would be rare for a government's decision-making to be 'juridified' without being 'judicialized', since nobody else is likely to see things like a lawyer if the lawyer is not involved. It would be possible, though, for it to be 'judicialized' without being 'juridified'. This would occur if lawyers, although thoroughly *organized into* the process, took a relaxed view of their government's powers or felt no special obligation to insert *law* into decision-making unless absolutely necessary.

Our council's initial review of the government's rate support grant announcement in December showed that cuts of at least 7% in real terms would be required to avoid penalty, and more likely of 10%, since the Treasurer thought the government had made inadequate allowance for inflation. On these figures it seemed extremely likely that the council would incur a grant penalty, and in January 1982, the Solicitor took his first judicializing steps into the rate-making process. He wrote to the Chief Executive, the Treasurer and the chief policy officer, with copies to the Leadership:

> If, as I apprehend, given the inadequate level of our GRE, the council is likely to favour a budget strategy which would involve some loss of grant, I think it would be as well to anticipate a legal challenge to the 1982/83 rate in some form or other. If this were to happen, our budget reports would be closely scrutinised and dissected by anyone seeking to establish that the council had acted unlawfully. With this in mind, it is even more important than usual that reports are thorough and objective.

He wrote in similar vein in February:

> Against that background, I need to see the drafts at the very earliest possible stage, so that I have a proper opportunity to consider and comment on them. I appreciate that the lawyers are not usually directly involved in the writing of budget reports (except to polish up the rate resolution), but I am sure you will agree with me that I am inevitably impelled into the area by recent events.

Evidently this was a conscious exercise of both judicializing and juridifying the council's budget-making process, of becoming more actively *organized in* for the purpose of ensuring that the council's budgetary decisions were legally *meticulous* and could be sustained in the event of challenge. It was against this background of a new-found urgency to do things demonstrably right that the council faced up to its 1982/83 budget decision.

B. A swift juridification

The two main budgetary decisions were, as ever, rents and rates, with the rents decision needing to be taken soon if an increase was to be brought into effect on 1 April. The Solicitor's injunction that it was 'even more important than usual that reports are thorough and objective' was certainly reflected in the paperwork presented. Not only was the level of information about different rent levels and different measures of comparison more extensive than ever before, but the Treasurer's report incorporated specific legal comment and was bolstered for the first time by a separate report from the Solicitor. This report was to become the basis of the standard legal advice for the budget-making of several years to come – a classic example of the 'once-for-all' legal decision-making that is common in government. Legal departments try to give, and client departments expect to receive, the same advice consistently, thus a legal conclusion that is formulated once will tend to stick, and advice on related issues will often use it as a foundation.

The basic principles that the Solicitor highlighted will be familiar to readers of this book. They included the relevant parts of the famous four 'W's, such as:

> (b) In exercising a statutory discretion, an authority must have regard to all relevant considerations and disregard all irrelevant considerations. A decision will not be reasonable (lawful) if it is one which no reasonable authority could have reached

and:

> (d) The council has a duty to its ratepayers to act (in the words of the leading case of Roberts v Hopwood) 'in a fairly businesslike manner with reasonable care, skill and caution, and with a due and alert regard to the interest' of those ratepayers to whom it 'stands somewhat in the position of trustees or managers of the property of others'. This duty is usually referred to as a 'fiduciary duty'.

They emphasized that the statutory discretion that was being exercised here was the council's, not the government's:

> 6. The fact that a local authority takes a different view from Central Government of the amount of money it should spend, does not in itself make any part of such expenditure unlawful. It is for the

> authority to decide the balance which should be between different sections of its community. Central Government cannot prejudge that decision by pronouncements of policy (although it could in theory do so by legislation).
>
> 7. But in the light of the way in which grant-related expenditure is determined, the fact that an authority's expenditure is above the prescribed threshold must clearly be a material factor in considering whether it is reasonable and pays due regard to the interests of the ratepayers as a whole.

In this newly juridified political process, moreover, the Solicitor underlined that these principles not only existed but must be actively observed:

> CONCLUSION
>
> 9. The combination of the current rate support grant scheme and the recent quashing of the GLC's supplementary precept means that any authority's rate decision for 1982/83 is more likely to be the subject of legal challenge than in the past. Against this background, it is essential that in its consideration of its budget and rate the council not only has objective regard to the material considerations, but is seen to do so. In particular, if the council were minded to adopt a financial policy which would result in a loss of grant, it must think long and hard before doing so and satisfy itself that it is striking a defensible balance between the interests of all concerned, including the ratepayers.

The rent decision was deferred twice in February when lengthy and rancorous meetings were taken up with other things, and was eventually taken at an extraordinary council meeting on 22 February. By then the process of *meticulous* juridified application of the *ultra vires* rule had been raised to even greater heights. The Solicitor had prepared an additional report directed to the specific rent options between which the council was deciding. He had also consulted Counsel, whose opinion was attached to the papers for the meeting.

Among the options put to Counsel the major ones were rent increases of £2.50, which would avoid any grant loss, £1.40, which was in line with inflation, and 'less than £1.40', which would include the Left's preferred option of £0. Counsel replied:

> (b) Against the financial background outlined in [the Treasurer's report] and the other papers before me it seems to me that it might

> well be considered that an average weekly rent increase of less than £1.40 (option 4) was a decision that no reasonable body of persons would arrive at, because there seems no reason (having regard in particular to the rebate system) to shelter all tenants from inflation at a substantial cost to ratepayers who are subject to the same inflation. At the other end of the scale an increase of £2.50 (option 3) avoiding any grant loss or deficit increase would not give rise to an objection on behalf of the ratepayers. Accordingly, in my view an increase of £1.40 (option 1) is the least that is defensible, and an increase of £2.00 (option 2) is more easily defensible. I use the expression 'defensible' because both option 1 and option 2 involve grant loss and deficit increase and may give rise to challenge. In my opinion, however, some grant loss (or deficit increase) would not be in itself a ground for finding that the council had exercised their discretion unlawfully or unreasonably. ...
>
> (c) Subject to following the proper procedures the risk of successful challenge for an average weekly increase is, in my view: less than £1.40 very substantial; of £1.40 much less but more than negligible; of £2.00 slight; of £2.50 nil. ...
>
> (f) Council Members who voted for an increase which was successfully challenged would in my view, on the basis of my estimates in paragraph (c) above, only be likely to face difficulty in discharging the burden under section 161(3) of the Local Government Act 1972 necessary to avoid personal liability or disqualification if they had voted for an increase of less than £1.40.

The Solicitor's personal opinion (offered when he commented on a draft of this chapter) was that Counsel was over-restrictive. Nonetheless, Counsel's advice was Counsel's advice, and the Solicitor provided it to council. He added a supplementary report of his own putting Counsel's advice into stark but readily understandable terms.

> 5. Against that background, I now set out a number of options for a weekly rent increase ... with my brief assessment of the risk element –

Option	Risk of Successful Challenge
(a) £2.50	This is the safest course which avoids any loss of grant or material increase in HRA deficit – Risk, nil.
(b) £2 }	
(c) £1 ([some dwellings]) } and £2 (the rest) }	Risk, very small.

(d)	£1 ([some dwellings]) } £1.50 (the rest) }	These options each approximate to an inflation-based increase. Risk, small but nevertheless material.
(e)	£1.40 }	
(f)	Less than £1.40	Risk, considerable, growing rapidly the lower the increase becomes.
(g)	Nil	Almost certain to be held unlawful.

6. ... my view is that the risk of surcharge to Members who might support options in the range (a) to (e), in the unlikely event that there were a successful challenge, is very small. But there would be a material risk at option (f) and a likelihood of surcharge at level (g).

The council did not take the legally safest option of the £2.50 increase; a motion recommending it, though moved by the Chair of the Housing Committee (and seconded by the Leader of the Conservative Group), was soundly defeated. A motion from the Left to make no increase was also defeated, by the solid margin of 29-11, and the council eventually settled for option (d) of the Solicitor's final summation, the combined £1/£1.50 increase depending on the properties in question. On the face of things, then, a majority of the council was prepared to accept a 'small but nevertheless material' risk of acting unlawfully, while a minority was prepared to take a decision that was 'almost certain to be held unlawful' and attracted 'a likelihood of surcharge'. However, a note of caution must be added, for on the rate-making front rapid changes were occurring. The council was becoming more and more determined on a *policy* of making the smallest rate increase possible, and the more successful its efforts in this direction were, the more comfortable it could be, as a matter of *law*, that a lower rent increase might still produce a legally justifiable 'balance' between rents and rates. The shifting context of the rates decision made the *operative law* of rent-setting a rapidly moving target, however much the Solicitor and Counsel might try to pin it down.

C. A swifter dejuridification

Strikingly, since the rent decision had been a case of juridification *par excellence* and the rate decision was being taken at virtually the same time, legal involvement in the rate decision followed a different and sharply diminishing trajectory. Over a very short time span, *policy* drove hard for a low rate increase, the Treasurer's financial assessments made this possible if certain decisions were made, and *law* receded in practical significance.

The first significant report following the block grant announcement in December 1981 was to the meetings in January and February 1982 at which the 1981 supplementary rate was revoked. At this time the Treasurer saw the government's target as requiring a 10% cut in real terms and the Leader's statement to council said this 'would mean savage reductions in the services on which many of the people of this Borough depend'. At that time, and taking into account the much increased precept the council was expecting to have to pay to the newly Labour Left metropolitan authority, a rate increase in the order of 32% was in store unless cuts were made.

In a remarkably short time, however, a mix of accounting ingenuity and adjusted spending decisions produced an apparently remarkable turnaround in the council's financial prospects. At the extraordinary council meeting at which the rents were set, the Treasurer produced a brief background note indicating that even without cuts or a rent increase the necessary rate increase would now be only 23.7%. That would come down to 19% if the £1.40 rent rise were adopted, and to only 15.4% if £2.50 were chosen.

Ten days later, after the rent increase had been decided upon but also after the metropolitan authority's increased precept had been set, the policy committee reviewed the implications of the three alternative rate increases, 25%, 20% and 10%, that the council had decided to exemplify. The figures showed that few cuts would now be needed if a rate increase of 25% were adopted. The policy committee noted, though, that 'real service reductions and staffing implications' would start to take effect with the 20% option, and that the 10% option 'carries very serious service reductions in all areas and would involve substantial staff redundancies.'

A mere two weeks later things looked very different again. The 10% rate increase was now what the Leader proposed, but 'very serious service reductions' and 'substantial staff redundancies' were no longer the order of the day. A further mix of cuts, deferred capital expenditure and revised estimates and provisions brought the rate increase down to the 10% level where the new majority on council had now become determined it should be. Their wishes ran into an unexpected bout of 'internecine hungness' at the council meeting, when the Conservatives abstained and six disgruntled supporters of the Leadership walked out before the vote was taken, but when the council reconvened on 26 March, all forces were properly mustered. With a couple of minor changes, the budget now passed by the narrow margin of 26-23.

Noticeable from the point of view of public law in the political process is that, compared to the abundance of legal advice that accompanied the decision on rents only one month earlier, the closing days of the rate-making decision proceeded remarkably unencumbered. Numerous legal opinions were in circulation at the time, as local authorities across the country faced up to their first budget since *Bromley LBC v GLC*, but most of these related to the legal implications of grant-losing budgets, and this was a prospect that became increasingly unlikely in this council as events unfolded. The Solicitor's general advice on levels of expenditure and rates, mentioned earlier as the first part of a much more comprehensive package of advice on the rent decision, was among the documents for the rate decision, but this advice had been prepared at the end of December 1981, when it had appeared inevitable that the council would incur grant loss in its rate decision. As a general statement of *law* the advice remained accurate late in March, but as the council's *policy* had consistently drawn it away from the legal danger zones, there was no need to supplement it with *meticulous* and focused analysis such as had accompanied the rent decision.

Even so, there were potential legal issues involved. In later years, even the kind of financial adjustments that occurred during March 1982 were sometimes felt to require a legal seal of approval, or would at least receive comment in terms of 'reasonableness' or 'relevant considerations.' In March 1982, however, in the context of a *policy* of minimal rate increases, these were not the legal issues that people were primed to identify and confront. Compared to the rents decision, taken only one month earlier, the rates decision was dejuridified, the very antithesis of the anxious process that Bridges *et al.* (1987) describe in the authorities they were examining in much the same period, the months after *Bromley LBC v GLC* (1981). Though the council's lawyers had indeed been, in the words of the previously quoted memorandum prepared by the Solicitor in January 1982, 'inevitably impelled into the area by recent events,' and though reports were certainly 'even more thorough and objective' than they had been in earlier years, the change of *policy* that followed the ousting of the Left in December 1981, and developed dramatically in March 1982, was easing the pressures between *policy* and *law*. The specific decisions that the council wished to take in March 1982 were simply not the kinds of decisions that were identified at the time as likely to cause legal problems.

Of course, the somewhat dejuridified format of the 1982 rate-making provides its own lessons on the functioning of the *ultra vires* rule. What it especially underscores, in addition to the interdependence of *law* and *policy* that has already been mentioned, is the similar interdependence of law and professional advice – here, financial advice. The fact that advice is or is not given, as well as the nature of that advice, can affect the legal range of action available to a local authority. If the Treasurer had advised strongly against elements of the 1982 budget, it would have been hard for the council to adopt them. To disregard unchallenged professional advice raises questions of law – of whether decisions are based on 'relevant' rather than 'irrelevant' considerations – as well as the possibility of liability to district audit action, since ignoring advice for no good reason may be a possible basis for a finding of 'wilful misconduct.' On the other hand, if the Treasurer does not question the financial wisdom of what is being done, it is unlikely that the Solicitor will have much of a basis for comment on the specifically *legal* ramifications of the council's financial judgments. The effect is to create an interdependence between legal, financial and political judgment. Each is a reality that the others must respond to, but at the same time, each is at the mercy of the others. What is or is not offered by way of professional advice can influence what can or cannot be done by political action, and conversely, the political situation at any given time will naturally affect the way in which professionals perform their advisory duties. These are among the 'paradoxes of dependency, interdependency, autonomy and bargaining' that Rosenberg (1989: 186) refers to in the context of local authority financial decision-making. Once more, therefore, the message is that when looking for the part that the public law plays in the workings of government one should not expect to find a simple picture. *Law* is one of several interdependent variables, with areas of flexibility both within itself and in its interaction with the other forces at play. Its contribution was modest in our council in the closing days of the 1982 rate-setting (as contrasted with the rent-setting of only one month earlier) because *policy* moved sharply away from the legal danger zones and financial advice was able to accommodate the switch. Shortly, though, all this was to change.

6
Leftward, Ho: The 1983 Budget

Local elections in May 1982 delivered firm control of the council to a Left-dominated Labour Party with a manifesto bearing all the marks of the 'local socialism' of the day (see Boddy and Fudge 1984; Gyford 1985; Lansley, Goss and Wolmar 1989). Race, women's issues, anti-poverty, decentralization of services – matters such as these were now firmly on the council's agenda. The manifesto also gave some important financial commitments: to protect jobs and services, to restore some of the cuts of the previous administration, and not to raise rents before 1984/85. That last promise naturally catches the eye in the light of the Solicitor's advice less than three months earlier that making no rent increase for 1982/83 would be 'almost certain to be held unlawful' and give rise to 'a likelihood of surcharge'. We will return to it later.

Elections are, of course, a central feature of the political process. Yet for governments of all kinds they only occur periodically, political control does not necessarily change, and even when it does, the change in political direction may not be dramatic. Thus the scenario that this chapter explores – how existing *laws* interact with the new and radically different *policies* of a new administration – arises relatively infrequently. It is, nevertheless, one of the essential possibilities of the democratic process.

A. Turning round the ship of state

The bureaucrat's first response to an election is to double-check the winning manifesto and decide how on earth to make good on its promises. Some are more troublesome than others. In our council the Solicitor distributed the manifesto to the Legal Department's solicitors and obtained comments on the new council's commitments, some of which were evidently problematic. (See Game and Skelcher 1983 on the subject of local election manifestos in this period.) In a memorandum to his staff he observed that there were interesting times ahead, and that in several areas legal advice would need to be fed into the council's decision-making at an early stage. Thus new directions in *policy* generated new issues of *law*, and the instinctive lawyer's response was that timely *information* was the way to avert difficulties with the *ultra vires* rule.

In relation to the council's financial affairs, a neat procedural move within a few days of the May 1982 election signalled the new council's impatience to undo the actions of the old. One of the latter's last acts, a formal precaution against the period of administrative uncertainty that an election brings, had been to delegate to the Chief Executive all of the functions 'of the council and every committee and subcommittee thereof which in his opinion do not admit of delay' and were not already covered by other delegations. Those functions were to be exercised with the approval of the Mayor or Deputy Mayor until the new Leader was nominated, and thereafter with the approval of the Leader or Deputy Leader. In a piece of deft management of the *who* and the *how* of the *ultra vires* rule the Chief Executive, most definitely with the approval of the new Leader and after brief discussion with the Solicitor, took the most unusual step of appointing a policy committee. The committee was thus able to hold a special meeting on 17 May, to receive properly 'relevant' financial advice from the Treasurer, and to submit recommendations to the first scheduled council meeting on 25 May for reversing some of the outgoing council's cuts. (Note that this occurred several years before *R v Brent LBC, ex parte Gladbaum* 1989 cast doubt on councils' ability to delegate their power to appoint committees.)

At the policy committee meeting the Treasurer presented a package of restored spending costed at £800,000. £500,000 was the actual cost; the remainder was the associated grant loss. He indicated that this amount would fall within the budgeted balances of £1.65m for 1982–83 but that this amount was already low. Having gone in with a package of £800,000, he came out with one of £1.2m, as members at the meeting restored an additional £250,000, attracting grant loss of some £150,000. This additional £400,000 was rolled back in council, but in July, when the next spending review came round, councillors showed less self-restraint. The Treasurer advised that he had revised several important budgetary estimates, producing a positive year-end balance of £2.5m, up to £2m of which was available for spending. However, 'it would be prudent to leave at least £0.5m' as a balance against contingencies.

The council thought otherwise, and decided to spend it all.

Where, through all of this, was *law,* and in particular the trustee of the rate fund? Certainly there is nothing in the formal council documents to indicate that the council's policies were thought to be running the gauntlet of the *ultra vires* doctrine, nor were there any obvious signs of juridified decision-making, even though *policy* had now turned in a direction which made *law* more problematic.

The explanation lies partly in developments in the *law* and partly in the internal dynamics of the running-in period of a new administration following an election. As to the *law,* both the *given law* of court decisions and the *operative law* of professional opinion and district auditors' rulings in the wake of *Bromley LBC v GLC* (1981) were coming down in favour of the less alarmist interpretations of the House of Lords's decision. Significant court decisions included *R v Merseyside CC, ex parte Great Universal Stores* (February 1982), where a transportation subsidy policy survived a similar challenge to the one that had succeeded in *Bromley,* and *Pickwell v Camden LBC* (April 1982), where the council's settlement of a manual workers' strike survived challenge by the district auditor as being excessive. *The Times* (30 April 1982) wrote that *Pickwell* showed that the test of reasonableness was 'a much broader principle than recent cases might have suggested'. Another important legal change, this one statutory, was the recent repeal by the *Local Government Finance Act 1982* of local authorities' power to levy supplementary rates. With the *given law* no longer providing this purpose-built means for local authorities to respond to major in-year financial changes, these had to be addressed through the *latitude* in other existing statutory provisions.

Within this council, meanwhile, there was the normal interplay of legal advice, financial advice and policy choice described in earlier chapters. The council's new political *disposition* genuinely changed its legal options, making it 'reasonable' for this council, with its own particular view of the importance of certain services, to take decisions that might well have been 'irrational' for its predecessor. The financial advice, moreover, was not strongly inimical to the council's spending preferences. It could well have been less accommodating; things like the Treasurer's revised estimate of housing subsidy were speculative. (The interaction between housing subsidy and block grant was 'extremely complex' – Kleinman, Eastall and Roberts 1990: 403 – so this was a fruitful area for malleable estimates.) However, these did not have to be any more than short-term expedients if the council had the will to put things on a more realistic footing at the 1983 rate-making, as it seemed that it did. In the circumstances, it was natural for officers to allow a certain generosity of financial judgment in favour of the new council until it could set its rate.

The administrative dynamics between officers and members were also changing in the wake of the election. There was, of course, a running-in period when new councillors and a new leadership would work out their roles, and the expectations made of officers might change. On the financial side, officers and members had not yet reached a point of understanding on their respective views of what made financial good sense. So far, members had generally seemed prepared to go beyond whatever the officers suggested, so all that was clear was that the boundaries, wherever they might be, had not yet been reached. A similar adjustment was under way on the legal side. Under the old council the desire to provide useful advice had been increasingly bedevilled by the council's 'internecine hungness' and the resulting unpredictability of its policy choices; this had made it hard to know exactly what the council would need advice about. Under the new council, with its clear new political *disposition*, there was the attraction of knowing what issues of *law* the *policies* were apt to generate. On the other hand, there was also the awareness that *law* was likely sometimes to cause problems. Boynton (1986: 63), a former local authority chief executive, has noted the need for officers to blend accuracy with diplomacy when giving advice as to the unwelcome implications of the *ultra vires* doctrine:

> When the chief executive decides that there are views to be put forward, he should do so in a way which will cause the least embarrassment to the council's leadership. Normally this means giving advice in confidence. The timing of that advice can often be crucial. It should not be given at a time which may result in cutting the ground from under the feet of the majority party, for example, or weaken their position in negotiations with the government.

The trick, of course, lies in working out where the point of accommodation lies. This was something that, in mid-1982, the key actors were feeling their way towards – predominantly in non-financial areas, in fact, for there were several other *policies* at the time that provoked more immediate risks of the council acting *ultra vires*. What was beginning to develop was something that the Solicitor was later to see as an 'enabling' or 'facilitating' approach to the advisory role, with lawyers being careful to ensure that the *ultra vires* rule did not become any more of a complication to the council's *policies* than it needed to be. Rosenberg (1989: 122) appears to imply that it is only 'other chief officers', as distinct from lawyers, who 'feel professionally that their duty to the council should not include such tactics as may narrow its options'. Lawyers, however, are no different from others. As events unfolded in our council there were to be times when the attempt to blend tact and accuracy in the way that Boynton advised would become an acute professional dilemma; explaining the relevant *law* while causing 'the least embarrassment' and avoiding 'cutting the ground from under the feet of the majority party' would not be easy. However in mid-1982 all that was happening was the first step of the process. An adjustment was taking place between a period of political instability, when advice tends to be more abstract and cover more options because a wider range of outcomes is conceivable, to one where the preferred outcomes were known and advice could therefore focus on whether or not specific proposals were *ultra vires*, with the council's *policies* probably receiving the benefit of the doubt in contexts in which there were reasonable legal arguments either way. In the immediate aftermath of the 1982 election the council's spending policies had not yet become so legally problematic as to require the Solicitor to caution against them.

B. Paving the way to a lawful budget

Meanwhile the council's budgetary inclinations for 1983/84 were emerging. In July the policy committee received its first official view of the rate forecast for 1983/84. The Treasurer's preliminary estimate was for a rate increase of 43%, allowing for a little over £3m of uncommitted growth (new spending initiatives that would be absorbed into the base budget for future years). It also assumed that there would be no rent increase, a matter which, in the light of the advice given the previous year that a 'nil' increase was 'almost certain to be held unlawful', was obviously going to demand legal attention at some point. The committee was not overawed by the size of the projected rate increase. Officers did, however, begin to lay down on paper what could become, if need arose, the council's justification in *law* for its expected decisions. The committee's report to council notes:

> We expressed the view that the increases in the rate forecast arise from the need to make proper provision within the budget for adequate levels of services, balances, wage settlements, interest and

> inflation rates etc. all of which have been reduced to an unacceptable level by the previous administration.

It has been noted already that the service-based justification for spending levels has, in law, a good theoretical founding. Indeed, the legal advice that the Department of Environment's lawyers had circulated less than six months before, analysing *Bromley LBC v GLC* (1981), had confirmed this approach.

By the time of the second rate forecast, in December 1982, the council's main expenditure option was for £88m, some £19m above the target that the government had set, generating a rate increase estimated at 62.2% and raising the prospect that grant might be lost entirely. Still the conundrum had not been answered of how far the council would go, nor of how far was too far in legal and financial terms. Elements of the Labour group, here as in other parts of the country (see Lansley, Goss and Wolmar 1989: 19–21), were striving for higher spending and a more generalized campaign of 'local socialist' opposition to the government's policies, and it was not yet certain which view would prevail.

It was, nonetheless, a time when official indications began to appear in council documents that there were constraints of *law* involved in the council's budget-making. The budget forecast in December had not made any provision for balances, but the Treasurer warned that this was a state that could not last, and that a minimum level would be £1.5m. The district auditor also pitched in, highlighting in his statutory report for a previous year that

> The general rate fund balance is the council's working balance and it is financially imprudent to make no provision for such a balance.
>
> It is moreover appropriate to remind the council of the duty imposed upon them by section 2 of the General Rate Act 1967 to make a sufficient rate. The section requires rating authorities to make such rates as will be sufficient to meet their total estimated net expenditure 'together with such additional amount as is in the opinion of the rating authority required to cover expenditure previously incurred, or to meet contingencies, or to defray any expenditure which may fall to be defrayed before the date on which the moneys to be received in respect of the next subsequent rate ... will become available'.

As the final stages of the budget-making process unfolded, with the rate support grant and penalty figures now known, the Labour group's internal debate about how far to take its opposition to the government resolved itself in favour of legal prudence. Those who had been arguing for the adoption of an *ultra vires* unbalanced budget lost the argument. Officers therefore never had to advise (as they had discreetly done in other political circumstances in both early 1978 and late 1979) that such a policy would be unlawful. This particular potential problem of *law* therefore receded into the background, and the council's formal documents carefully paved the way for a high budget to be adopted by means that would withstand potential legal challenge.

C. Rents: a 0% increase?

One part of this was the decision on rent levels. The council's manifesto had promised a 0% increase. The government was assuming, for housing subsidy purposes, an 85p increase. The difference between the two was £4.7m, made up of £1.8m in loss of rent income and £2.9m in associated loss of block grant. For the policy committee meeting on 22 February 1983, the Solicitor reworked the advice he had given the previous year, making a few minor changes and one striking omission: the explicit assessment of the degrees of legal risk attached to various rent options. The report still said that 'if the decision were to lead to a loss of central government grant or a material increase in the Housing Revenue Account deficit, then there would be some risk of a successful challenge to the legality of the decision'. It also still said that 'The extent of that risk would increase the greater were any grant loss or increase in the HRA deficit'. Notable for its absence, though, was the statement that with an increase of less than £1.40 (equivalent to inflation) the risk of unlawfulness was 'considerable, growing rapidly the lower the increase becomes', and that a 'nil' increase (the council's current preference) was 'Almost certain to be held unlawful'.

Why was the *operative law* of rent-setting, the *law* as presented to councillors, so different in 1983? Why was a 'nil' increase 'almost certain to be held unlawful' in 1982, but apparently acceptable now? Obviously the *policy* had changed – which for some may simply lend itself to the cynical interpretation that local authorities make sure they receive the legal advice they want. This interpretation would be inaccurate, however, for the change of *policy* had generated other changes in the ever-unfolding interaction between *law* and *policy*.

First, as a matter of form, there was no need this year for legal advice to compare alternatives in terms of their *vires*. In 1982, the political situation had been volatile; which of the rent options the council would choose was unpredictable, so the advice compared them. In 1983, however, there was only one real option on the table and only one legal question to be asked: is a decision not to increase rents this year *intra vires*, yes or no? If the answer was yes, nothing else mattered. According to the Solicitor the answer was yes, as long as the council approached the decision correctly.

One key factor in this was that the financial facts had changed since 1982. The large rent increases of previous years had made a difference, and the Treasurer's Department made no particular effort to have the 1983 policy changed; it was financially manageable. As for the legal issue of the 'balance' between rent and rates, the policy committee's report to council in March 1983 made a special point of noting that increased rents in recent years 'had been an important element in forcing inflation to be higher for council tenants', and that

> (5) No rent increase would restore the balance between income from rents and rates to that which existed prior to 1978/79 when the Conservative Government began reducing housing subsidy to local authorities. We feel that that is the correct balance and that any additional expenditure arising should be met from the rates.

By inference, this countered Counsel's inflation-based argument the previous year that an increase of less than £1.40 was suspect because 'there seems no reason ... to shelter all tenants from inflation at a substantial cost to ratepayers who are subject to the same inflation'.

It is also interesting that the committee's minuted justification for its decision does not refer to the manifesto commitment not to increase rents. Lawyers who had followed the decision of the House of Lords in *Bromley LBC v GLC* (1981) and the grounds on which it had been distinguished in *R v Merseyside CC, ex parte Great Universal Stores* (1982) cannot have been unaware that blindly following manifesto commitments was a sure route to an *ultra vires* decision. This commitment, important though it must have been to councillors, was simply not mentioned.

At the end of the day, though, the fact is that the Solicitor was comfortable with a 0% increase in 1983 as a one-off decision. He would not have been surprised if it had been challenged (it was not), but he *would* have been surprised if the challenge had succeeded.

D. Rates: the shell game

The 1983 rate decision was taken at the same meetings as the rent decision, and with similarly elaborate documentation of the council's reasoning. The minutes of the policy committee record that at its meeting on 22 February the Leader 'drew attention to a number of major issues to be taken into consideration' and that the Treasurer 'emphasised the need for the council to take into particular consideration the reasonableness of the level of rate to be levied' in the light of the various factors set out in his report.

The spending plans outlined in February 1983 were slightly more ambitious than the December ones that had produced an estimated rate increase of over 60%, for spending of £88m. Now, however, their estimated cost had reduced to £74m, and the necessary rate increase to only 29.4%. The policy committee's report to council on 8 March 1983 complained vigorously that one-third of the rate increase was due to the 'plundering of the balances by the last administration to produce an artificially low budget in an election year', and that 'having established an artificially low budget, that then acts as the base on which government targets for 1983/84 are calculated. Consequently our penalties are among the highest in the country'. A similar situation was to confront a newly elected Labour majority in Liverpool a year later, and evoked the sympathy of commentators such as Midwinter (1985: 26–7), Parkinson (1985: 87–99) and Carmichael (1995: ch. 4).

The policy committee unashamedly pronounced 'the introduction of imaginative accounting procedures' as one of the means adopted to keep the rate increase down, and detailed a particularly clear example. Four large year-end accounting measures – 'Allow for shortfall in spending'; 'Further allowance for back years housing subsidy'; 'Revised method of calculating interest credited to the Rate Fund for use of money to fund capital expenditure during the year'; 'Transfer to General Rate Fund of capitalised interest on loans to housing associations' – increased the council's closing balance for 1982/83 to almost £4m. This allowed £3m to be paid into a newly established 'housing repairs account', as to which: 'The Solicitor has advised that the creation of such a fund is legal'. This, in turn, saved the council more than £3m overall, because the payment into the fund at the end of 1982/83 attracted penalties at a much lower rate than payment of the money on repairs in 1983/84. It is worth pointing out, incidentally, that though the Solicitor's advice on the housing revenue account was uncontroversial according to the *operative law* of the day, and was consistent with the government's view at the time, the government was later to change its mind, leading to corrective legislation in the *Local Government Finance Act 1987* and to the council's thoroughly complicated rate-making exercise that year (below: Ch. 9; see also Loughlin, 1996: 292–7).

Another significant element in the council's efforts to maintain its overall spending plans while keeping its rate increase closer to 30% than to 60% was referred to as 'capitalization of revenue spending'. Driven again by the different treatment of capital and revenue spending under the *Local Government, Planning and Land Act 1980*, a concerted effort was under way to identify items that were capital in nature (the Treasurer's working definition was 'expenditure which results in the creation of a capital asset which will be of benefit beyond the year in which the expenditure is incurred'), and could therefore be funded out of capital resources. For a council facing the level of penalties that this one was in 1983, re-classifying the spending had dramatic effects. Every £1 that could be capitalized would reduce revenue spending by £1 and generate (in rough figures) an additional £1.50 in grant. Parts of this spending on the council's housing programme would, indeed, attract government subsidy rather than penalties once capitalized. Capitalized payments still had to be funded, of course, but compared to revenue spending capital spending was highly cost-effective.

Capitalization was not new to the 1983 budget. The old council, the previous year, had used it heavily in its drive to keep its pre-election rate increase down to 10%, and the new one this year expanded the practice. Salaries of staff like architects, valuers and conveyancers whose work had a 'capital' element was already being capitalized, and some employees were required to apportion their time and segregate the 'capital' element from the 'revenue' element. Newly identified for capitalization this year were several items relating to the council's major housing repair programmes. The revenue saving, net of debt charges, would be £2.5m, with the additional block grant benefit not specified in the report, though presumably in the £4m range. The Treasurer added, though, the reminder that under the *Local Government, Planning and Land Act 1980* there was an overall finite limit to the council's total capital expenditure in any one year. The council's capital expenditure (more accurately, its 'prescribed expenditure') could not exceed a sum derived primarily from its government allocation and its capital receipts. The more 'revenue spending' the council capitalized, the less money would be available within that finite limit for its preferred spending on bricks and mortar.

E. Applied ingenuity

Was that 'finite limit', however, really quite that 'finite'? Or was there legal *latitude* by which the limits could be stretched? In theory the limit was finite, in the sense that actual cash figures could be attached to all of its constituent parts. However, there was some potential *latitude* available within the legal theory. The most obvious was that the formula under the *Local Government, Planning and Land Act 1980* was partly based on the volume of the council's capital receipts. By generating capital receipts, therefore, the most straightforward method being by selling property, the council could increase its spending power.

This council, however, found this option unattractive as a matter of *policy*. Though sales of council houses were mandatory under the right to buy provisions of the *Housing Act 1980* (much though the council disliked the fact), and were to be a large and steady source of capital receipts, other sales were discretionary, and the new council had moved quickly, in June 1982, to cancel the previous administration's policy of discretionary sales. The council would now sell only to housing associations and co-operatives.

There were other assets, however, towards which the council was less tenderly disposed, among them its holdings as a mortgage lender. These were residential mortgages, most of them advanced in earlier years to assist residents in buying houses, some of them now being advanced in connection with 'right to buy' sales, and in November 1982 the finance sub-committee approved in principle an arrangement for the transfer of £4m of these to a building society. The arrangement was straightforward in legal terms. The council would invite the borrowers to switch their mortgages to the building society, and, as the transfers occurred, the building society would buy out the council's interest. This was clearly an *intra vires* transaction which was good for the council (which wanted the money), good for the building society (which wanted the business), and good for the purchasers (since the building society's interest rate was lower than the council's at the time). The council's lack of legal *autonomy* in relation to this exercise was compensated for by the availability of a willing financial partner and by the real prospect that the borrowers, around whom everything else revolved, would have good reason to co-operate.

As things were to turn out, it was to be another two years before the transfer of residential mortgages occurred, by which time the scheme had developed several 'creative' features. First came a variant in which a bank would purchase the mortgages and would guarantee at the outset the total payment to the council – a great improvement from the council's point of view. Then came several versions in which the council would get a better financial return, but the disposal would not be absolute and the council would remain responsible for managing the mortgages on the funding source's behalf. The best of these variants, finally adopted in February and March 1985 in a flurry of conveyancing paperwork and buttressed by Counsel's opinion as to its *vires* and financial effect, was one promoted by the ever-resourceful Company B, with whom the Treasurer had continued to deal, to mutual advantage, since the groundbreaking 'happy accident' of the new municipal offices.

Let us return, though, to 1982, when another initiative that Company B was assisting was the creation of a council-owned development company (henceforth 'Council Co.'). This company had its nominal origins in the local Labour party's 1982 manifesto proposal for an 'Economic Development Board' (Cochrane and Clark 1990 describe local authorities' early economic development initiatives), but in late 1982 and early 1983 the preoccupation had come to be the part that such a company might be able to play in relation to capital financing.

The first question, of course, was whether it was *intra vires* at all for the council to set up the company. The Solicitor (and Leading Counsel) said yes, relying primarily on the 'free 2p' provision in s.137 of the *Local Government Act 1972*, the power to spend money on things not permitted by other Acts, rather than the 'incidental powers' provision in s.111 that others sometimes relied on (see Department of the Environment and Welsh Office 1989: 5; Sharland, 1997: 42). Recent *given law*, in the compelling form of the House of Lords's decision in *Manchester City Council v Greater Manchester Metropolitan County Council* (1980), had approved the use of s.137 by the county council, which was not an education authority, to create and fund a trust to cover private school fees, and the parallels to establishing Council Co. seemed clear.

Next came the conundrum of control. It was 'essential', the Solicitor advised, that Council Co. be in law and fact an independent entity, and not just a 'puppet', if it was to serve its intended purpose within the capital controls. Practically, though, the council also wanted to be assured that Council Co. would act as the council wished. With the assistance of a leading firm of City solicitors a management structure was devised that reconciled these conflicting imperatives.

What, then, were the transactions in which Council Co. was expected to be involved? The plan in early 1983 was for the redevelopment of two industrial sites, one for letting, the other for occupation by the council's direct labour organization. The central legal elements were some interconnecting leases. The first was from the council to a merchant bank at a peppercorn (nominal) rent; the bank would finance the development on the site and lease the completed development back to the council. The council would then sub-lease the site to Council Co., but Council Co. would appoint the council as its agent to let and manage the site, with most of the rent accruing to the council under its management agreement with Council Co.

The full legal intricacies do not need to be explored. Suffice it to say that they built on the lessons learned with the new municipal offices and added some refinements. One element that does need explanation, though, since it recurs several times in this book, is the idea of the 'notional capital receipt' under leasing arrangements.

A notional capital receipt was one that the *Local Government, Planning and Land Act 1980* deemed to arise when a long lease was granted, whether or not a payment – an 'actual capital receipt' – was received at the same time. The practical value of notional capital receipts was to increase the council's ability to spend its actual capital receipts. Under the legislation, only a specified portion of a council's capital receipts was 'useable' each year. If the portion was 40% and the council had £1m of capital receipts, £400,000 was useable. If, though, the council had £1m of actual capital receipts as well as £1m of notional capital receipts, it now had £2m of capital receipts, and could spend £800,000 of the actual £1m it had received. If enough notional capital receipts were available, actual capital receipts could be fully spent in the year they were received. Leases were adaptable instruments for this purpose. A lease of 20 years plus a day (remember that number?) produced a notional capital receipt. A lease of 20 years minus a day did not. Actual cash could be timed to be received when it was most needed, as long as the non-*autonomous* council and its financial source could come to terms. Careful planning of the length of leases and leasebacks and the timing of payments could affect the council's financial position significantly.

Another essential element in the Council Co. arrangement was the council's power to make grants and loans for specific statutory purposes. This was important because most disposals of land by the council to Council Co. had to be at open market value, and grants or loans from the council enabled Council Co. to pay the market value that the council had to obtain. This was obviously a convenient alignment of Council Co.'s needs with the council's powers, and there may well have been some within the council who were more impressed by the convenience than the legal logic. For the officers most closely involved, though, the *law* of the arrangements was critical. Making sure that dealings with Council Co. were *intra vires* in all respects was an essential part of living with the annual finite limits of the *Local Government,*

Planning and Land Act 1980. Especially if Council Co. arrangements were extensively used (as was contemplated at the time, though events turned out otherwise), the whole edifice of the council's capital programme might come to grief if the details of particular transactions were not done right. The technicalities were also important to the council's funding sources. The council could not act *autonomously* in any of its capital transactions. To act *intra vires* in its own mind was not enough. It also had to recognize that its potential financial partners had a legitimate interest in ensuring that whatever was done was justified in law. Properly structured and properly implemented procedures were necessary in keeping the funding available.

With that thought in mind, let us turn to another major step forward in the council's rapidly evolving engagement with the *operative law* of the *Local Government, Planning and Land Act 1980*. It occurred swiftly and unexpectedly in response to a most unlikely stimulus.

In mid-1982, the Department of the Environment became concerned that local authority capital spending was, of all things, too low. Lewis and Harrison (1983: 60) write, with bemusement, that 'Ministers were apparently surprised, but not grateful. On the contrary, they thought something should be done about it'. In October, therefore, local authorities were invited to submit fresh bids for capital allocations. This was doubly odd since, as the Audit Commission (1985) was to point out, 'because of the nature of capital expenditure and the long lead-time required for implementation, large additional allocations late in a financial year can rarely be used effectively'. With the able assistance of Company B, however, our council (and at least one other; see Audit Commission 1985: 13–14) found a way. Enter the so-called 'advance funding scheme', an arrangement under which, in a great rush before the end of the financial year, the council applied for and received additional capital allocations of £12m from the government, borrowed the money these allocations permitted, and paid the whole amount out to a company jointly established by itself and Company B (henceforth 'Jointly-owned Co.') for use on capital projects. Legally, a wholly independent company would have been preferable, but for members, once more, having substantial influence over the company that was handling the money was important, and the Solicitor considered that joint ownership was acceptable.

Again a brief explanation of the advance funding scheme is useful, for it shows once more the way in which the legally, the financially and the politically possible were evolving together under the *Local Government, Planning and Land Act 1980*, and each new step gained more ground for the council as its new political majority tried to take it in a radically different direction than its predecessor.

Compared to the new municipal offices and the Council Co. arrangements a major difference was that the advance funding scheme would now include a whole programme of capital works, not just specific major projects. The first step, though, was that for each separate contract in the programme, the council would accept a tender in the ordinary way. Each time this was done – and all £12m worth of tenders had to be accepted by 31 March 1983 – the council would pay the contract price to Jointly-owned Co. Jointly-owned Co., pending the need to pay contractors, would pay the funds to an investment company (wholly owned by Company B) for investment until payments to contractors were due, at which time the investment company would return the money to Jointly-owned Co. and Jointly-owned Co. would pay the contractors. A legal twist which made it easier for the council to ensure it spent all the money by 31 March 1983 was its general ability under contract law to 'novate' existing contracts – that is to say, to have the builder under an existing contract with the council agree that Jointly-owned Co. would take over the council's rights and obligations under the contract. A further refinement, this one emerging in the dealings with the investment subsidiary of Company B, was that while the money was being held by the investment company, interest on the investments was covenanted to the council, to be paid into the general rate fund. Tax considerations originally prompted this, but (excuse the pun) the outcome was income, and thus the discovery of another area of *latitude* and potential flexibility in the tools available to the Treasurer in negotiating the swiftly evolving *operative law* of the *Local Government, Planning and Land Act 1980.*

F. Progress report, 31 March 1983

Clearly the council was by now well and truly into the realms of 'creative' financing. It is worth standing back for a moment, though, to analyse the various financial decisions that it was taking in late 1982 and early 1983, for they illustrate a variety of different dimensions to the ways in which *law* was sustaining the results that the council's *policy* demanded.

Underlying everything was the proposition of *law* and of *policy* that the council's budget had to balance. Some in the Labour group had argued against adopting a balanced budget, but they had lost the argument. The fundamental premiss that a budget must balance was therefore driving much of the financial action, but this year (things began to change the following year) the notion of the balanced budget was still operating at an *intuitive* level, without people considering closely what it really meant, as a matter of *law*, to say that a budget must 'balance'.

Another key premiss, this one carefully *reasoned*, was that the council's budget would not become *ultra vires* simply because it incurred a loss of grant. Here the *operative law* as the Solicitor had outlined it both before and after *Bromley LBC v GLC* (1981) had been reinforced by the subsequent *given law* of *R v Merseyside CC, ex parte Great Universal Stores* (1982). Loughlin (1985: 67) seems to suggest that the impact of *Bromley LBC v GLC* (1981) should be seen as limited both in time and in scope: 'Although this decision has been confined to its facts and has not been followed by the lower courts, for a critical period in 1982/83 it exerted an influence over certain aspects of local authority policy-making'. In our particular council, however, and presumably elsewhere also, its effects were widespread and enduring. *Bromley* had identified a problem: potentially *ultra vires* budgets. Other cases had validated the antidote: *meticulous* legal decision-making. In order to avoid the problem one had to keep taking the antidote, and our council was to continue to do so for years to come.

Set against this general background, the major items that have been described in recent pages – capitalization of revenue spending, accounting adjustments and special funds, the sale of mortgages, council-sponsored companies, lease/leaseback development funding, the advance purchase scheme – display a variety of different characteristics.

Capitalization was probably the area in which the law was least actively involved. Though *law* determined the financial consequences that flowed from both capital and revenue spending, the decisions on what could be capitalized were entirely those of the financial officers, based on *their* interpretations of the concepts.

Law was, by contrast, more directly involved in several of the accounting adjustments and special funds on the revenue side. On the surface there were features like the specific advice about the legality of the 'housing repairs account'. Operating beneath the surface, though, was the fact that these kinds of adjustments, though 'creative' and no doubt contrary to what the government had expected from the *Local Government, Planning and Land Act 1980*, were the natural working out of the legal and financial logic of the legislation. This was highlighted by the Audit Commission's comment that the Act created a 'perverse incentive' (Audit Commission 1984: 52) for local authorities to spend up to their expenditure targets, whether they really wanted to or not, in order to preserve their grant entitlements, and that by using devices such as special funds to optimize their spending levels for particular years, local authorities were responding 'rapidly, predictably and (from their point of view) sensibly to the pressures induced by the uncertainties ...' (Audit Commission 1984: 23). Other authors (Smith 1983: 47; Midwinter 1985: 32) made much the same point.

On the capital side, the council's varying ways of managing the theoretically finite limit on its annual capital spending showed even greater diversity. The sale of council mortgages, at least in its original 1983 form, went thoroughly with the flow of the *Local Government, Planning and Land Act 1980*. The Act clearly contemplated the sale of council assets to fund capital spending. By contrast, the lease/leaseback transactions that were then envisaged went very much against the flow. From the point of view of *vires* they were analysed more closely, the more so because they relied in part on another legal innovation, creating and dealing with a council-owned company.

The large advance funding scheme, by contrast, fell somewhere in between. It was an intriguing and successful attempt to do the virtually impossible, to incur major capital expenditure in a hurry, yet it was done in response to urgings from the government and was based upon an expansion of the council's capital spending power by entirely conventional means: the receipt of an additional allocation from the government.

One way or another, though, the end result was that by March 1983, only ten months after the Left gained proper control, the council had not only made a major change in *policy*, it had also identified major elements of the legal building blocks with which it might be theoretically possible to sustain that *policy* against the seemingly inhospitable framework of the *Local Government, Planning and Land Act 1980*. The complicated relationship between the capital and revenue accounts was being established, each being exploited alternately for all possible benefits they could produce. A preparedness to enter into novel, and potentially complex, legal relationships had also developed. The council was treading delicately, for it and others like it were breaking new legal ground, and there was no firm understanding of what was *ultra vires* and what was not. The atmosphere was one of secretiveness, partly because of the uncertain legal situation, but partly also out of concern that if local authorities were successful in finding legal vehicles that worked, the government might step in to take them away.

It must be said, however, that this exploration of the legal borderlines of the council's powers was, in a sense, something that its officers had a positive obligation to undertake. Given the mismatch between the council's needs, as the new majority saw them, and its resources, the council and its officers were duty-bound to investigate the merits of potentially attractive financial and legal schemes, and when they found an idea that worked, the council was fully entitled to squeeze it for the last drop of legal or financial advantage. The caveat, of course, was that the council should not cross that uncertain line that separates the *intra vires* from the *ultra vires,* but as things stood in March 1983, it had not done so. More *latitude* had been identified than had previously been recognized, and as long as nothing happened to upset the apple-cart of *operative law* that had developed, the key questions for the future would revolve less around whether the council had the statutory power to do these things – it already considered it did – than around whether it would be able to find the financial partners it would need, since it did not have the *autonomy* to proceed alone.

All in all, then, though the *given law* had changed little in the preceding 12 months, by 31 March 1983 the *Local Government, Planning and Land Act 1980* had begun to look very different, and far more varied and accommodating to the incoming council's *policies* than had once seemed likely.

7
Pressing Ahead: The 1984 Budget

The financial pressure continued, and grew, in the 12 months leading up to the 1984 budget. Bad news came in April 1983, when the government decided against funding £258,000 of Partnership schemes, leaving the council to find £194,000 to replace the government's 75% contribution and £316,000 to cover the associated grant loss. The policy committee's report to council notes that 'Our officers are pursuing alternative ways of avoiding the penalties, so that the increased funding is limited to the £194,000'.

Worse news came in June. Another general election was held that month, and the Conservatives were re-elected. Clearly there was no hope of relief from existing central policies for the foreseeable future. The Conservatives' manifesto, moreover, included the controversial proposals to abolish the GLC and the metropolitan county councils and to introduce what would become known as rate-capping. Most local authorities would rightly have seen themselves as extremely unlikely candidates for rate-capping. Though they may have disapproved of this prospective new *given law* – most local authorities did (see Lansley, Goss and Wolmar 1989: 35) – they did not have to be preoccupied with what to do about it. For our council, by contrast, which immediately and equally rightly identified itself as a likely target, the situation was entirely different. Its *policy* had to be to prepare for the legislation in ways that would make the impact as manageable as possible.

Preparing for this new *given law* was in principle the same 'in with the new' exercise described in Chapter 4, but in practice it had some important differences. Though it still involved the mechanical process of feeding new *law* into the council's activities in accordance with the four 'W's of the *ultra vires* rule, the exercise in 1979 and 1980 had been the archetypal one of understanding the new rules so as to be able to live by them. With rate-capping, by contrast, the aim was not merely to understand, but to deflect its impact as much as possible.

Attempting this would produce a year of contrasts that emphasized how the *ultra vires* rule can affect closely related issues differently, even within a single government at a single time within a single context of *policy*. On the one hand the council found itself gearing up for the unfamiliar and unwelcome new *given law* that was to become the *Rates Act 1984*. On the other hand, the existing *law* of the *Local Government, Planning and Land Act 1980*, though still evolving, was beginning to settle down in the new contours established in the wake of the vigorous *policy* change of the previous year.

A. Intimations of a rate-cap

As Young (1983b: 5) has pointed out, the attempt to impose central control on local authorities can often be self-defeating, because it 'elevates the subversion of central directives to a major goal for implementers'. Indeed so. Baldwin (1994: 161) comments that 'Using a rule to control discretion at one point ... will ... often result in the displacement of the discretion to another point in the process.' True again; Baldwin calls this 'displacement of discretion'. It would take time, however, for the government to put those rules in place, and as McBarnet and Whelan (1999b: 107) rightly say, 'The inevitable lag between recognising an issue and implementing a regulation can provide a temporary gap, or indeed, be treated as a *pre-implementation licence*', an opportunity to take full advantage of the old law before the new law bites. Our council was to do just that. Soon after the 1983 general election it became clear that the government's hopes to have rate-capping in place for 1984/85 were unrealistic (*The Times*, 26 June 1983). The council therefore had one more budget at its disposal, and almost two full years, before its legal *latitude* was restricted by the yet unknown new *law*.

During this period, however, our council was far from a free agent. Unlike the private sector bodies that Baldwin and McBarnet and Whelan studied, the council was a government operating under public law. Rules about *what, why, who* and *how* applied to every potential measure of displaced discretion it contemplated and to any attempt to enjoy its pre-implementation licence. McBarnet and Whelan's discussion of 'good faith' (1999b: 99–100) can be used to highlight the difference:

> Companies may look to the law to decide what they ought to do or to assess what they might get away with doing. They may believe in

> good faith that their approach is legally the right one. They may take a more pragmatic approach, adopting what they see as a not unreasonable reading of law or regulations, which suits their interests. They may see themselves as sailing close to the wind – or even in their own judgement as on the wrong side of the line, but find some basis for arguing a case in the hope of getting away with it. All, however, are likely to present their arguments in good faith.
>
> Distinguishing genuine good faith from a presentation of it is not easy to do. In both cases the same evidence is produced – pointing to statute and standard, to auditor support, to accountants' and barristers' opinions. Supporting opinions might be easily found, or they might have been accomplished only after extensive 'opinion shopping'. Only the supporting opinions, not the adverse ones, or the shopping for them, will be disclosed. Good faith may be presented, but not in good faith.
>
> Whether companies are arguing in 'real' good faith or not, however, the issue is the same. Are regulations breached or not?

For a local authority, though, the *why* of the *ultra vires* rule makes that closing paragraph a contradiction in terms. Unless a council is acting in actual good faith, the regulation *is* breached, regardless of what the regulation says. Motive counts, and the only acceptable motive is one that derives from statute.

Procedure also counts, and this, too, presents challenges for a body operating under public law rules. For the most part the council would want to act discreetly in preparing for rate-capping. At least, this would have been the officers' preference, though the Treasurer has commented (at interview) that members sometimes had an inconvenient urge to spread the good news to their friends elsewhere if a successful scheme was developed. To act completely discreetly would be hard, though, when the *who* and the *how* of the *ultra vires* rule required some decisions to be taken in public forums, such as committees, on the basis of 'relevant considerations', and with the Opposition present. Acting discreetly, moreover, can sometimes shade into secretiveness, and secretiveness into furtiveness. The more one hides things, the more one may feel one has something to hide, and things which, in happier times, might be done without a second thought take on the aura of the questionable. At the same time, though, one must not to be too distracted by the mere *aura* of questionability. Things may be done furtively yet still be legitimate. The time was one when difficult judgments would have to be made in sometimes delicate situations, and for the council's officers, maintaining their professional objectivity would be at a premium.

B. Running silent

The council's tight-lipped approach to its 1984 budget was evident at the first review of income and expenditure for the current financial year in July 1983. This gave few details and concentrated on the uncertainties. While approving £475,000 of new spending (plus £775,000 of grant loss) for 1983/4 as being within its estimated closing balances, the policy committee adopted an interim guideline of 'net nil growth' for 1984. That is to say, any new spending initiatives, or 'growth', for 1984/85 would have to be offset by savings. Noting the likelihood of tight expenditure targets in 1984/85 and the strong possibility of rate-capping in 1985/86, the committee reported to council that 'Because of the lack of detailed information it is extremely difficult for us to develop a financial strategy for 1984/85 and 1985/86 at this time'. The reference to 1985/86 is worth noting. It was unusual for the council to plan two years ahead. The prospect of rate-capping was casting a long shadow.

The second review of income and expenditure, in October, was similarly opaque. By this time the government's target figure for the council's spending was known: £70.5m, derived by applying a 6% reduction to the current year's budget. The report stated that the implications of this were severe, though they could not be assessed in detail before the government announced other key elements of the financial puzzle. The council confirmed its 'net nil growth' strategy for the 1984 budget, and for the current financial year approved a mere £245,000 of additional spending (plus £400,000 grant loss).

Further information on the expected grant and penalty for 1984 emerged later in October. The national total of rate support grant was to be lower in real terms than in 1983/84, and the penalties were to be more severe. At the upper levels of the council's spending, every £1 spent would cost ratepayers £3.40, since the government would deduct £2.40 in grant. The council's spending plans were clearly in the range at which rate support grant would be lost entirely, yet still there was no concrete rate projection for 1984/85. Two months later, in response to a question from a member of the public at the December council meeting, the Leader casually mentioned that the council's projected spending for the coming year was about £15m over the government's target, and that even with a standstill budget rates could rise by over 27%. A passing comment like this, though, was far less than the formal rate forecast that the Treasurer had produced in comparable circumstances the previous year. The Leader also remarked at that meeting that the council was 'at an early stage in the budget process to determine next year's rate'. Given that the date was now 13 December, it might seem rather late to be still 'early in the process'. What that comment reflected, though, was not so much a matter of uncertainty about the budget as about what the blend of *intra vires* financial measures and transactions would be that would permit the council's spending plans to be funded.

C. Deflecting the pressures

'We are also examining our budgets line by line', said the Leader, 'and will be investigating ways in which we can limit as far as possible the impact of this Government's action on the people and business of [the area] through their services and rates'. One exercise that was under way, a public sector version of displaced discretion, was an attempt to find new statutory means of achieving existing objectives, and thereby deflecting the pressures of the council's financial predicament. The decisions the council was considering were not the central components of its financial decision-making, but they deserve brief mention as complementary explorations of the *latitude* under other statutory powers that could be pressed into service to relieve the financial strain.

One example was the sale of vacant substandard properties to housing associations and co-operatives, who were to convert and improve them for special needs housing. The proposed terms of sale were to include a right for the council to nominate the future occupiers where appropriate, restrictive covenants preventing the properties being used for unapproved purposes, and rights of pre-emption under which the council could buy the properties back if the associations ever sold. The combined effect was that the properties would remain in the public rented section indefinitely. The council obviously did not have the legal *autonomy* to make this happen by itself, but in this case willing and politically sympathetic purchasers were at hand in the form of the associations, and by November projects amounting to roughly £2.5m were being negotiated.

Inconveniently, though, even the combined *autonomies* of the council and the associations were not enough this time. The council's right of pre-emption required Department of the Environment approval, which was not forthcoming, and the restrictive covenants were unacceptable to the Housing Corporation, which was the source of the associations' funding. The council's finance sub-committee decided to swallow hard, to 'place on record its serious concern at the attitude of the Housing Corporation', and to proceed with the sales anyway, being reasonably confident that the housing associations and co-operatives would not sell unless they ran into severe financial difficulties.

A second example of the council attaining its objectives while deflecting the financial pressures was its 'co-operative homesteading' scheme, a method for getting dilapidated properties rehabilitated at minimum cost and maximum benefit for the council. Referring to it briefly at the council meeting of March 1984 the Chair of Housing said: 'It is a relatively simple scheme but for reasons of its survival I am not particularly anxious to talk about it at great length ...'. From the details he gave, though ('a scheme like this where we can co-operate with people buying, them putting in a small sum of money and the council giving them grants to bring the house to a habitable standard for families or groups of people sharing'), one gathers that the basic elements were that the council sold the property at a low price, the new owners applied for improvement grants (which were heavily subsidized by the government and were generously treated at the time for rate support grant calculation purposes), and the council retained enough control over who subsequently occupied the property to make the exercise worth its while. Each of these three elements raised possible issues of *law*, but overall it was accepted as a means of getting some properties repaired, and back into the kind of use that the council wanted for them, with a substantial part of the cost being paid by the government.

D. Judicial review?

For the first time this year, the council also seriously investigated another *law*-based avenue to deflecting the pressures of the government's spending targets and penalties: judicial review proceedings challenging their legality. Several authorities were contemplating this. The targets and penalties were so severe as to lead people to consider whether they were 'unreasonable' in the legal sense, whether they were, essentially, asking local authorities to do the impossible, and then punishing them for not doing it. A similar suggestion was that the courts might hold a target to be unlawful if it was so low that a local authority could not even carry out its statutory duties if it observed the target.

Contemplating litigation had a clear impact on the way in which the council conducted itself. If the council chose to 'judicialize' matters by turning to the courts, it would also have to 'juridify'. If it did not wish to prejudice its chance of success in litigation, it would have to proceed in a *meticulous* way that would withstand scrutiny in court.

The process started in late November, when the Solicitor advised the Chief Executive that if the council was serious about taking legal action, which he thought it should be, it had to do something soon. The deadline for responding to the government's October consultation document on rate support grant was approaching, and the council had not yet responded. The legal danger here was that if the council did not take its opportunity to improve its position through consultation, the government might have a defence to a legal action. The Leader was consulted and representations were duly made.

They were unsuccessful. When, in mid-December, the government laid its rate support grant report before Parliament, the effect was even more severe than anticipated. The Solicitor was instructed to challenge it if possible. Counsel advised that a claim could be brought on the basis that the rate support grant target had to be attainable, and that the Secretary of State had wrongly failed to have regard to this. He did not think the prospects of success were large, but he considered that the potential gains if the case was won justified bringing it.

If this part of Counsel's advice sat well with the council, another part would not. Success in the case, Counsel suggested, would depend on showing not only that the Secretary of State had wrongfully failed to have regard to the attainability of the target, but also that the target was in fact unattainable. Counsel emphasized that for this purpose, all options should be considered to be open – rent increases, privatization, service reductions, anything. The Solicitor stressed Counsel's views to the Leadership: 'The appraisal really must be an objective one, not a political one'. It should include the possibility of making cuts. 'If the appraisal were less than objective, then the credibility of the unattainable claim could be readily undermined'. Compelled to proceed by juridified method to preserve any prospect of a judicial remedy, the Leader agreed that the politically distasteful attainability exercise should proceed.

Ultimately, adding insult to injury, it failed. Though the Treasurer's Department had originally advised that the target was indeed unattainable, subsequent analysis suggested that it *might* be attainable if – and this was a highly significant if – Counsel were right in saying that success depended on showing that the target required unacceptable reductions *in traditional services*. However, the council was also much involved in untraditional areas, and its study found that if the council limited itself to preserving traditional services and complying with its statutory duties, this could probably be managed within the target.

In the face of this, the potential legal action petered out. The council watched as Hackney LBC took the government to court on the basis of the unattainability of the target, and eventually, two weeks after our council had made its rate for 1984/85, lost (*R v Secretary of State for the Environment, ex parte Hackney LBC* 1984, appeal dismissed 1985). The new *given law* of the Hackney decision was a setback; the Solicitor considered that it was even more favourable to the government than the government's own argument had been. According to Forbes J it would be open to the Secretary of State 'to issue guidance indicating a level of expenditure which he knew was impossible to achieve... . It had not been Parliament's intention that the guidance level should necessarily bear any relationship to actual expenditure.' The judgment did, though, contain a silver lining. In deciding that the target did not have to be attainable Forbes J also mentioned that 'It was clearly in the secretary of state's mind that any shortfall in revenue could be made up by levying a higher rate', a comment that emphasized that it was up to local authorities, whatever their target, to determine their own spending needs and rate levels. For the council under examination here, though, this silver lining came a little late. For 1984/85, its budget had already been set; for later years, rate-capping, rather than target, was to be the problem.

E. Budgets: the evolving legal analysis

5 March 1984 was the date the council reached its budget decision. The budget was for £85m. Block grant would be lost completely at £83.5m, so the budget assumed there would be no block grant, though the hope was that events might turn out more favourably (as in fact they did). As the various pieces of the budgetary puzzle had fallen into place, nonetheless, the Treasurer had managed to turn the rate increase of 27% or more foreseen in December into one of only 13%, remarking in his report that 'all local authorities were now investigating accountancy adjustments to maximize block grant, and this had been done to the greatest extent possible'. Another remark indicated just how much this approach was colouring the budgetary process: 'because of the strategy of maximising block grant resources it was not possible to make valid comparisons between the 1983/84 and the 1984/85 budgets'.

What those accountancy adjustments had produced (once again) was what the Treasurer called an 'apparently very high level of balances'. For the 1983/84 financial year that was now ending, the original estimate of balances had been £1.5m. The revised estimate was £16.5m. The £15m difference was mostly block grant, roughly £9.5m of it, which had been attracted by approximately £5.5m of budgetary adjustments. These included, in roughly equal proportions, some genuine savings, some accountancy devices (notably 'a transfer of £1m out of the provision for bad debts into the General Rate Fund at the 31st March' which was then immediately 'reversed out on 1st April 1984 in order to attract additional block grant'), and £1.5m of interest generated by the funds in the advance funding scheme involving Jointly-owned Co.

As for the 1984/85 spending plans, the highlights included the following: £4m for uncommitted growth (a change from the initial 'net nil growth' assumption); a rent increase of 75p (the government guideline figure, adopted late in the day and despite dissension in the Labour ranks); an 'abatement' of £3m (this was a figure for unspecified savings to be found during the year, and thus a tacit acknowledgment that resources did not yet match projected expenditure); and a working balance provision of £0 (this despite the obviously deliberate recording in the minutes that the Treasurer recommended a balance of at least £1m). The council also implemented, mere days before the 1983/84 financial year closed, a covenant arrangement for the construction of four neighbourhood offices under its decentralization plans, with the arrangements anticipating a lease/leaseback with Council Co. to generate notional capital receipts. This new covenant, along with the notional capital receipts, was an important part of the Treasurer's juggling act as the council's 'prescribed expenditure' for 1983/84 threatened for a while to exceed its allocations considerably.

These spending plans included two significant new steps in the evolving *operative law* of budget-making. One was whether an 'abatement', or unspecified savings item, was lawful, or whether it made the budget unbalanced and therefore *ultra vires*. Though different opinions on this question were available at the time, the stronger one, the Solicitor thought (he had encountered this issue once before when working in another local authority), was that as long as the abatement was a genuine estimate of savings that were actually expected to be made, it was acceptable. The other was whether a £0 working balance was legal, bearing in mind not only ordinary *ultra vires* principles but also the requirement in s.2 of the *General Rate Act 1967* to levy a rate sufficient to meet both the council's total estimated net expenditure and 'such additional amount as is in the opinion of the rating authority required ... to meet contingencies' (among other things). On this second issue the fact that the Treasurer advised that a balance of at least £1m should be provided, but that the Solicitor did not say it must be, highlights the fact that although legal advice and financial advice do feed off each other, there is nevertheless a difference, and financial advice that a decision is imprudent will not necessarily generate a legal opinion that it is *ultra vires*. In the particular circumstances of March 1984 one thing to note is that the council's plans for £4m of uncommitted growth – new spending that the council was not obliged to incur – was equal to the total of the £3m 'abatement' and the missing £1m working balance. Unspecified savings to meet the £3m 'abatement' could therefore be identified by simply deciding not to incur additional spending. The Treasurer's financial assessment of what was 'prudent' had to be premissed on the council's declared intent to incur £4m of uncommitted growth. By contrast, the Solicitor's legal assessment of what was *intra vires* or *ultra vires* could pay greater attention to the fact that the council always had the discretion, and might even in some circumstances have the obligation, to change its mind.

The two new issues of *law* just mentioned, the 'abatement' and the £0 balance, had something in common. Both were reflections of a new range of legal questions that were coming into focus in connection with the *Rates Act 1984* – questions relating to what, exactly, made a budget 'balanced'. Previously, though the idea that a budget had to 'balance' had been axiomatic and had provided the legal underpinnings for a number of the budgetary decisions already described in this book, it had operated as an *intuitive* proposition rather than as a carefully *reasoned* one. The *Rates Act 1984*, looming large though not yet enacted, was changing that. For councils such as this one, rules of thumb about balanced budgets (among other things) were being replaced by more *meticulous* legal analysis as local authorities sought to determine exactly how much legal *latitude* they might retain under the new legislation.

Nevertheless, a notable feature of the 1984 budget itself is the absence of any sense of legal concerns. In some ways this is remarkable. In less than two years, the council had increased its budget by some 60%, and had gone from 100% grant to 0% grant. It was now proposing to enter 1984/85 with no working balance, and spending at a level, the Treasurer advised, that could not be sustained into the following year unless similar balances were available, which was most unlikely, or unless there were a 32% rate rise, which the prospect of rate-capping made even more unlikely.

What had happened, essentially, was that over the period since the Left took control political and financial pressures had combined to raise new legal questions and to generate a variety of new understandings. Within the general framework of the *ultra vires* rule, new *policies* had sought, and had for the most part found, the legal *latitude* that was necessary to sustain them. The legal conclusions reached had been tentative in some cases, but unless and until something happened to change them, they were conclusions upon which the council would continue to act and from which other trains of thought would evolve.

In relation to council rents, for example, it had been established by the decision taken in 1983, without adverse legal comment, that a 0% increase could be *intra vires*, and this would be sufficient for the council's policy purposes for the foreseeable future. In relation to rates and grant, the decisions reached in 1984 added that the council could lose 100% of its grant, have no working balance and budget for £3m of unidentified savings yet still be acting *intra vires*. For lawyers, one must clarify, the operative word here is that all of these things 'could' be *intra vires*. For members, however, the lesson learned was probably that they simply 'were' *intra vires*.

The comparable development on the capital side was that the search for answers to the revenue difficulties had produced some financing methods, primarily covenant schemes coupled with leasing arrangements, which were sound according to the *operative law* of the day, and which had obvious value as instruments in financial planning under a system of annual capital allocations. In an ideal world, the schemes adopted would not have been the Treasurer's preferred financing methods, but for this less than ideal reality they were good vehicles.

In many ways, then, budget-making in 1984/85 was, despite its financial challenges, in the process of settling down from the point of view of the *ultra vires* rule. It was moving back towards the realms in which it could operate by rule of thumb rather than rule of law, where people had acquired a familiarity with what they could and could not do, and would conduct themselves accordingly. The legal aspects of the major budgetary decisions had been fully explored, and the financial considerations were once more becoming the dominant ones, though often expressed in a framework in which, as part of the enduring aftermath of *Bromley LBC v GLC* (1981), much more care was being taken about the quality and the content of the paperwork presented to members. Some elements, the legal details on the margins and any novel ideas for deflecting the financial pressures, would still need careful examination as new suggestions were presented, yet even here a degree of familiarity was emerging with the experience and the processes of decision-making in areas of legal uncertainty.

There were, though, broader and stronger disruptive forces at large. In Liverpool a whole new range of legal questions was about to be confronted as the council first threatened to adopt an unlawful deficit budget, and then entered the 1984/85 financial year without adopting a budget or making a rate at all. (See Parkinson 1985.) For 1985/86, meanwhile, the prospect for our council was the ominous one of rate-capping, and of budget-making with some important legal differences.

8
Rate-Capped and Resistant: The 1985 Budget

'If Mrs. Thatcher is returned to Downing Street, the prospect for the next few years is for a direct and possibly bloody confrontation between the Department of the Environment and a small but vocal array of Labour city councils'. So *The Times* (2 June 1983) had said when the Conservative manifesto for the 1983 general election was published, and so it was to be. The main items behind this grim prediction were the Conservatives' pledge to abolish the Greater London Council and the other metropolitan county councils, and their promise to curb 'excessive and irresponsible rate increases by high-spending councils'. Rhodes (1992: 55) writes that both abolition and rate-capping were inserted into the manifesto by Mrs. Thatcher, who 'wanted to "do something" about local government' and 'disregarded all known opposition within the government and the party'. Our council was obviously one it was intended to 'do something about'.

The previous chapter dealt with one important aspect of our council's preparations for rate-capping: its attempt to rearrange its financial affairs to deflect the impact so far as possible. That story continues here. Most of the chapter, though, will focus on the so-called 'rates rebellion' that broke out as the authorities most affected mounted a 'united strategy of non-compliance' with rate-capping.

These events were exceptional, and of all the public administration scenarios described in this book, they are perhaps the ones most closely tied to the specifics of an *ultra vires*-based central-local relationship in which the centre holds *all* the legal cards. Their political aspect has been described by writers like Grant (1986) and Lansley, Goss and Wolmar (1989). Here, though, the focus of attention is both legal and internal, examining the way in which the *ultra vires* rule intertwined with our council's problematic *disposition* to both enable and confine the council in its attempt to realize its political goals. This was the art of the possible at its most difficult, yet sustaining it was built on the same basic mantra as applies in simpler times and unexceptional contexts: provide the legal inputs so that outputs can be legal.

A. The challenge of *law* and *policy*

Rate-capping changed the legal framework for budget-making enormously. As a joint report of the Chief Executive, the Solicitor and the Treasurer to the policy committee in November 1984 stated:

> The Rates Act 1984 ... effectively reverses for rate capped authorities the usual process involved in making a rate. Until now the council had a wide discretion to decide on its level of spending and was not under any specific statutory constraint when setting a rate sufficient to meet that level. For 1985/86 at least, instead of working from spending level to rate, the council needs to consider setting the spending level in the budget against the background of a rate levy ceiling. Rate income will become the fixed element in the budget/rate equation.

Note, incidentally, the appearance now of joint reporting by the Chief Executive, the Solicitor and the Treasurer – a small change of *organization* designed to ensure that the three chief officers spoke with all the combined authority they could muster. There had also been a change in personnel. In June 1984 the Chief Executive – who was a lawyer, and a 'first class' one in the Solicitor's view – had retired. The Treasurer became Chief Executive, and the Assistant Treasurer became Treasurer.

Being rate-capped injected new procedural elements into the normal course of budget-making. The first step was the Secretary of State's determination of the total expenditure level for an authority that was to be rate-capped; the authority could then apply to have this redetermined. Subsequently the Secretary of State was to convert the total expenditure level into a maximum rate that the authority could levy; the authority could then say whether it accepted this limit, and if not, attempt to agree a different one. Finally, if no agreement was reached, the maximum rate limit would become binding when approved by the House of Commons. (See Grant 1986 for a full explanation of the process.) For rate-capped authorities, therefore, the budget-making process became one with several legal fixed points: redetermination, acceptance, and potentially an opportunity to seek last-minute adjustments.

At its end, moreover – unless a council was prepared to reduce spending, which ours was not – was a new financial exercise: bridging the gap between spending plans and finite rate revenues.

Adding to the complexities was the fact that all of these budgetary decisions would be taken against the background of a concerted campaign of opposition to the legislation. This council, like others, opposed the *Rates Act 1984* and everything it represented, and wanted to have as little to do with the legislation as possible. This took the council beyond the mere tension between *law* and *policy* described in previous chapters and into the realms of direct incompatibility, where there was a distinct possibility that, whether by accident or design, the line might be crossed into *ultra vires* action and the prospect, at that time, of surcharge by the district auditor. In terms of the internal operation of public law the possibility of accident is probably the greater preoccupation. Some accidents are preventable, and the function of the lawyer is to prevent them. If, though, a government which has been properly advised as to the law acts unlawfully by design, there is little a lawyer can do.

The comprehensive way in which the four 'W's of the *ultra vires* rule regulate local government means that the potential for accidents abounds. Obviously important in a highly charged political atmosphere will be issues of motive, of *why* a council acts. Even the most innocuous of actions, such as deciding what newspapers to buy for public libraries (*R v Ealing LBC, ex parte Times Newspapers Ltd* 1987) or who to buy oil from (*R v Lewisham LBC, ex parte Shell UK Ltd* 1988) can be *ultra vires* if done for an improper reason. However, issues of person and process, of *who* takes decisions and *how*, are every bit as important; they are just as capable of making a decision *ultra vires*. Indeed, the more evident it is that councillors' various *dispositions* raise unavoidable risks of *ultra vires* action, the harder lawyers will try to ensure that the risk is not compounded by inattention to issues of person or process.

The previous chapter has mentioned the professional challenge for lawyers of maintaining objectivity in circumstances such as these – the challenge of giving legal advice in circumstances in which one knows that an *intra vires* decision is possible, but only if decision-makers can see the world as lawyers present it, segregating the legally 'relevant' considerations from the legally 'irrelevant' ones that are, in reality, an inescapable part of the context. Also involved is the challenge of diplomacy, which was mentioned previously in connection with Boynton's observation (1986: 63) about not causing 'embarrassment to the council's Leadership' nor 'cutting the ground from under the feet of the majority party'. The twin challenges of objectivity and diplomacy were to be a continuing theme of the year leading up to the 1985 rate-making, recurring at each of the fixed points at which *intra vires* decisions had to be taken under the new procedures of the *Rates Act 1984*.

B. A productive almost-moratorium

Although much of this chapter deals with rate-capping, there was also a hugely important parallel story unfolding quietly on the capital front at the same time, as the council's officers and Company B between them continued to identify new areas of *latitude* under the *Local Government, Planning and Land Act 1980* and to put together the legal wherewithal for the council to achieve as many as possible of its political objectives.

The spur to this was the government's long-running consideration of imposing a moratorium on local authority capital expenditure. Early in the 1984/85 financial year the government was reported to be contemplating this, but in July it called for voluntary restraint instead, with a moratorium held in reserve if needed. Enough authorities obliged voluntarily (though our council was certainly not among them) that in September 1984 the government lifted the threat of a moratorium for the current financial year, though perhaps not for 1985/86. Finally, in December 1984, the government announced that there would be no moratorium for 1985/86 either, but that capital allocations would be reduced and the 'useable portion' of housing capital receipts would go down to 20%.

This long-running almost-moratorium had a variety of effects within our council. The immediate response was, of course, for the council to take full advantage of its 'pre-implementation licence' and try to enter binding commitments for as much of its capital programme as possible before any moratorium took effect. The previous council had done the same in 1980 when the government had also announced a possible moratorium. By mid-1984, however, the evolving *operative law* of the *Local Government, Planning and Land Act 1980* had placed new options at the council's disposal. It was not long before officials (and Company B, of course) were considering whether the existing advance funding arrangements involving Jointly-owned Co., designed to enable additional capital allocations to be used up quickly before the end of a financial year, could be expanded, repeated or otherwise adapted to the very similar purpose of outrunning a moratorium. Both the Legal Department and Company B concluded that, with minor adjustments, or perhaps even without them, they could be. Plans therefore proceeded with as much speed as could be mustered – plans for entering conventional arrangements as soon as possible, plans for substantial advance funding arrangements, and subsidiary plans for emergency 'beat-the-moratorium' arrangements that would allow the primary contracts to be put in place quickly if and when word came that the moratorium was imminent.

At the same time, in a deliberate act of *policy*, the council expanded its 1984/85 housing capital programme rapidly. Faced with the prospect of a moratorium either later in 1984/85 or in 1985/86, it brought forward as much of its programme as possible into 1984/85. The added projects would cost £19m, taking the programme roughly 40% over the capital resources that the Treasurer had so far identified as being available.

When the threat of the moratorium reduced in September and vanished in December, the new arrangements involving Jointly-owned Co. were put to one side as no longer required. However, the new *operative law* they had engendered remained: the council now had a more refined understanding of advance funding arrangements and of emergency methods for entering them if needed. More important than this, though, was that the train of thought that the almost-moratorium had set in motion continued. The council and Company B had been developing an advance funding scheme (pay first, build later) for a large programme of housing works that would be sheltered, as far as legally possible, from the prospect of future moratoriums or reductions in government allocations. From there it was a short step to contemplate setting up similarly large housing programmes on a deferred purchase basis (build first, pay later). This, too, would protect the council's housing programme from the vicissitudes of future government policies, and the deferred purchase approach, with the council's first payments delayed for a couple of years, could substantially ease the financial crunch that the council was expecting in the early years of rate-capping.

By early 1985, then, as the controversy of the first year of rate-capping was inching towards its very public climax, the Treasurer was discreetly pursuing arrangements under which the council's entire housing programme for the next two years would be funded under deferred purchase agreements. In April 1985 the housing committee approved this £137m programme, noting in properly circumspect terms that 'The Treasurer has confirmed to us that he is currently undertaking discussions on funding for the proposed two-year programme and that he has no reason to doubt that the resources required will be available'. In June 1985, the Treasurer provided updated detailed estimates of what would be needed in the deferred purchase arrangements – £55m for 1985/86 and £67m for 1986/87, for a total of £122m. Knowing a good thing when they saw it, members wanted more. Though the first instalment (slightly revised to £57m) was duly put in place in August 1985 much as expected, the second, seven months later, was to balloon to £143m. Thus a total housing programme of £200m, probably three times the expected amount of the government's allocations and twice what the council would have contemplated until fears of a moratorium prompted officers to revisit the *operative law* of the *Local Government, Planning and Land Act 1980*, was to be 'safely stowed away', as it was put at a meeting of the council's capital programme working party in late 1984.

There was, though, still a problem for the current year. While the 'beat-the-moratorium' rush of 1984 was developing into the 'safely stowed away' capital programmes of 1985 and 1986, there was still the additional £19 million of accelerated capital spending in 1984 for the Treasurer to deal with. The response combined the *intended latitude* of the *Local Government, Planning and Land Act 1980* with the *unintended latitude* that had previously been identified, and was topped off with another fresh realization of *operative law*. The *intended latitude* was the use of capital receipts from the sale of council properties, mostly but not exclusively council houses. The *unintended latitude* included the generation of notional capital receipts through transfer and leaseback arrangements with Council Co. in relation to more new neighbourhood offices. The last-minute realization of *operative law* related to the sale of council mortgages that had been under discussion in various forms for the past two years. For some time the Treasurer had intended to complete the transaction in 1985/86. Now, however, the £4m receipt was needed in 1984/85, partly because of the council's greatly increased housing programme, and partly because of the government's decision to reduce the useable portion of housing capital receipts to 20% in 1985/86. What emerged, however, when the final form of the transaction was analysed by Counsel, was that the £4m fell outside the rules that made 'capital receipts' only partly useable for 'prescribed expenditure', and was, in the circumstances, fully useable. Just when it was most needed, therefore, the Treasurer had £4m available to balance spending and resources in 1984/85, rather than the £1.6m (40% of £4m) that had been assumed for so long.

Achieving that balance was essential now that the 'rates rebellion' was nearing its climax. It was mentioned in Chapter 4 that one possible *consequence* of a capital overspend was that the Secretary of State could step in and issue a binding direction. Indeed, he could issue one if he merely considered an overspend was likely. Giving the Secretary of State this opening to control any part of the council's finances was something the council was absolutely not prepared to risk, and it was therefore a great relief that, amidst *meticulous* and politically fraught internal discussions of exactly what the legal implications of a capital overspend might be, Counsel's opinion on the mortgage sales allowed everything to fall into place.

Also falling into place at around the same time was another useful piece of the *operative law* of capital controls. The trigger was the government's eventual decision that it would not impose a moratorium in 1985/86, but would reduce the 'useable portion' of housing capital receipts to 20%. One thing that the Act did not say, however, was what could be done with the 'non-useable portion'. The government and local authorities had disagreed over this in the past, but the local authorities had convinced the government that its own view was untenable. (See Audit Commission 1985: 34; Davies 1987: 30; Gibson 1992: 73.) The accepted wisdom now was that if, say, 40% of the receipt was useable, 40% of the balance was useable the next year, 40% of the remaining balance the year after that, and so on. This was sometimes called the 'cascade' principle. The Deputy Solicitor, incidentally, was never convinced that this 'national consensus' was correct.

The coming reduction to only 20% useable in the first year and only 20% of the reducing balance in subsequent years would make a big difference to the council's finances. So it was very convenient that the Deputy Solicitor, in correspondence with the Treasurer, commented that the non-useable portion was not *completely* non-useable; it was simply not useable in any given year *for prescribed expenditure*. It could of course be spilled over to later years under the 'cascade' principle; but it could also be used on what was to become referred to as 'non-prescribed capital expenditure', spending that was capital in nature but did not fall within the regulations defining 'prescribed expenditure'.

Here, then, the change to the useable portion brought back into focus, with newly important practical implications, a point of *law* that had been allowed to remain fuzzy in earlier years. It was mentioned in Chapter 4 that in the early days of the *Local Government, Planning and Land Act 1980*, there had been a tendency for officers and members to talk of 'prescribed expenditure' and 'capital expenditure' as though they were synonyms. (The Deputy Solicitor recalls resisting that habit from the start.) Now, though, that 80% of the council's housing capital receipts were no longer to be useable for 'prescribed expenditure', the more literal frame of mind was to reap its rewards. Expenditure could be 'capital' even though it was not 'prescribed'. Note, therefore, the expression 'non-prescribed capital expenditure'; it is one we will meet again as the mysteries of the locally possible continue to unfold.

C. The 'united strategy of non-compliance'

In any normal year, the events described so far in this chapter would have provided quite enough legal excitement. This year, however, was anything but normal. It was the first year of rate-capping.

The first element in the council's preparations for rate-capping was, of course, the question of *disposition*. How would it respond to its new and detested legal obligation to set a rate that did not exceed the government's limit? Its options would be few, since the Act was 'drafted on the assumption that those to whom it was directed would ... explore all available avoidance routes' and was 'competently constructed' (Loughlin 1996: 92).

The Labour group's *disposition* was to have as little to do with the *Rates Act 1984* as possible. However, the Labour group's views must for the rest of this chapter be clearly distinguished from the *disposition*, or the *policy*, of the council, for one of the dominant features of the year leading up to the 1985 budget was a clear and deliberate attempt by the council's lawyers to do what common sense (as opposed to *law*, that is) would tell us cannot be done: to differentiate the council as a corporate entity from the councillors who constitute it. The key dividing line was that councillors as individuals, as a group, and even as holders of non-statutory political office such as Leader or Deputy Leader, could say or do virtually whatever they liked, but that when those same individuals acted as or for the council, there were limits. They should not indicate in any way that the council would choose not to comply with the law; and they could not act for a party political purpose, since this in itself would lead to the council acting *ultra vires*. (See *R v GLC, ex parte Bromley LBC* 1984 and *R v Bromley LBC, ex parte Lambeth LBC* 1984.) This theoretical distinction between the council and its members was reiterated in Grant's contemporaneous *Rate Capping and the Law* (1984: 11–12), which emphasized the importance of 'the structure of the decision-making process and the extent to which the authority's decision-making is seen to be divorced from that of the controlling party group'.

The process began early. In April 1984, even before the *Rates Act 1984* had received the royal assent, arrangements were made for a workshop in London, in May, for the likely candidates for rate-capping. Our Leader planned to attend and to present a paper. The Solicitor examined the nature and composition of the meeting carefully to make sure that it could not be construed as 'party political'. The Solicitor also reviewed drafts of the Leader's paper, suggesting several things that would be better left unsaid or said differently. The potential legal delicacy of the approaching situation was evidently well recognized.

A couple of weeks before the London workshop, our council's Labour group met to discuss its general approach towards rate-capping. Deciding between two options – either confrontation or manoeuvring its way through the legislation by financial and legal devices – it decided on confrontation. It also decided that if it was rate-capped, as expected, it would not apply for redetermination of its designated expenditure level. Both of these decisions were reinforced at the well-known Sheffield Conference in July, where a 'mood of determination ... stemmed from a sense of outrage shared by most sections of the Labour Party' (Lansley, Goss and Wolmar 1989: 35). In the face of this emerging 'united strategy of non-compliance' (the precise details of which remained unknown), the Solicitor found himself assigning a variety of novel and semi-novel legal questions to his staff for research. 'What legal status does a budget have?' 'Does a budget have to be agreed at or near the start of the financial year?' 'What is the position of various kinds of creditors – money lenders, staff, contractors, etc.?' 'What is the role of officers in such a situation?' 'What if any role does the Audit Commission have?' 'What is the personal position of councillors who do not vote against an unbalanced budget?' 'Are there legal devices which can slow down the reconciliation of expenditure with income?' 'Can a local authority go bankrupt in law?' 'When and with what mandate would Commissioners be likely to come in – if at all?' 'How would an authority's powers and/or ability to borrow money be affected?' The answers to questions like these, which bore on the council's legal *latitude*, its *autonomy* and the *consequences* of certain actions would provide key legal *information* determining how and where the coming confrontation would play itself out. These were at the time, and remained when Grant (1986: v) revisited them two years later, 'complex legal issues to which there were no easy answers'.

The issue that needed addressing most immediately was the Labour group's decision that it would not apply for redetermination. Redetermination was the first of the major legal fixed points in the scheme of the *Rates Act 1984*, and was in the Solicitor's view a particularly important one. It provided a possibility of improving the council's financial situation, and if the council did not take the opportunity it seemed unlikely that the courts would grant a remedy if it challenged its rate limit later. (See Grant 1986: 51.) Furthermore, the decision on whether or not to apply for redetermination had to be taken by *the council,* not by the Labour group; it had to be based on a proper description of the legal and financial ramifications, which the group's decision had not been; and it could only be taken after the council's designated spending level had been set, whereas the group's decision had been taken before the Act was even passed. Failure to consider the matter properly and at the proper time might generate one of those entirely avoidable risks of acting *ultra vires* in the preparations for the council's eventual budget decision, with potential further implications in terms of the possibility of surcharge.

The Solicitor therefore suggested to the Leader and the Chief Executive a possible way out of the redetermination box: to make detailed representations on the council's spending needs for 1985/86 *before* the Secretary of State made any rate-cap announcement. This, it was hoped, would put the council in a similar position to an application for redetermination, and would present the Secretary of State with 'relevant considerations' which, when setting the council's limit, he would disregard at his legal peril. S.2(2) of the *Rates Act 1984* required him to act on 'the best information available to him', and disregarding information provided by the council might therefore be risky. Despite the group's decisions on confrontation and on redetermination, and giving credence to the idea that there can indeed be substance to the legal distinction between the council and its members, this non-statutory submission of the council's spending needs went ahead. For a while, indeed, serious thought was given to taking things a large step further, and actually using the submission as a basis for adopting the council's budget and rate for 1985 nine months early, in June 1984, when there was no legal limit to the council's rate. Legally, it appeared, this was possible, but unfortunately the Legal Department advised that if the rate was made early and the subsequent order was for a lower rate limit, the rate would probably be invalid. The idea was abandoned.

The council sent its financial submission to the Department of the Environment in July 1984, later than planned but still within the time frame (just) that could make it a 'relevant consideration' that the council could later argue the Secretary of State had unlawfully ignored. The submission criticized the government's rate support grant decisions in the past, and argued that the council needed to spend at least

£94m in 1985/86. The Secretary of State did not respond until after the rate-cap announcement, in which, to no-one's surprise, the council was named, with a spending level of £86m. The Secretary of State's subsequent reply to the council's letter rejected its criticism of the government's past decisions, and said that if the council thought its spending needs were greater than £86m, it could raise this with him through an application for redetermination.

The council was therefore back in the situation its informal financial submission had been intended to avoid. Would it or would it not apply for redetermination of its rate-capped spending level?

The Labour group, in May, had said no. Nevertheless, within the council, whatever may have been the position within the group, the possibility of applying for redetermination was still a live issue.

In August the question was whether the council could obtain undertakings from the Secretary of State that would remove from the redetermination process the risk that he might reduce the spending limit rather than increase it, or might impose conditions. These were among his statutory options. Reflecting on them Grant (1986: 47) comments that 'The price for seeking a redetermination could be high.' The council therefore wrote in September asking the Secretary of State to undertake not to reduce the rate-cap level and not to impose requirements if the council applied. The Secretary of State responded in the kind of nuanced terms that public lawyers tend to use when they see themselves as trying to give as much assurance as they can without 'fettering their discretion', saying that he could not bind himself to exercise his discretion on redetermination in a particular way, but that '... generally speaking, I find it hard to envisage circumstances in this round in which I would seek to require a bigger reduction than that which I have originally proposed' and that he had made clear in Parliament that the power to impose requirements was only designed to cover 'a very specific set of circumstances .... While therefore I cannot rule out the use of the power, I can assure you that, contrary to suggestions that have been made, I have no intention of using it for the purpose of detailed intervention.' However, this was not the clear undertaking the council had wanted.

While this was going on, a draft report on redetermination was being prepared for the policy committee, and a further line of internal questioning was under way. Was redetermination really the *only* way in which the Secretary of State could vary the original decision on the council's expenditure level? The underlying question was whether the council was really going to have to bite the bullet, and decide by the rapidly approaching deadline of 1 October 1984 whether or not to apply. The legal response was that the Act gave the Secretary of State no express power to extend the deadline, and that whether or not he nevertheless *could* do so, it would be most imprudent for a local authority to miss the deadline in the hope that he would.

In the light of this obviously sound advice, a special meeting of the policy committee was called, reluctantly, a few days before the deadline expired, and the decision was taken not to apply. It must have been galling, then, that the Secretary of State did, in fact, assume exactly the implied power in question, and as late as 10 November 1984, six weeks after the 1 October deadline, *The Times* reports Mr Baker, the Local Government Minister, as saying that appeals for redetermination would still be accepted, and even as offering broad hints that some might succeed. By that time, though, the council had moved on.

If there was one thing that was not in short supply at this time, it was legal advice. Academic specialists were advising local authorities and meetings of local authorities. Information was being exchanged through bodies such as the Local Government Campaign Unit. The Chartered Institute of Public Finance and Accountancy was supplying advice to Treasurers and providing a facility for inter-authority discussions. Treasurers, in turn, were in touch with the Audit Commission, who were attempting to work towards a degree of consistency in the approach auditors would take to the issues thrown up by the authorities' likely responses to rate-capping. The solicitors of the rate-capped authorities were also meeting periodically, aware of the difficulties that would arise if their respective councillors were given substantially different legal advice. Yet to come in our council was the decision of the Labour group to involve a solicitor in private practice in advising them – a development which, though technically appropriate in the light of the theoretical divide between the council and the group, was nonetheless a complication from the Legal Department's point of view, since it made it hard to know what advice the group was receiving or whose advice it was taking. In due course the Opposition retained solicitors, too, in their case to proceed against the council for its failure to make a rate.

Through all of this, one thing that is very clear is that there was never any doubt or real disagreement on the major elements of the council's legal position. Any differences were of detail or nuance – though these could be of major importance. One QC, for example, had advised another authority that it could only budget for uncommitted growth, which our council was proposing to do, if there was an 'overwhelming need' for it. Was the legal test really this exacting? What about balancing the budget through an 'unidentified savings' item? The Solicitor had accepted this in the past, and the council might well need to rely on one again, but it was being questioned by others. In due course, when the council came to take its final decision, opinions on matters like these might become critical. For the time being, however, what was clear was that the legal *issues* were well mapped out, as was the range of opinions that might be expected to be expressed when it finally came time for decisions to be taken.

In November and December 1984 the Solicitor reported to the policy committee and council on some basic legal issues surrounding the 1985 budget. The timing offered a convenient lull in the main action, with the redetermination issue closed but the maximum rate limit not yet set, when the Solicitor could discharge his professional responsibility to provide members with general legal *information*, but without there being an actual, and unavoidably controversial, decision that needed to be taken. Specific decisions that were touched on at that time included the council's decision, along with other authorities in the 'non-compliance' camp, to refuse statutory requests from the government for information about the council's finances and services, and the tricky little legal issue of consultation with the commercial sector about the council's 1985/86 rate and budget. Under the *Rates Act 1984*, the council now had a duty to consult. Consulting, however, did not sit well with 'non-compliance', yet not consulting opened the door to a possible legal challenge to the rate. The council resolved this conundrum by carrying out a borough-wide consultation that included commercial ratepayers as well as others. A wide public consultation was not politically unacceptable to the council, and making sure that commercial ratepayers were included (along with everybody else) protected the council's flanks from possible legal challenge.

Later in December came the second of the major procedural fixed points the *Rates Act 1984* imposed. The Secretary of State made the general rate support grant announcement for 1985/86 and converted the rate-capped authorities' designated spending levels into maximum rate limits. Our council's limit was within the expected range, and at this level the council would be eligible for £21m in block grant, substantially more than the £16m that the Treasurer had mentioned as possible in a report in September. The Secretary of State then asked each authority, as the Act required, whether it accepted the rate limit, and gave them until 15 January 1985 to reply. The authorities could now accept this limit or argue their case for a different one.

This, though, was still the era of the united strategy of non-compliance. Shortly before the rate support grant announcement the authorities involved had decided that they would meet on a common date in March and vote simultaneously to postpone making a rate until the government addressed their financial grievances (*The Times*, 10 December 1984). In January 1985 the national Labour Party's local government committee resolved that the rate-capped authorities should seek collective negotiation with the government (*The Times*, 8 January 1985). On 10 January 1985, at a special meeting called for the purpose, the council's policy committee considered and adopted a standard form resolution. It began with two paragraphs critical of the grant system in general and addressed acceptance of the rate limit in the third:

> ... this Council resolves to ... (c) Re-iterate its rejection of the Rates Act as an undemocratic means of controlling local expenditure by central government. It is therefore not appropriate for this Council to accept any proposed limited rate as we do not accept the premise upon which such a limit is based. Any variation of that limit makes no sense unless it deals with the fundamental attack on local democracy and the provision of local services.

Given that the overall message of the resolution was that the authorities involved rejected rate-capping and would have nothing to do with it, one thing that deserves comment is that they nonetheless felt the need to hold a meeting to give this message. In our council, indeed, it was a special meeting, called principally for the purpose of passing that resolution. Underlying the meeting, at least in part, was the *ultra vires* rule. If the council were to avoid the risk of *ultra vires* action and a possible charge of 'wilful misconduct', it had to consider properly, as a council, the question of whether or not to accept the proposed rate limit. They could not simply ignore the legislation; they had to hold a meeting in order to decide to ignore it. At that meeting, moreover, they had to base their decision on the 'relevant considerations', which were duly referred to in our council's documents. Overall, nonetheless, the legal logic of the council's situation drew them into the procedural scheme of the *Rates Act 1984*, like it or not. To have failed to respond to the Secretary of State's statutory request as to whether it accepted the maximum rate limit would have raised the danger of avoidable *ultra vires* action.

The solidarity shown by the rate-capped authorities in January, though, could not hold much longer. It had always been vague in its details;

ever since the Sheffield conference in July 1984, where there was agreement that there should be a united strategy of non-compliance, it had never been possible to decide on the specifics (see *The Times*, 9 July, 26 October and 6 December 1984; Lansley, Goss and Wolmar 1989: 44–5). Now events were about to reach a point of no return for the precepting authorities. 8 March 1985 was the last date on which they could adopt their precepts, and the prevailing legal view (though Grant 1986: 72 disagrees) was that they could not adopt one later. The rating authorities, by contrast, were subject to no specific date for making a rate, and a rate made late in the year would be *valid*, even though the delay might cause loss and thus incur the risk of surcharge. It had long been anticipated that the precepting authorities would 'go legal' when the deadline for making precepts finally arrived. They did.

For rating authorities like our council, solidarity became even more important once the preceptors had 'gone legal'. However, the strong but subtle forces of the *ultra vires* doctrine were at work to undermine it. The remaining rate-capped authorities had all agreed to hold meetings on 7 March, and one of the things they wanted to do was pass a resolution in common terms expressing their combined opposition to rate-capping and the grant system within which it operated. Legally, though, in this course lay danger. If each authority passed a resolution in the same words, this might suggest that all of them had come to the meeting with deliberately closed minds, that they had 'fettered their discretion'. The importance of this, at least in our council, was accentuated by the fact that there was no other council meeting scheduled between 7 March and the beginning of the new financial year. This meant that the Treasurer *had to* treat the meeting as a potential rate-making meeting, and present an appropriate report to the policy committee. The report did not have to recommend the making of a rate by the end of the financial year; it could, as it did, comment that

> There are always problems and uncertainties at Budget time in any year. This year these problems are even more significant and the Committee may feel that they are not in a position to make a recommendation to the Council. If this is the case the Committee should carefully consider all the advice and information in this report before coming to a decision.

What the report did have to do, though, was ensure that before the new financial year began on 1 April 1985, when, as the report put it, 'legal and administrative difficulties would begin to arise and these would get progressively more serious as time went on', the council had a proper report, setting out 'relevant considerations', on which an *intra vires* decision could be based. This report, incidentally, indicated that the council's spending plans for 1985/86 now totalled £101m, a £7m increase from the £94m that the council had submitted to the Secretary of State as its assessment of its spending need in July 1984 when trying to provide 'relevant considerations' without applying for redetermination.

At the meeting on 7 March 1985 the council deferred the making of a rate, the operative part of its decision being that the council 'considers it impossible for the Authority to make a rate at this meeting for the financial year 1985/86'. The fine details of the resolution had received considerable scrutiny in point of *law*. Could the resolution simply say that the council found it 'impossible' to make a rate, or was it safer to say 'impossible at this meeting', or even to use some milder term than 'impossible'? Should the resolution set another time before the end of the financial year to reconvene, or was it sufficient if the Leader simply mentioned at the meeting that it was the intention to meet again, or might it be all right to say nothing? To what extent, if it was 'impossible' now to make a rate, should the resolution state the legally 'relevant considerations' that might indicate why making a rate was likely to become any more 'possible' at some later date?

Much of the discussion and (considerable) tension that issues such as these generated might well seem faintly preposterous. Given the facts at the time, could it really make much difference whether the council determined that it was 'impossible' to make a rate rather than 'impossible at this meeting'? Could it really matter that it did not set another date for a meeting, bearing in mind that there was always the possibility of calling a special meeting, even if none was specifically predetermined? Certainly the Secretary of State made light of the decision, dismissing it as an empty gesture that carried no immediate risk (*The Times*, 15 March 1985). From the council's position, however, it was not that way at all. Of the fact that the council *could* lawfully decline to make a rate at that meeting there was no doubt. On the other hand, there were equally possibilities that the council *might*, by the way it handled the matter, create risks of acting unlawfully, or even of 'wilful misconduct', where none needed to exist. In a situation like this a few poorly chosen words in the wrong places can spell the difference between success and failure, and the costs of failure would be high. Shortly before the 7 March meeting the district auditor had begun officially drawing the council's attention to its obligation to make a lawful rate and to the possible *consequences* for councillors personally – surcharge and disqualification – if they failed to do so.

Council next met on 28 March 1985. This was a special meeting called to consider the making of the rate, and even its timing had received anxious consideration. By common consent, 1 April 1985, the opening of the new financial year, was the time when *some* risk of loss arose if a rate was not made, and this loss *might*, depending upon the circumstances, be attributable to wilful misconduct. Since the 7 March meeting had simply deferred a decision on the rate, it seemed necessary to hold another meeting no later than 31 March at which a proper and *intra vires* decision on the 1985 rate could be taken.

Numerous legal uncertainties and difficulties surrounded the start of the new financial year. One major and immediate one was that council house rents were charged inclusive of rates, but if, as of 1 April no rate was set, it was unclear what level of rent could be collected. Equally important and immediate was that the government had said that if no rate was set there would be no 'person liable to make payment in respect of rates', and that it would therefore have to withhold its contribution to the housing benefit the council paid to tenants. The council thought the government was wrong in law, but the government's position nevertheless compelled the council to consider both the lawfulness and the level of housing benefit it wished to continue paying.

Procedural items, too, were important, among them the question of what the legal duty of officers was at the 28 March meeting. Were they obliged to present an actual budget or budgets for members' consideration, as the GLC's officers had apparently decided some three weeks earlier? Or was their duty the lesser one of merely presenting members with enough information to adopt a lawful budget if they chose? The answer would determine whether things had yet reached the point where officers' individual legal obligations and members' preferences came into direct conflict. More subtly it might also affect the legal logic of the decision that members would be facing. The 'relevant considerations' necessary to support a decision not to adopt a lawful budget presented by officers might be rather different from the ones that could support a decision to defer if officers merely presented information.

The legal advice within our council was that officers could simply present information. The Chief Officers' report to the 28 March meeting therefore went forward without specific budgetary options attached, but with enough information to enable the council to make a valid rate if it chose to do so. Based on the figures provided, the members' situation was this. If they thought that a rate no smaller than the maximum rate limit was necessary, they should vote for a rate at that level. However, 'A decision on the rate must include the approval of a budget which is consistent with the rate decision', and a budget had not yet been approved. If members were unable to agree the exact details of a budget consistent with the maximum rate limit, it would be lawful for them to approve one that provided generally for a 'specified level of reduction in spending' and 'a procedure which would ensure that during the course of 1985–86 decisions were taken to achieve that budgeted reduction.' But if members still concluded that 'it will not be possible for them to adopt a legal budget at this stage', they must at least establish an interim budget, based on non-rate income, to allow continued spending after 1 April 1985.

Equally important for the 28 March meeting, the Treasurer had managed to plan a rescheduling of payments that would fall due in April so that no loss was immediately in prospect (and therefore in the council's view no 'loss caused by wilful misconduct' and therefore no surcharge). The figures actually showed a net saving in the short term, though with the caution that 'this net saving may be more notional than real'.

As the 28 March meeting approached, the Leadership decided it was time for the council to take advice from a QC on its own specific circumstances and on the resolution that it was contemplating to defer making a rate. In a matter as serious as this, with the potential for charges of wilful misconduct in the air, acting in accordance with a QC's advice was going to be important.

Counsel's opinion was received on the day of the meeting, and was appended to the Chief Officers' report. It set out the relevant legal principles in a summary form that is worth quoting in full. Nothing here can have come as any surprise:

1. A rating authority is under a duty to make a rate in respect of each period of twelve months beginning with 1st April.
2. A failure to perform this duty would amount to wilful misconduct within LGFA [the *Local Government Finance Act 1982*] Section 20.
3. The rate must be within the limit prescribed by a Rate Limitation (Prescribed Maximum) (Rates) Order.
4. There is a discretion to be exercised as to where within that limit the rate should be set, having regard to the fiduciary duty to ratepayers.
5. There is no specific time by which the duty must be performed.
6. It must be performed within a reasonable time.
7. The authority must address itself to the question when will be the reasonable time to make the rate.

8. In considering that question the authority must have regard to all relevant considerations and to no others, weighing in the balance the factors for and against the immediate making of a rate.
9. When the reasonable time will be may vary from year to year or authority to authority depending on circumstances.
10. If the authority has addressed itself to the question and given it due consideration its decision should not be interfered with unless it is perverse.
11. In most authorities in most years a reasonable time would be by 1st April.
12. There is, however, no absolute rule that the rate must be made by that date.
13. Among the powerful arguments for the immediate making of a rate is any substantial loss that would be incurred by a deferment.
14. Members should therefore be informed inter alia of the timing and scale of any such loss, and of any off-setting savings.
15. Such loss might be on a scale so substantial and so rapidly escalating as to be virtually decisive (at any rate in conjunction with other matters) against deferment.
16. There is, however, no absolute rule that if the postponement of a decision will occasion some cost that decision should not be postponed in order to improve the quality of it or for some other potential benefit.

These being the principles that framed the council's steadily narrowing legal *latitude*, what was the *operative law* of its current situation? Counsel's view was this:

> In my opinion the council could, if it saw fit upon properly directing itself in accordance with the principles to which I have referred, properly defer the decision until 23rd April 1985, [the date of the next ordinary council meeting] on the basis that the estimated cost and other disadvantages, on the information before me, of such a deferral could be regarded as reasonable to be borne in relation to the potential benefits, on the information before me, of such a deferral.

The main benefits referred to in the material before the council were the possibility that discussions with the Secretary of State might bring some concessions and the greater possibility that other negotiations the council had been pursuing with a third party might increase the council's income in 1985/86 by several million pounds. This, though, had to be taken together with a warning earlier in the opinion:

> Only the most cogent reasons could justify any deferral of the rate decision substantially into the financial year to which the rate relates. I find it very difficult to conceive that there could prove to be any justification for deferring the decision beyond the council's meeting on 23rd April 1985.

The council's decision on 28 March was to defer the making of the rate, its resolution carefully pointing out the unsettled questions that made it impossible to finalize the budget on which the rate was to be based. And if there was no budget, there could be, according to the advice that members had been given, no rate.

23 April approached, and with it the sting in the tail from Counsel's comment that it was 'very difficult to conceive that there could prove to be any justification' for deferring the decision further. Over the intervening four weeks, it had become apparent that it was virtually inconceivable that the Department of the Environment would have the slightest change of heart. The third party negotiations about further income were looking promising, but no detailed figures would be available until May. Legal action was threatened by the Opposition, but had not yet been taken. Courts had pronounced in cases involving other authorities, most importantly in Hackney, where the court had surprised everybody by allowing the council until the end of May to make its rate; a shorter time had been expected. Further litigation involving other authorities was in progress.

The district auditor had also sent the council a particularly strong letter, highlighting not only the council's collective legal obligation to make a lawful rate but also each member's individual duty to ensure that this was done and the personal legal *consequences* that duty entailed:

> Dear [Chief Executive]
>
> I am very concerned at the council's continued failure to make a valid rate for the financial year which commenced on 1 April 1985. ...
>
> The council's duty in this matter and my responsibility under the Local Government Finance Act 1982 have been clearly set out in reports by officers and also in my letter of 1 March which you circulated to all members. ... it is vital that there is no doubt at all in members' minds as to their lawful duty and the circumstances that will inevitably follow if they fail to discharge their duty. ...

> A deliberate failure to perform the duty to make a lawful rate would amount to wilful misconduct. Further, any expenditure or deficiency incurred as a result of an unlawful resolution would of itself be unlawful.
>
> ... It is clear ... that there is no question on the Government's part to reconsider the rate limits or the RSG settlement for 1985/86. The council can therefore have no cogent reason to delay further and I would urge the council in their own interests as well as those of individual members, employees and the local community that a rate should be made at the earliest possible date. ...
>
> ... each member has a duty to oppose a known illegal resolution; a member cannot divest himself of his responsibility either by abstention from voting or by absence from the meeting. In short, each individual member must do everything in his power to ensure that the council makes a lawful rate. ...
>
> ... There is one further point to which I feel bound to refer. Neither the council nor individual members should assume – as I believe some may have done – that I will issue any further advice or warning before considering action. There can be no possibility now of any misunderstanding about my position.

Against the background of this clear and forceful warning, the chief officers prepared a joint report for 23 April, setting out essentially the same options that had been presented a month before, and once more the Treasurer's figures showed that in the short term, by rescheduling payments, loss could be avoided. Again, the intended significance in *law* was that as long as there was no 'loss' there could not be a 'loss arising out of wilful misconduct'. Despite the district auditor's warnings, the council decided to defer once more, though this time six Labour members broke ranks. The six were only a small fragment of the party's large majority, but they included the Chair of the finance sub-committee, who resigned.

In the delicate situation arising out of the council's continued decision to defer, the Leader took the sensible step of writing to the district auditor, setting out explicitly the council's views on why this renewed deferral could not possibly be typified as 'wilful misconduct'. The letter emphasized that the council was doing its very best to take good decisions under extremely difficult circumstances. It pointed out that the decision to defer making a rate on 28 March 1985 had been in accordance with Leading Counsel's advice, and that there were indeed, in the terms of that advice, 'the most cogent reasons' for the subsequent deferral on 23 April. The letter ended:

> I wish to emphasise that there is no question of the Council intending to wilfully misconduct itself so as to justify your intervention. You may not have understood this and your letter indicates that the information on which you may have based on information [*sic*] otherwise than by direct contact with this authority. I would be most happy to meet with you to discuss the matter further and to satisfy you that there is absolutely no need for your intervention in relation to this Borough.

That meeting was duly held. After it, the district auditor wrote again, in the form of a formal report under s.15 of the *Local Government Finance Act 1982*. The report gave a clear warning that a surcharge was imminent, but offered councillors one last chance to act:

> In my letter of 19 April I advised that the Council had no cogent reason to delay its decision further … .
>
> The Council has also received firm and unambiguous advice from its officers that there is no lawful reason to delay further the making of a rate.
>
> … I must now give the Council notice that unless it makes a lawful rate at the earliest opportunity and in any event before the end of May I shall forthwith commence action under section 20 to recover losses occasioned by the failure to make a rate from the members responsible for incurring them. …
>
> Yet again and for the last time I urge the Council most strongly to comply with its statutory duty to make a lawful rate and to do so with the utmost speed.

Actually, one thing that the council had not received from its officers was 'firm and unambiguous advice … that there is no further reason to delay further the making of a rate'. Even the report that officers provided to the next meeting of the council, late in May, did not give this advice, for the Solicitor was not certain it was necessarily correct. Again the officers' report provided an interim budget for April, May and June, in case members were once again unable to adopt a legal rate at the meeting. The report's conclusion was in terms of the risks of the situation rather than of legal obligation:

> CONCLUSION:
>
> 18. It is clear from the District Auditor's report that he intends to issue surcharge certificates if a legal rate is not made by 31st May. The figures in paragraph 12 show that the loss of interest at 31st May is greater than the saving achieved by the rescheduling of payments and that this loss becomes very substantial if a rate is not made before the middle of June.
> 19. Members are now undoubtedly at risk and should consider the consequences very carefully before deciding on any action which would prevent the council making a rate at the earliest possible date.

Finally, though, the council was ready to make a rate. The council meeting was preceded by a meeting of the policy committee which lasted all of four minutes. The Leader came with a proposed rate resolution that was evidently not intended for debate. The rate was set at the rate-cap level, and the measures adopted to bridge the £15m gap between this and the council's budget of £101m did so, according to the wording of the resolution, 'without any cuts in services or jobs, without the need for a rent increase but with the inclusion of the full provision of £2m of committed growth and £1.5m of uncommitted growth'. They included £4m of income obtained through the negotiations with the third party, and a number of accounting adjustments, the major ones being the provision for bad debts (£2.5m), financing housing repairs from reserves (£2m), capitalization of housing repairs (£4m) and further financial adjustments to be determined (£2m).

When a member of the Opposition asked for legal advice on some of the measures that bridged the gap between the rate-capped rate and the council's budget, the Leader stated that the items in question were items in the motion, not part of the officers' report. According to Standing Orders, therefore, officers could only be questioned on them if the committee so decided, which it did not. The committee resolved that the Leader's motion be put to council (where officers could not be questioned either without suspension of Standing Orders), and after 2½ hours of discussion in council the motion was adopted by 39 votes to 10, with one abstention. An earlier amendment under which the council would have resolved 'not to set a rate at this time' was defeated by 34 votes to 10, with 6 abstentions. Finally, therefore, the rate-capped rate was made.

D. The district auditor's verdict: a very close call

The final verdict on all of this was delivered four years later; a different district auditor conducted the investigation and hearings. By what must have been an uncomfortably narrow margin, councillors escaped a finding of wilful misconduct.

The process unfolded in two stages. First there was an initial hearing at which officers gave evidence but members did not participate. From this the district auditor formed the provisional view that wilful misconduct had indeed occurred, and that a loss of almost £150,000 should be recovered from the councillors who voted to defer making a rate on 23 April 1985. That sum would have been only the first instalment if subsequent audit investigations had identified other losses as flowing from the same misconduct. Councillors were informed of the district auditor's provisional view and given an opportunity to make representations before he reached a final decision.

Representations were made, and a further hearing was held. The councillors were represented by Counsel, and the Leader gave evidence on their behalf. On balance, and by a very narrow margin, the district auditor was persuaded to stay his hand, with the reasoning taking some twists and turns along the way.

A central feature of the earlier provisional view had been 'that the dominant motive in the minds of the majority of Members voting for the resolution passed at the council meeting on 23 April 1985 was to use the non-making of the rate as a weapon, or as a lever in an attempt to prise additional money from Central Government'. The 'weapon' or 'lever' terminology came from *R v Hackney LBC, ex parte Fleming* (1985), where Woolf J had held that acting in this way was unlawful. At the second hearing, however, Counsel for the councillors, in a nice exercise of legal semantics, carefully submitted that what the councillors had been doing was actually something entirely different, namely 'deferring the making of a rate while seeking by lawful means to persuade the Government to provide more resources', and that there was nothing objectionable in that.

The distinction may be rather subtle for those of a non-legal temperament, but it persuaded the district auditor, who decided, on the evidence, that the 'weapon' or 'lever' approach, though it may have been 'contemplated by many of the Respondents at an earlier date' and 'among the motives of some of the Respondents on 23rd April 1985', was nevertheless not, on that date, 'the principal or dominant motive on the part of the majority of the Members voting for the resolution to adjourn making the rate'. He accepted, instead, that 'the dominant reason motivating these Members in voting to delay making a rate on and after 23 April was to try to ensure that a balanced budget, consistent with the prescribed maximum rate, was achieved which would enable the council to maintain preferred levels of expenditure, avoiding cuts in jobs and services, if legally able to do so.'

The councillors were not in the clear yet, though. While the district auditor accepted that the decision of 23 April was not unlawful on the 'weapon' or 'lever' basis, he found it unlawful on other grounds. By that date, he held, the council did have 'sufficient information' to enable it to set a lawful rate, and there was 'no reasonable explanation or excuse for the delay'.

The crucial question, though, was whether this *ultra vires* act was or was not wilful misconduct. According to the accepted interpretations, this depended upon whether the councillors had either known that the act was unlawful or been recklessly indifferent about it. It was relatively easy to show that they did not *know* that the decision was unlawful, but harder to refute the claim that they did not *care*. Eventually they succeeded ... just. The district auditor wrote that a charge of wilful misconduct was serious and the consequences grave, and 'it should take a lot of evidence to tip the balance in favour of a positive finding of wilful misconduct'. On balance, and 'after much deliberation', he concluded that the charge was not made out. The threat of surcharge and disqualification was therefore finally lifted by the district auditor's studiously anticlimactic punchline 'Accordingly my decision is that I have no duty to perform under section 20 of the 1982 Act.'

How sweet the words must have sounded.

Two things particularly influenced the district auditor's conclusion. One was that the Solicitor had never advised members that he considered that the decisions they were taking were necessarily unlawful; in his evidence, moreover, he had confirmed that he would have said so if he had been certain that they were. The other was that the Chief Executive had indicated to members – wrongly, in fact, but in good faith – that Counsel had approved the resolution of 23 April 1985 as capable of being a valid exercise of the council's discretion at that time.

As one reflects on the auditor's decision, one thing which becomes evident is that a number of apparently silly arguments that took place during the making of the 1985 rate, generated by the continuing injection of public law elements into the council's decision-making, were not so silly after all. Things like the precise words in resolutions did turn out to matter, as did the consistent effort to differentiate the council from the group and to avoid any suggestion that *the council* might violate the law. The frustration, considerable at times, that was caused by the attention paid to these issues as events unfolded was natural. They were, after all, small details, and the probability at the time must have been that they would make little difference one way or the other. But in a case as marginal as the district auditor eventually considered this one to be, they did, and the subtleties of the legal *information* fed into the decision-making process do seem to have had subtle, but ultimately important, influences on the outcomes.

It is right to point out, though, that despite all the care and attention involved, there was also a random element to some of this. This was not just in relation to the flow of events – try as they might, nobody could control or predict exactly what would happen – but on the legal side too. Though the *law* was, in general, well known and not disputed, there were times at which pure chance as to the way in which it was expressed could open or close small but significant avenues. Different ways of formulating what was essentially the same legal question could affect the legal advice and thus the practical result.

One example that seems to have been important was the slight blurring in the legal advice between the ideas of 'unlawfulness' and 'wilful misconduct'. The district auditor's final conclusion that the council had acted unlawfully, but without wilful misconduct, emphasizes the fine distinction between the two. Legal advice in the period leading up to the rate-making, as well as the district auditor's interventions, had concentrated on the issue of wilful misconduct. If, though, it had also focused separately on the *vires* of the decision, as the final district auditor's report did, the answers might have been different. This is not to say that treating unlawfulness and wilful misconduct in the context of the 23 April decision as a combined entity rather than as two separate ones is either better or worse as an analytical approach. It is merely to say that they are slightly different, and that the fact that the emphasis was on one rather than the other was more a random element than a conscious choice. A different style of analysis might have been enough to tip the delicate balance the district auditor found in another direction.

Another small expression that carried enormous weight was the single word 'certain'. The Solicitor's evidence to the district auditor was that he would have advised the council that it was acting *ultra vires* if he was 'certain' that it was doing so, but he never was, and he never did. Applying less stringent tests than 'certainty', however – for example, 'probability', 'more likely than not', 'a real possibility' – would progressively advance the point at which a solicitor would feel obliged to warn his or her council about the doubtful lawfulness of its actions, with all this would imply in terms of the council's ability to proceed without 'wilful misconduct'. The adoption of the certainty standard was, of course, anything but random. It was 'a very challenging decision', the Solicitor now writes. 'I wrestled with it for some time.' And bear in mind that he, too, like all other officers involved, was potentially liable to surcharge if his contributions to the rate-making exercise were anything but his objective and professional best. In the end, though, and taking into account the comparable exercises of professional judgment that were taking place at the same time in other rate-capped authorities, 'certainty' was the standard the Solicitor identified, and the council therefore never received the advice that would have made its *policies* far more difficult to sustain.

The importance of the legal advice that was or was not given emphasizes just how central *law* was in both confining and enabling this council and others through the turmoil of the 1985 'rates rebellion'. Their *disposition* of vigorous objection to the *Rates Act 1984* made *law* the source of enormous difficulties. At the same time, however, it was their only hope of salvation, since only a carefully legal decision-making process could protect them from the risk of surcharge. Thus was born the paradox of the 1985 rate-making: blending a 'united strategy of non-compliance' with *intra vires* decision-making. Deciding how and when to feed legal *information* into this process will have been a challenge, not only for lawyers but also for members across the country, who would be well aware of the difficulties the law presented. At times, no doubt, there was an element of calculation involved, since it would be hardly credible that authorities involved in this kind of crisis, and with the extensive knowledge these ones had of the range of plausible opinions available, should have sabotaged their efforts by asking what they thought was the wrong question at the wrong time to the wrong Counsel. Nonetheless there are limits to the extent to which, by an effort of will, one can turn the law as it is into the law as one would like it to be. Officers will have found the same. They will have been in no doubt as to what their respective councillors wanted to hear, and each will probably have gone as far as his or her individual sense of professional objectivity allowed, saying what needed to be said while trying to act with as much diplomacy as possible. To advise both objectively and diplomatically is, of course, simply a rule of everyday good practice. But in times as awkward as those described in this chapter it can develop into an acute dilemma, its resolution unpredictable. And if, at the end of the day, after everyone's best efforts, one's fate comes down to such refined distinctions as whether one is 'using the non-making of the rate ... as a lever in an attempt to prise additional money from Central Government' or whether, on the other hand, one is merely 'deferring the making of a rate while seeking by lawful means to persuade the Government to provide more resources', perhaps all one can do is cross one's fingers.

9
Aftermath: The 1986 Budget

The year leading up to the 1986 rate-making provides an instructive comparison with the year before. The legal framework was broadly the same. The council would be selected for rate-capping in the summer, and would then pass through the same rites of passage. In the autumn there would be a decision on redetermination, in the New Year a decision on whether to accept the maximum rate limit, and at some point, if all else failed, a decision on whether to apply for judicial review of the Secretary of State's actions. With the rate expected to be set at the legal maximum, financial efforts would concentrate on identifying non-rate means of sustaining the council's plans.

Within that overall framework, however, the years show various contrasts. The council's *policy* was different, uncertain at times, but not dominated by a direct clash with the government. As noted in the council's earlier years of 'internecine hungness', uncertainty of policy leads to uncertainty of legal focus. In the months leading up to the 1986 budget, the council's ambivalence about whether it was prepared to come to terms yet with the *Rates Act 1984* made it hard to know what specific legal questions would need answers.

The more important changes, though, related to the council's internal administrative dynamics. Severely strained by the previous year's tempestuous developments, the internal administrative process evolved in their aftermath in ways that gave *law* a more modest role. The contrast illustrates how, within a government, the functioning of public law responds to the pressures of events and is influenced by individual choices: advisors' choices about how to advise, and advisees' choices about whether, when and about what to seek advice.

A. Induced dejuridification

One thing that changed, and produced in effect a change in *organization*, was that the Solicitor assumed a less active posture in providing advice on the 1986 budget as compared with those of recent years. This was a natural response in both human and bureaucratic terms to the previous year's events, which had imposed enormous strains on working relationships – within the council, within the Labour Party locally and nationally, with the government – and among the relationships that had suffered were those between the Leadership and both the Solicitor and the Treasurer. What had been damaged was what Rosenberg (1989: especially ch. 10) calls the trust relationship, the intangible acceptance of roles, competencies and commitment that oils the wheels of local authorities' internal workings. As Rosenberg points out, the trust relationship 'is not a static quality', and 'once questioned, even on a relatively minor issue, it can lead to a lengthy chain reaction and undermine role authority even in a context where such authority apparently has been accepted for a lengthy period' (186). The controversies of the 1985 rate-making, of course, had been far from a 'relatively minor issue'. For both the Solicitor and the Treasurer the immediate aftermath was a time for keeping a lower profile, for discharging their responsibilities in a proper professional manner, yet doing so in a way that would give time for the wounds to heal.

The result in terms of the political process was to reduce the contribution of *law* to the 1986 budget. Rather as, by common consent, the *ultra vires* rule had been *organized into* the budget-making process immediately after the House of Lords's decision in *Bromley LBC v GLC* (1981), it was now being *organized out*, at least for the time being, by equally common, though tacit, consent. This was a form of 'dejudicialization' induced by the pressures of the previous year's events, and with it came 'dejuridification' of several aspects of the rate-making process.

An added complication was that members continued this year, as they had the year before, to make use of their own external sources of legal information. Early in the year this was through leading members' continued cooperative involvement with other rate-capped authorities, and from time to time throughout the year they continued to involve the solicitor in private practice who had advised them during the delayed rate-making. Such use of outside sources is another change of *organization*. It alters who is talking to whom on issues of *vires*, and produces a change in, or at least uncertainty about, the nature of the legal *information* that is available to the council as it exercises its statutory powers. For the internal legal advisors of a body like a local authority, the distinction between being *the* source of a council's legal *information* and being just *a* source is important, especially if, as in our council at this particular period, the demarcation between the internal and the external roles was unclear. If it is not clear who is advising on what, some items will fall through the cracks, others will lead to duplication, and some to inconsistent advice that the internal advisors are unaware of.

B. Rate-capped again

It came as no surprise in July 1985 when the council was again designated for rate-capping. The designated expenditure level was the same as before, £86m for the council's own spending, with no increase for inflation, and a further £20m to cover the cost of services that were to be inherited when the metropolitan authority was abolished on 31 March 1986, for a total of £106m.

From the outset, however, events unfolded differently. The first step was taken by the Secretary of State for the Environment, who decided this year to give more encouragement to the redetermination process. Unlike last year, he gave firm undertakings in Parliament, and reiterated them in a letter, that if rate-capped authorities applied for redetermination he would not reduce the expenditure level or impose conditions if the application was made 'principally on the grounds of inadequate allowance having been made for functions inherited from the GLC or Metropolitan County Councils' or 'on the ground that primarily because of budgeted use of special funds or similar accounting devices in 1985/86 the expenditure levels imply unachievable economies'. The letter also set out the comprehensive financial information that he required with an application for redetermination.

The Treasurer wrote to the Leadership in August comparing the council's projected expenditure to the government's much lower £86m and suggesting 'how this might be presented in any appeal for redetermination'. The council's *policy* at the time, however, was still one of concerted action of some sort with other rate-capped authorities, and rather than take this thinly-veiled hint that redetermination was relatively safe, the Leadership held off, pursuing instead correspondence with the Department of the Environment jointly with other authorities and through the local authority associations.

Their first effort was, in form, an attempt to clarify the meaning of the Secretary of State's undertakings, but in substance it was an effort to interpret them in the most favourable way possible from the rate-capped authorities' point of view. The undertakings had spoken of applications based 'principally' on inadequate provision being made for the transfer of metropolitan services or 'primarily' because of the use of special financial or accounting devices. In a letter of 16 August 1985 the Association of London Authorities said:

> We take the view that if either factor, or a combination of both, forms the largest single proportion of any application (although less, even much less, than 50% of any increase sought in the expenditure level), then the undertakings given by the Secretary of State would be operative ... . Please confirm that this interpretation is correct.

The new Secretary of State (Kenneth Baker had recently replaced Patrick Jenkin) declined, responding blandly that 'I do not believe that in practice authorities will have any difficulty in recognising the circumstances in which the undertakings would apply', and referring once more to the government's view that the much-feared powers to reduce expenditure levels and impose conditions were only designed to be used in a very limited set of circumstances.

Next the leaders of ten of the rate-capped authorities wrote in the most tentative terms to see whether a risk-free approach might be available on a narrower basis. Would the Department consider an 'early collective meeting' to 'explore ... the implications' if they were to 'enter discussions' dealing only with creative accounting and the costs of abolition, and only providing the financial information that was relevant to those two things? The authorities were suspicious of the Department's motives in requiring all the information it did. In reply, the Secretary of State stood pat. He declined the request for a collective meeting (as opposed to individual ones), gave no indication of what his reaction would be if an individual authority did in fact submit a limited application, and insisted that any application must provide all of the financial information originally listed.

There had been little involvement from the Solicitor in any of this. This year, in marked contrast to last year, he was observing the discussion rather than guiding it or actively participating. Yet even in this more limited role there was a certain basic minimum of *information* that had to be fed into the council's deliberations, normally by way of discreet discussion with the Chief Executive. One element was concern at the passage of time, since the deadline for an application for redetermination was approaching fast. This year as much as last year, and for all the same reasons, an *intra vires* decision on redetermination needed to be properly taken by the council before the deadline passed. Another concern was that the documentation the Legal Department had seen was slightly missing the point, legally, in the argument the council needed to make to the Secretary of State. Yet another was the suggestion that, if the council's objective was, as the correspondence appeared to imply, to make an application within the terms of the Secretary of State's undertakings but provide only limited information in support, the best approach might be to make a conditional application on the council's terms, but ask the Secretary of State to treat it as withdrawn if it was not accepted as coming within the undertakings. The Solicitor's main concern, however, was to make sure that when the report for the policy committee was finally prepared, there was an opportunity for the proper legal input that would help ensure that the council reached an *intra vires* decision on redetermination, based on the legally 'relevant considerations'.

In the event this did not happen. The Treasurer's supposed 'draft' report for the policy committee in October reached the Solicitor too late for comments to be added. The Treasurer, too, was adopting a lower profile in the interests of reestablishing the equilibrium that the events of the previous year had destroyed, and was not inclined to send out a document on a sensitive issue like redetermination unless requested by the Leadership or until it became absolutely necessary. The report was simply the Treasurer's report, drawn in part from the previous year's joint report, but not saying everything that, in the Solicitor's view, it should this year. In council, the Leader and the Chair of the finance sub-committee both took the opportunity to vent their anger at the current Secretary of State, who had, in their view, reneged on his predecessor's promises that it would be possible to negotiate on some issues relating to the council's budget but not on others. The minutes duly recorded this, their political tone and content being an apt reflection of the dejuridified, rough and ready decision-making of the present year rather than the legally *meticulous* minute-writing of the year before. The council resolved:

> That the council does not apply for re-determination of its expenditure level but that a letter be sent to the Secretary of State for the Environment specifying the cost of abolition of the [metropolitan authority] and the special funds the council has used.

There followed a futile exchange of correspondence with the Secretary of State, the Leader trying to engage the Secretary of State in discussions of abolition and special funds without making a formal application for redetermination, the Secretary of State saying that it must be a formal application or nothing.

In December came the announcement of the rate support grant and the council's maximum rate limit. The limit was calculated to fund a budget of £86m for the council's own services and £20m for services to be transferred when the metropolitan authority was abolished. The council, however, had already decided on a much larger budget of £118m for its own services alone, based on a policy of no cuts, no job losses, no rent increase and £2m of uncommitted growth, and considered it premature to take decisions about the new services it was to inherit. There was obviously a huge difference – £32m – between the council's assessment of its spending needs on its existing services and the government's. The council now had until 22 January 1986 to say whether it agreed with the proposed maximum rate limit before this was finally confirmed.

The council's rate support grant figure was not as bad as it might have been. In July, a distribution favouring the counties had been expected (*The Times*, 26 July 1985), but later that year – after riots in places such as Handsworth, Brixton and the Broadwater Farm Estate – the government reconsidered its inner city policy, and the announcement in December favoured the cities at the counties' expense (*The Times*, 19 December 1985). The result for our council was that, assuming it set its rate at the rate-capped limit, it would now be eligible for £46m of block grant. A further £12m was available under a rate equalization scheme that was to operate after the abolition of the metropolitan authority, for a total of £58m in grant and a rate reduction of almost 20%.

Reflecting this year's less *meticulous* observation of the *ultra vires* doctrine, with a member-led administrative process and with key officials adopting a lower profile than in the recent past, no formal council or committee decision was ever taken about whether to accept the rate limit proposed by the Secretary of State. Instead, after a reminder by the Treasurer in January 1986 that time was running out, the Labour group met and decided on a strategy with two components. The council would reject the maximum rate limit and try to negotiate an increase with the Secretary of State, its first grudging step into the procedures of the *Rates Act 1984*. It would also take Counsel's advice on the prospects for judicial review proceedings if the negotiations were unsuccessful.

Both parts of the strategy failed. The negotiations that the council had in mind were not of the kind that the Secretary of State considered germane to this stage of the statutory process, and he declined to increase the maximum rate limit. The council then directed the Solicitor to bring judicial review proceedings, arguing on the basis of *R v Secretary of State for the Environment, ex parte Hammersmith and Fulham LBC* (1985) that the Secretary of State was obliged to negotiate with them but had failed to do so. However, the rough and ready approach the council had adopted this year in its dealings with the Secretary of State made this an uphill struggle. The court proceedings failed at the first hurdle, the judge's initial decision, based on the court documents only, of whether the case could proceed to a hearing on the merits. The judge's written note stated:

> I am not satisfied that it is arguable the Secretary of State failed to negotiate: he had put forward a figure ... : why should he put forward a higher figure before you put forward an alternative figure which you did not do. Nor am I satisfied that he failed to provide or seek the exchange of relevant information.

The council pressed on to the next step, at which it could supplement its documents with oral argument, and managed to get the initial ruling changed. At the hearing on the merits, however, the application was dismissed. The judgment confirmed that the Secretary of State did have the discretion to review the maximum rate level late in the process before prescribing it, but stated that the weight he gave to representations at that stage was a matter for him. 'The short message here', the Solicitor noted in a memorandum reporting the outcome of the case, 'seems to be that it is only by making an application for redetermination that an authority puts the Secretary of State in a position where material weight must be given to representations' – a comment which might be loosely interpreted as 'I told you so'.

Losing the judicial review proceedings was not a major blow. To win would have been nice, but the prospects had always been poor, and it had always been expected that the council's rate would have to be at or close to the rate-cap level. More important was whether, as a matter of *policy*, the council was prepared to allow this to determine its spending levels, and the answer was a resounding 'no'. Group and council decisions in January, February and March 1986 confirmed the £118m figure the council had established for its own services and added £26m, instead of the government's £20m, for the services inherited from the metropolitan authority. The financial gap, therefore, for 1985/86 was £38m. The *policy* was to be one of financial defiance, of finding means by which, if possible, to hang on until the next general election. The only option, said the Leader in a Labour Party document that was subsequently obtained by the local newspaper, was to 'borrow against current spending and hence mortgage our future'. This is a form of words that would not have commended itself to the council's lawyers at this or any other time. As a matter of *law*, borrowing against current spending was exactly what the council was making sure it did not do.

C. Capital: the battle of wits

In the meantime, the year leading up to the 1986 budget had proved active on the capital front. Its bookends were the two large covenant agreements totalling £200m that were mentioned in the previous chapter, but there was much other activity in between.

The covenant arrangements themselves added a few new twists to what was, by now, a tried and true legal model. Central to each of them was a specially created private company, wholly controlled by Company B. Each of these companies (henceforth 'Company B.1' and 'Company B.2') was to be, technically, the main contractor for an extensive list of housing projects. The council would select projects from this list and would approve and supervise the builders. The company would engage them and pay them, borrowing from financial institutions for the purpose. In due course the council would make payments to the company; these would reflect the cost of the works, plus the interest due from the company to the financial institutions on the money it had borrowed. The council's first payments were due in 1989/90.

A feature worth noting is that Companies B.1 and B.2, unlike their forerunners Council Co. and Jointly-owned Co., were not even partially owned by the council. The council was now sufficiently confident in its dealings with Company B to allow this. Indeed, when the Company B.2 covenant was being put in place at great speed late in the financial year amid fears that the government might soon ban these transactions retrospectively (see Davies 1987: 31), and a member of the legal staff pointed out some weaknesses in the terms of the arrangements, the Deputy Solicitor's response was that the Treasurer should be informed, but if he assessed the risks as though Company B were a partner not a stranger, that would probably not be unreasonable. Eventually, the Company B.2 deal was done just in time for the 31 March deadline, and Treasurer commended the Legal Department for its achievement. 'Yet again', commented the Solicitor in a note passing the compliment on to the officers involved, 'Legal Department staff have worked the miracle of the March "panic"'.

Meanwhile, the government had already clamped down on sales of mortgages like the well-known one between Liverpool and Banque Paribas (Carmichael 1995: 181; Loughlin 1996: 379) and the one our council completed in March 1985. This was done with almost immediate effect, the Secretary of State announcing in July 1985 that as from 24 July, under legislation that would be introduced later, local authorities would no longer be able to sell their 'Housing Act mortgages' *en bloc* without the prior consent of the individual borrowers. Other possible changes that were announced included applying the same restriction to non-residential mortgages and requiring that any mortgage sale had to transfer the entire risk to the purchaser, a potential problem for our council, since its mortgage sale had not done so. When the Bill was published in November 1985, the Treasurer was swiftly back in touch with the Solicitor about a mortgage sale that the Bill did not seem to block. This would be of mortgages that the council had granted to housing associations. The Bill did not seriously impede these as sales *en bloc* because the only borrower whose consent was needed for each sale was the housing association involved, not the individual occupiers. Counsel concurred; the sale was duly concluded; and an extremely welcome £4m was received.

The large covenant schemes and the sale of the housing association mortgages were just two of many ideas in circulation at the time as a cottage industry developed in identifying and employing the legal *latitude* still available to local authorities under the *Local Government, Planning and Land Act 1980* and its various offshoots in other Acts and regulations. As a brochure that a finance company circulated to potential local authority clients in June 1985 put it:

> The City and Local Authorities have an impressive and well deserved past record of working well together in responding to the constraints which have been placed over public spending. It appears to us that the ever-tightening expenditure controls require that our past joint inventiveness in dealing with these problems needs to be continued and, where possible, improved upon.

The council, too, was all in favour of 'joint inventiveness'.

Numerous proposals were in circulation at the time. Their normal trajectory was that finance companies would send them to the Treasurer, he would consider them and pass to the Solicitor those that seemed promising both in *law*, as the Treasurer understood it, and in the light of the physical assets available to the council. The Solicitor would then seek Counsel's opinions on the ones that were serious possibilities both practically and legally. The proposals tended to concentrate on capital transactions. Some, like the covenant schemes and the mortgage sales, the council had already done. Others included different versions of sale/leaseback or lease/leaseback transactions designed to produce real capital receipts rather than, or as well as, the notional capital receipts mentioned previously in this book. There were also schemes designed for their revenue effect, especially attractive, perhaps, to a rate-capped authority, such as a proposal that a local authority might transfer income-producing assets to a charitable trust on terms that the trust would use the income for such of the local authority's purposes as were charitable. There were also other schemes, rather like the co-operative homesteading initiative outlined in Chapter 7, that were not financially oriented in their own right, but aimed to provide *intra vires* means by which councils could accomplish their policy goals within the context of the legal and financial constraints of the *Local Government, Planning and Land Act 1980*. In our council, for example, schemes were considered for acquiring high priority development sites through a carefully structured set of leases and underleases involving a financial institution, or by 'landbanking', under which a financial institution would buy the site and agree to sell it to the council later when resources became available.

With any of these transactions, particularly asset sales, there were also various potential niceties as to how and when money available to the council might be used. Should the price simply be accepted as a cash payment, and if so when? Or might it be better if the payment were invested, with the council receiving interest over time rather than a lump sum? Might the buyer be prevailed upon, instead of paying the council, to pay a third party, who would then do something for the council? Might the buyer be prepared to pay some of the council's bills as they came due?

Not all of these ideas, by any means, were productive. One, for example, was described as a 'useless idea' by the Deputy Solicitor. Another was 'demolished' at a conference with Counsel. The exercise overall, nonetheless, was an informative exploration of the *operative law* of the *Local Government, Planning and Land Act 1980*, as a variety of ideas were examined, conclusions were reached that reflected the collective wisdom of the day, and a range of financing possibilities was either accepted as *intra vires* and available if required by the emerging realities of the council's political position, or rejected as *ultra vires*.

D. Bridging the gap

In March 1986, something was definitely needed. The council's *policy* was for spending of £143m. (The amount had changed marginally from earlier figures.) The revenue available at the council's rate-capped level was £106m. The gap was £37m. The strategy was financial defiance, with the council doing whatever it could to hold out until the next general election in the hope of a Labour victory. What were the *intra vires* financial measures that would convert these mismatched elements into the balanced budget that was legally required?

This was the point at which all the lessons learned, and deals done, over the recent and not so recent past came together, feeding off each other in several cases. For example, £3.5m was covered by capitalizing housing repairs that were currently charged to revenue, paying for them from the proceeds of sale of the housing association mortgages. £1.5m was covered by leasing, with no payments falling due until 1987/88. Another £3m came from 'non-prescribed capital expenditure' (remember that term?) on housing repairs. The Treasurer's report carefully explained that 'Capitalised housing expenditure is only classed as "prescribed" expenditure (i.e. it counts against the council's capital allocations) if it is financed by borrowing. The council can therefore capitalise housing repair expenditure, if it is financed in some other way, outside of the capital controls.' That other way was by using the 'non-useable portion' of the council's capital receipts.

Add another £12m of deferred purchase arrangements, £3m of capitalized repayments on covenant schemes, £6m of estimates of sums due from the government and £2m taken from the provision for bad debts at the end of the 1985/86 financial year ... and the Treasurer was still adrift by a substantial £5.5m.

All he had left to offer was a very large 'unidentified savings' item, coupled with the urgent warning that 'it is essential that proper mechanisms are in place to identify those required savings'. Legal advice the previous year had emphasized that an unidentified savings item was only acceptable as the final element in balancing a budget if the council genuinely intended to make the savings, and that it was preferable if a proper mechanism was set up to identify them.

In relation to capitalization and deferred purchase schemes, moreover, which had recently been so useful to the council, the Treasurer warned

> 57. ... there are two constraints on the continued use of deferred purchase schemes:

a) an upper limit which the money market would impose as being the maximum that could be prudently raised by this arrangement,
b) the council will have reached the limit on identifying revenue spending which could conceivably be capitalised.

The fact that deferred purchase arrangements were *intra vires*, in other words, would be tempered by market assessments of the nature of the items involved and of the council's overall financial situation; both were constraints on the council's *autonomy*. There was, furthermore, a limit on the council's *latitude* to classify spending as being capital in nature; at some point the council's working definition would have gone as far as an honest professional opinion could conceivably take it.

Clearly there was much in the 1986 budget report that might well have been thought worthy of careful legal comment. Items like a 0% rent rise, the increased provision for uncommitted growth and the largest reliance ever on unidentified savings catch the eye, given the legal discussions of these items in the past. Likewise, the proposed new £12m deferred purchase scheme seemed far from being a done deal, and questions might well have been raised about how reliable a bridge it was for such a large gap. In fact, however, the legal input was limited. When an Opposition member asked at the policy committee meeting immediately before council whether the report contained any legal observations, the Chief Executive answered that the legal implications were incorporated into the Treasurer's report and that Counsel's opinion had been obtained on all of the financial adjustments. He undertook also to provide the member with a copy. It is not clear what Counsel's opinion was being referred to; it does not appear to have been obtained through the Legal Department.

E. A semblance of normality?

A number of factors influenced the more modest contribution of *law* to the budgetary decision this year of aftermath to the 'rates rebellion', some of them natural, others not. The natural part of this was that in any government there will be, over time, an ebb and flow in the explicit legal involvement in decision-making. It bears repeating that the *ultra vires* rule, which applies not only to *what* local authorities do, but also to *who* does it, to *how* and to *why*, potentially has some bearing on everything that anybody in local government ever does, and is capable in any situation of being more or less *meticulously* applied. Practically speaking, though, it is not possible for the doctrine to be applied equally *meticulously* to everything, all the time. High-water marks such as the 1982 rent decision or the advice on the process leading up to the 1985 rate-making cannot be the norm. After them things settle back to a new or an old state of balance. There is also a natural tendency that, however careful lawyers may be to emphasize that a particular decision *can be* lawful if taken in the right way, what decision-makers tend to remember is that such a decision *is* lawful, without any of the riders that lawyers try to add. Thus it was natural that some of the financial decisions that had sometimes had much emphasis placed on their legal dimensions might, in time, revert to being more purely financial in nature.

What was less natural about the process in 1986, though, was that part of the reason why there was relatively little legal input was the conscious self-restraint exercised by the Solicitor (among others) in the interest of re-establishing equilibrium (or 'trust') in the aftermath of the hugely disruptive rate-making controversy of the previous year. In fact the Solicitor strongly felt in March 1986 that the council's budgetary decisions would be placed on firmer legal ground if the Treasurer's report were more thorough and detailed, and if the council's attention were more deliberately directed to the 'relevant considerations' surrounding the key decisions that the report was to present. This was discussed at length with the Chief Executive, who was insistent that the legal aspects of the report should be more condensed. The Solicitor searched his professional conscience closely, wondering whether his duty to the council required him to supplement the Treasurer's report with an additional report of his own, which would of course have done nothing to help re-establish equilibrium. Ultimately, however, he decided to accept that the version that the Chief Executive preferred presented an accurate summary of the principal points, and should proceed alone.

At the end of the day, though, and strange though it may seem, there was a form of normality about the circumstances of the 1986 budget, though it was probably not apparent at the time. What was normal about it was that out of the combination of natural and unnatural causes described above there emerged a budget in which the major financial decisions were to be based substantially on financial judgment, with the *ultra vires* rule playing only a limited and broadly contextual role. *Law* was reverting to being a *peripheral* factor in the council's actual budget decision, as opposed to the *explicit, determinative* or sometimes *contested* contributions it had so often made in the recent past. What was on display, though, was an odd and somewhat precarious version of normality. Partly this was because there was not at this time a common understanding within the council of how active a part *law* should be playing in the process (witness the disagreements about the legal component of the Treasurer's report for the 1986 rate-making). Partly, also, it was because in 1986 it was only by dint of enormous legal effort at the staff level, and with careful attention to many potentially destructive legal details, especially in relation to the deferred purchase and similar arrangements, that the breathing space was established in which financial judgment could enjoy this relative freedom to operate. The writing was on the wall, though, for even this distorted version of financial normality. The Treasurer's warning that further deferred purchase measures alone could not 'bridge the gap' for next year meant that something else would have to be found, and this would bring *law* back into focus as the council was forced to identify some new *intra vires* measure that would generate new resources. The deferred purchase approach, in any event, was expected to be eliminated by the government at any time, even in advance of the new system of capital controls it was by now developing. Holding out until the next general election, which was the council's overarching *policy* goal at the time, was not expected to be easy.

10 Victim of Circumstance: The 1987 Budget

The following year was one of convoluted events and a flurry of activity. Viewed in broad outline, it probably played out much as one might have expected: another rate-cap; a continued determination to maintain services; a growing 'gap' to be 'bridged'; and a need to identify new legal *latitude* as the government sought to control the use of deferred purchase arrangements. Examined more closely, however, the council's continued financial travails in 1986–87 were not wholly of its own making. Though the council began a *policy* shift towards firmer financial ground, events conspired against it to force it back into the hole it was now ready to start digging out of.

Responding to the pressures of events is more difficult for a government like an English local authority, whose only public law resources are statutory powers, than for one that has an inherent capacity to act and may be able to legislate away some its problems. Nonetheless, events confront them all, and public law will constrain their response. A small-scale example involving the Crown, in the form of the Canadian Department of Fisheries and Oceans, is *Larocque v Canada* (2006), where the Department had tried, but failed, to negotiate a co-management agreement for the snow crab fishery and to get a stock survey done as part of the agreement. Its reaction was to fund the survey creatively, through an allocation of fishing quota, but doing so was held to fall foul of the rules on appropriations in the *Financial Administration Act*. In a far more serious context, Cooper (2007: 288–9) describes the difficulties President Bush initially encountered trying to set up the Department of Homeland Security by executive order in response to the 2001 terrorist attacks in New York and Washington. The appointee, Governor Ridge,

> found himself without statutory authority, technical capacity or appropriations to carry out the mammoth task of bringing order

> and coordinated operations to the plethora of well-established agencies that had jurisdiction over or another aspect of the field of homeland security elements.

Governments, in short, have to respond to the hand fate deals them with the legal resources that public law allows. For a purely statutory body like our council these are statutes and statutes alone, but even for governments with non-statutory powers there are public law constraints.

A. Seizing the moment

The new financial year began where the old one had ended. The council's financial situation was bad and expected to get worse. Its legal options were limited and expected to become more limited. It was better to act sooner rather than later, taking advantage of *intra vires* financial options while they were available.

The government, at its capital spending review in mid-April 1986, did not impose the legal restrictions the Treasurer had feared, and by the end of the month he was investigating a further refinement of the step-by-step evolution of the *operative law* of deferred purchase arrangements. This was an early draw-down of the funds available under the Company B.2 scheme. Spending under it had been scheduled over several years, and Company B.2 could draw on the resources that the financial institution made available whenever they were wanted. 'Early draw-down' meant drawing on them before the works were done, rather than as they progressed. The funds would in fact be drawn not by the council but by a further *ad hoc* private company, Company B.3, which would invest them and pay the interest to the council. An attraction of this was that it converted covenant arrangements into a source feeding the revenue accounts. Company B.3 was expected to produce income to the council of about £3m in the current year and £4m for the 1987/88 budget that the Treasurer was beginning to look towards, though it did so at a price; the earlier the money was drawn, the higher the eventual repayments would be. Nonetheless, the £3m expected for the current year would take care of a large part of the unspecified savings the Treasurer had to find, and for 1987/88 also the benefits were considerable. The Legal Department was satisfied that this 'advance funding/deferred purchase' combination, a new twist in the *operative law* of the *Local Government, Planning and Land Act, 1980,* was *intra vires* and did not amount to borrowing. So was Counsel.

Similar in theme was advance leasing – entering leases in 1986 for items which would actually be provided and paid for in later years.

Leasing had become in our council an increasingly important *intra vires* method of meeting the financial challenges of the *Local Government, Planning and Land Act 1980.* Items that were now leased included not only conventional things such as vehicles and computers, but also, building on the lessons learned with the 'happy accident' of the new municipal offices in 1981, major items of fixed equipment such as lifts, boilers and central heating systems. More recently smaller items such as television aerials, entryphones, kitchen and bathroom fittings and library books had begun to be leased. Leasing had become, in short, an increasingly useful element in sustaining the council's policies in the existing framework of *given law.*

Advance leasing was a further adaptation of these already expanded leasing activities, designed to protect them from the prospect that the government might change the rules and require some or all of them to be dealt with as 'prescribed expenditure'. This might happen either under the new system of capital controls discussed in the January 1986 Green Paper *Paying for Local Government* or under the administrative restrictions that were feared in the meantime. Company B, in response, developed advance leasing proposals, and by August 1986 the Treasurer was reporting that three years of advance leasing was under discussion. When the government did indeed clamp down on leasing, announcing in October 1986 that any expenditure on leasing arranged on or after 1 April 1987 would count against capital allocations in the year the expenditure was incurred, the five month 'pre-implementation licence' was too good to be missed. In January 1987 the leasing programmes for the next three years were finalized. By 31 March a further two years had been added, and advance leasing arrangements were in place for amounts ranging from £13m to £15m per year for the next five years. The arrangements could be technically complex, and were decided upon as the *given law* of advance funding (though not advance leasing) was clarified in several cases examining the advance funding schemes that metropolitan councils had adopted in anticipation of their abolition on 1 April 1986. (Loughlin 1996: 161–5 discusses several unreported cases.) Both Counsel and the Legal Department were satisfied that the advance leasing arrangements were *intra vires.* The Treasurer was therefore able to pin down an important part of the council's future equipment needs while the legal *latitude* still remained.

B. Policy shift: local elections and the 'new realism'

At the same time, though, that the council was trying to 'DoE-proof' its finances as far as possible, it was also developing a different, and more restrained, *policy*. At the first meeting of the policy committee after the 1986 rate-making there were decisions taken to approve a further £600,000 in uncommitted growth, but only on the basis that off-setting savings would be identified and that 'there will be no further uncommitted growth in 1986/87'. The committee also considered a management letter from the district auditor which mentioned such things as rent arrears, rate arrears and empty properties as representing revenue potential that was being lost. The letter also calculated that a rent increase of a little over £1 per week would generate more than £6m in income, £4m of it from the government in rate support grant, at a cost to tenants of only £600,000 once rebates were taken into account. In May, local elections were held (the Opposition group expanded from 4 to 19 members, but a Left-leaning Labour Party remained in firm control of the council), and in July the Leader put to the council a strategy proposal that reflected several of the district auditor's themes:

> 14. We also need to look at other areas of the council where we can raise more resources to improve other services. Examples include voids, management of ... non-housing assets, rent and rate arrears ...

A rent increase was notably absent from this list, but even this was to be remedied later. In October, in what the local newspaper described as a 'bombshell' disclosure to a tenants' association meeting, the Leader revealed that a rent increase in 1987 was likely.

Even without that final element, though, the Leader's proposal after the May 1986 local election reflected a recognition that time was running out for the financial policies of recent years. The focus now was on holding out until the next general election, due within two years, and then undertaking a 'mid-term review in the light of the financial, service and political circumstances' at that time. If a Labour government were elected it would need to be persuaded of the urgency of the council's situation. If the Conservatives won, the prospects would be 'dire'.

Meanwhile, and during the struggle to survive until the next general election, a change of direction was being proposed. The controversies of recent years were presented as almost having been a distraction from the real business of the council:

> 12. The 1982–86 council was forced to give priority to the issues of ratecapping and abolition. The manifesto also set us the priority of

> decentralisation. These issues prevented us from reviewing our services in a detailed and systematic way to ensure their relevance and effectiveness. Such a review is time-consuming, but is essential if we are to restore public confidence in the worth of public services. We need to establish new priorities for examining the effectiveness of our policies. In the end things like a better repair service and a more polite response by our officers in dealing with the public, will ensure continued confidence in the council's ability to deliver good services.

Though there was dissension in the Labour ranks, the Leader's proposal prevailed. This change in the council's *policy* orientation was one of the defining events of the financial year. Though the proposal still mentioned 'tapping into new sources of external finance' as part of the agenda, this was a subsidiary theme in a bigger picture of providing good local government and high quality services in the struggle to hold out until the next general election.

In terms of the *ultra vires* rule and the interaction between *law* and *policy*, this new strategy, the 'new realism' as it was known, had the important but subtle effect of redefining the benchmark of 'reasonableness' against which specific financial decisions would have to be measured. It has been mentioned previously that to some extent a local authority's political preferences can influence the range of options that the *ultra vires* rule leaves open to it; the local authority's own view of what is reasonable, of what it should be doing, helps define when 'unreasonableness' in the legal sense arises. Thus the council's recognition in July 1986 that it had to pull in its horns would make it harder to justify in legal terms actions that did not fit easily with its revised financial orientation.

C. 22 July 1986: the fateful day

The second defining event came with the government's rate support grant announcement on 22 July 1986. It not only dealt with grant and with rate-capping – the council was again selected for rate-capping for the coming financial year, with its designated expenditure level of £106m unchanged – but also imposed the long-anticipated capital controls. The Secretary of State said that the government was going to introduce legislation which would effectively put a stop to advance purchase and deferred purchase as means of avoiding capital controls, and would require expenditure to be charged to the year in which the local authority received the benefit of the works. The legislation, he announced, would be retroactive, and would apply to all schemes entered into from midnight that night. This combination of rate-capping and new capital restrictions placed the council in a particularly unfavourable legal position: rates were to be limited at the same time that the best measures so far identified for dealing with rate limits and other restrictions under the *Local Government, Planning and Land Act 1980* were to be removed. Rhodes (1992: 57) refers to this period from early 1986 to mid-1987 as a period of 'stand-off', a 'lull before the storm' while the government was 'waiting for a third term of office before mounting its next attack on the "problem" of local government finance'. This may be true at the level of broad legislative policy; Rhodes had the government's poll tax proposals particularly in mind. In the trenches, however, at least as far as our council was concerned, the period was anything but a 'lull'. This was instead the height of the 'storm', and the government's attack was in full flood.

Interestingly, the two elements of the government's announcement on 22 July 1986 generated very different kinds of legal activity. Rate-capping was by now a relatively familiar legal framework from which experience had removed many of the uncertainties. The council's response this year was to lock horns with the government by thoroughly conventional means. The capital restrictions, by contrast, impelled the council vigorously in the direction of the unfamiliar and the unconventional as it strove to identify resources to fund its commitments. Between these contrasting responses there was a direct connection. If the rate-cap were eased so that rates could be increased, there would be less need for legally 'creative' responses to the capital restrictions. If, though, the rate-cap stayed as originally announced, the council could only preserve its programmes by identifying and taking advantage of unfamiliar areas of legal *latitude*, for the familiar ground had now been cut away.

D. The rate-cap fiasco

That the council was to be rate-capped again for 1987/88 might not appear surprising to the outside observer, but to the council it was a shock and a disappointment. On the basis of past practice the council would have been rate-capped if its total expenditure was more than 20% above the government's assessment of its spending need. This year the margin was 12.5%. Had the Treasurer known this in advance, rate-capping could probably have been avoided, since even at 12.5%

the council was only fractionally above the limit (0.02%, to be exact), and on the basis of actual figures for the year rather than the budgeted figures, the council would be below the limit. Some in the council suspected that the 12.5% figure had been deliberately chosen to ensure that our council was caught.

The council's first reaction was a perfectly ordinary one for a local authority that was finally prepared to come to terms with the *Rates Act 1984*: it tried to get the Secretary of State to change his mind. The Chief Executive wrote explaining the council's situation and suggesting that the council should be removed from the rate-cap list. The Solicitor was not *organized into* this approach, which was not seen at this stage as having major legal connotations. The Department replied in tones that suggest it was playing its cards close to its chest in anticipation of a possible legal challenge. It said that the Secretary of State had no power to make the change requested, but that in any event the Secretary of State, having considered the Chief Executive's comments, 'does not consider that your authority should be omitted from the list of those designated for rate limitation in 1987/88', a broad, bland response that gave nothing away.

Persuasion having failed, the next step was again a perfectly conventional legal fall-back: to consider whether the council had grounds for a legal challenge. Here the Solicitor was *organized in*, for litigation was, of course, archetypal lawyers' work. This year the Legal Department felt that there were credible grounds and a genuine possibility of success. Its contention was that the Secretary of State, having the statutory obligation to act on the basis of the 'best information available to him', (s.2(2) *Rates Act 1984*) had not done so, since better information than the 1986/87 budget figures was readily available, namely the council's revised estimates based on actual rather than projected figures. Counsel considered this argument had real possibilities, though certainly no guarantee of success. In October the judicial review proceedings were commenced.

During this time frame, the council was also considering another perfectly ordinary step under *Rates Act 1984*: applying for redetermination. In the rate support grant announcement on 22 July 1986 the Secretary of State for the Environment had again given an undertaking that where redetermination was requested because special accounting arrangements in the past meant that the proposed expenditure levels implied unachievable economies, he would not reduce the expenditure level or use his power to impose conditions.

Though the council remained highly suspicious of the Department of the Environment and of its motives in requiring much of the information that it insisted accompany the application, the Treasurer saw little danger, and ultimately the Leadership agreed. Crucial to this was the experience of the six authorities who had applied for partial redetermination the previous year, and had received increases ranging from £3m to £9m, with no conditions or restrictions. Moreover, the gap between the council's designated expenditure level of £106m and its projected spending of £154m was an enormous, and currently unfunded, £48m. Even so, the council proceeded cautiously. The Treasurer's report to the policy committee advised that there was still a 'considerable risk' in making an application that did not come within the scope of the Secretary of State's undertakings, and that, to be confident of remaining within their shelter the council's request for redetermination should be limited to £12m.

The Legal Department, one should note, played virtually no role in the preparation of the decision to request a redetermination. Partly this was because it had not yet emerged from its lower profile of the previous year, though it was beginning to do so, but partly also it was because the particular *policy* of applying for redetermination did not call for anything more than a passive legal role. It was one of those situations in which one can enable one's local authority to act *intra vires* by doing nothing: when outputs can be legal even without legal input. This year, for the first time, *policy* was running with the grain of the *law* in the *Rates Act 1984* rather than against it, and appeared to offer genuine prospects of an improvement in the council's financial predicament. The letter that accompanied the council's application asked for assurances that it would be treated as within the undertakings and would not lead to a reduction in the limit or the imposition of conditions. In reply, the Department of the Environment agreed.

At this point, exit the Solicitor, who took up an appointment as Chief Executive elsewhere. The Deputy Solicitor took over the reins for the next seven months. Enter, meanwhile, a cruel blow of fate that totally disrupted the council's planning for its 1987 budget.

For a little while, meetings with the Department of the Environment on rate-capping, redetermination and the council's judicial review proceedings had been strangely hard to arrange. On 16 December, the explanation emerged. The Secretary of State for the Environment announced in Parliament what the headline in *The Times* the next day called the 'Minister's £65 billion rates blunder' – that the Department's entire approach to calculating rate support grant under the *Local Government Planning and Land Act 1980* had been based on a legal error, and that the government was going to have to correct this by retroactive legislation. The error had to do with whether transfers between certain funds within a local authority's accounts should or should not be considered 'expenditure' for purposes of calculating rate support grant. The government had previously accepted local authorities' opinion that they should (see *R v Secretary of State for the Environment, ex parte Birmingham CC* 1987: 54), but now, revisiting the *operative law* of rate support grant calculation in response to litigation involving Birmingham and Greenwich (see Loughlin 1996: 290–9), it changed its mind.

The effect for our council was dramatic. At the time the '£65 billion rates blunder' was announced, the council was challenging the lawfulness of its rate-cap in judicial review proceedings, with real hopes of success, and there was every likelihood that, whether or not it won its judicial review, its designated expenditure limit would be increased through the redetermination process. All of that was now lost. The government's plans for remedying its past errors included a special statutory régime for determining, among other things, this year's rate-caps, and it soon emerged that these plans would not only correct the government's self-identified error but would also make it impossible for the council to pursue its legal challenge, even though it was based on a different ground. They would also render abortive the redetermination process that the council had entered for the first time this year, and would impose, substantially, the unamended spending limit that the government had originally announced.

The Bill that was to become the *Local Government Finance Act 1987* did all of these things. Various efforts were made to amend it, some failing by only a handful of votes in Parliament. Hoping that one or another of them might succeed, the Legal Department attempted various manoeuvres in its judicial review proceedings, all with a view to preserving its legal challenge to its 1987/88 rate limit if amendments to the Bill made this possible. But all efforts were to no avail. As the council's rate-making in March 1987 approached, all the indications were that the rate-cap figures were to be set by unchallengeable law, and that any attempt in the meantime to set a higher rate would be rolled back.

The Deputy Solicitor's advice to the policy committee set out the council's frustrating legal situation in stark terms:

> <u>Rate-capping: where we stand now</u>
> 16. I need to explain to members where the Council now stands on rate-capping for 1987/88. Legally, we are not at the time of writing (13th March) rate-capped. The Secretary of State has admitted his

> July 1986 rate-capping designation to have been unlawful because of the [rate support grant] error mentioned at paragraph 7 of the main report and paragraph 10 of this Appendix. Indeed, he insists they are unlawful. The High Court has furthermore declared the council's rate-cap to have been unlawful, in the consent order obtained in our judicial review challenge (see paragraph 13 of this Appendix).
>
> 17. However, the Local Government Finance Bill is highly likely to receive the Royal Assent during March, and we can be in little or no doubt that it will be enacted in the form described above. The effect is that we shall be re-ratecapped for 1987/88, and there is no sensible alternative to proceeding on that basis at this stage.

This advice – 'my suicide note, as I sometimes think of it', writes the Deputy Solicitor – was obviously not what the council wanted to hear, and at some times the abruptness of its closing sentence might have proved controversial. This, though, was not one of them. Unwelcome though the message was, there was a greater preparedness under the *policy* of 'new realism' to accept it as *determinative* of this aspect of the council's legal *latitude*. The Deputy Solicitor certainly examined the Bill closely to see if it left any openings, but it did not. The Leader also brought in once more, apparently for the last time, the solicitor in private practice who had advised the group, and later the council, on rate-making issues at times in the past. No gaps, however, were identified, and the rate was set at the rate-cap level. On this front, therefore, the sheer bad luck of the 'Minister's £65 billion rates blunder' and of the way it was corrected had deprived the council of the likelihood that redetermination would have improved its financial position markedly, and of the small but real hope that success in the judicial review proceedings would have also brought financial relief.

E. The capital calamity

Bad luck on the revenue side, however, translated into severe strain on the capital side, where the implications of the announcement of 22 July 1986 had already been entirely different. Instead of playing by the book, which on the revenue side seemed to hold out genuine prospects of success, the council was forced to consider breaking new legal ground, and the only statutory powers available were ones that had already been available before 22 July but had not been the council's preferred options.

Three strands of the council's response to its unpleasant legal predicament can be differentiated. First, it had to deal with the direct consequences of the government's announcement for the schemes directly affected. This part of the picture was unavoidable, and was simply the process of coming to terms with changed, and in this case unwelcome, *given law*. Second, it had to find new means of financing its programmes. This was a matter of choice. As a matter of deliberate *policy*, the council had decided that it must at least struggle on until the next general election, and this in turn meant finding new areas of legal *latitude,* now that the council's tried and trusted covenant arrangements had been taken out of play. Third, there was the effect of the 22 July announcement at the level of the intangibles. Until now, in the financial struggle between the council (and others like it, of course) and the government, the council had been making most of the running, relying on ever-expanding *operative law* in which, over time, it had developed increasing confidence. From now on, though, it was to be embroiled in a rearguard action, using unfamiliar legal mechanisms which had not previously found favour. The legal self-assurance that deferred purchase schemes had brought was to begin to fade; the council felt itself to be on the defensive, as indeed it was, since the government had announced in July that its attack on creative financing methods was not necessarily going to stop with deferred purchase schemes.

As to the first of these strands, the need to deal with the direct consequences for existing deferred purchase schemes, the most immediate effect was to constrain their operation. The council, Company B, and Companies B.1, B.2, and B.3 started taking special care to ensure that nothing was done that might prejudice the schemes' protected status under the 22 July announcement. This was complicated by the fact that there was an element of guesswork involved, since the details of the proposed retroactive legislation giving effect to the announcement would not be known for several months. The consequences of error, furthermore, might be severe. Though it was thought likely that if a particular building contract was dealt with in a way that removed its protected status the result would only affect that particular contract, it was not inconceivable that the entire covenant might be affected. Caution was clearly the order of the day.

More generally, the announcement of 22 July 1986 also contributed to a difficult nine months for the Treasurer on the capital side, with fluctuating figures producing a projected capital underspend of £4m in September which then transformed itself into projected overspend reaching £10m by January 1987. This year, however, in sharp contrast to the year of the 'rates rebellion', the Treasurer approached the overspend with equanimity. There was no concern about whether it was, technically, *ultra vires* or about the Secretary of State's power to impose financial conditions. Instead the Treasurer managed to boost the council's allocations by borrowing unused allocation from a nearby authority, and as to the rest of the overspend he reported that he was 'confident, based on the experience of other authorities which had been in a similar position, that the DOE [Department of the Environment] would allow the council to gross up its resources for 1986/87 and 1987/88'. Evidently this part of the system, too, like the redetermination process, was settling down to one where people 'knew the ropes' and had a shared understanding of how *law* would be implemented in practice. No doubt the fact that this year the council was not actively embroiled in a 'united strategy of non-compliance' assisted the Treasurer's equanimity.

The second strand of the council's reaction to the announcement of 22 July 1986 was the one that could have been avoided if the council's *policy* had been different. This was the search for ways of circumventing the government's action. The local government grapevine lost no time in passing on possibilities for investigation – with the caution, of course, that it would be wise to be extremely discreet. The government had, after all, said it would act against other arrangements than deferred purchase if necessary. Publishing one's intentions was therefore likely to be legally counter-productive.

As was mentioned at the beginning of this chapter, the government did indeed take action in October 1986 to bring more leasing within the prescribed expenditure rules, but only prospectively. Local authorities across the country, the Secretary of State subsequently stated, rushed through over £2bn of leasing deals in the period of grace allowed (*The Times*, 10 March 1988). Our council's share was £72m, taking advantage of and expanding the advance leasing arrangements that Company B presciently had on hand. The council's legal *latitude* was therefore fully exploited while it still existed. Deferred purchase, moreover, was still potentially the source of a useful *intra vires* transaction or two. The announcement of 22 July 1986 had only imposed controls on deferred purchase for prescribed expenditure. It occurred to the Treasurer that deferred purchase for non-prescribed expenditure might still be a possibility. In November 1986, he asked the Legal Department what they thought of this. The response was that it appeared to be both *intra vires* and financially effective, and that it would be interesting to see what Company B thought. The Treasurer then asked Company B, who naturally thought it a splendid idea. By March 1987, then, when the council's budget was set, negotiations were well under way for a £19m deferred purchase arrangement with a new company, Company B.4, to cover the estimated cost of the council's capitalized spending on housing repairs and maintenance. Inconveniently, though, it was already known by then that this particular device was not likely to be worth repeating in the future, for reasons which had nothing to do with the *vires* of the arrangements. The government had noticed that the combined effect of its rules on housing subsidy and on debt charge subsidy meant that capitalized housing repairs attracted both. It was therefore changing the rules in a way that would make future capitalizations of this sort pointless. It would also make the council £11.5m worse off in revenue terms the following year, 1988/89, a blow that the Treasurer recommended softening by making provision for the first £5.5m of it in the 1987 budget. Nonetheless for the specific purposes of bridging the council's 1987 budgetary gap, the £19m capitalization of repairs and maintenance and the related Company B.4 deferred purchase arrangement could proceed and was extremely useful.

F. The 'Sale of the Century'

Even £19m for housing repairs, however, pales by comparison with the major initiative that the council was now increasingly investigating in consequence of the 22 July 1986 announcement: a £150m lease/leaseback transaction. The transaction involved new *operative law* for the council, for this was not the kind of lease/leaseback that had once been contemplated as a means of financing a specific development like the new municipal offices. Nor was it a lease/leaseback of the kind involved with the neighbourhood offices, designed to raise notional capital receipts. This time what the council was looking at was a lease/leaseback transaction that would produce money. Here, then, was another example of the council taking a familiar and lawful device, the lease/leaseback transaction, and examining it closely to see if it could be adapted to serve as an *intra vires* vehicle for meeting other needs.

The idea of this adapted form of lease/leaseback transaction had been in circulation in the local government financial world for some time, but initially the council had not been particularly interested, financially or legally, since other options were more advantageous. By the time of the previous year's budget, however, such a scheme had been under very discreet consideration as a fallback if the deferred purchase arrangements proved impossible to conclude, and for the current year, 1987, it was very much on the table. 'I cannot stress strongly enough how confidential it is bearing in mind the Secretary of State's announcement on 22nd July 1986', wrote the Treasurer in October 1986 when instructing the Solicitor to begin serious work on this. The work began shortly before the council took its ill-starred decision to apply for redetermination, and it is very noticeable that if the council had been successful in its redetermination application, which had requested an increase of £12m in the council's designated expenditure level, there would have been, in March 1987, no remaining gap to be bridged between the council's spending plans and an *intra vires* balanced budget. As things had turned out, however, the 'Minister's £65 billion rates blunder' had put paid to the council's hopes of a redetermined spending limit, and the £12m gap that the council now faced was large.

So was the proposed lease/leaseback transaction. At the time of the rate-making meeting in March, a package of properties that had grown from smaller beginnings to an enormous and ambitious £150m in response to members' continuing requests for more, was expected to be involved. The arrangement had been receiving consistent and considerable attention over the preceding months. It was not yet settled, but it was close. As an alternative, however, the Treasurer identified a package of possible savings comprising an immediate recruitment freeze (£5m), a £3 rent increase as from July 1st (£4.5m), and the elimination of the allowance for inflation on running expenses (£2m). This was in the context of a budget that already provided for a 7% rent rise, no uncommitted growth and £6m in unidentified savings.

The Treasurer summarized the basic terms of the lease/leaseback arrangement (the 'Sale of the Century', as the local newspaper called it) in his report:

> 47. Lease/leaseback of council property. The council has substantial property assets in its holdings of administrative, operational and commercial buildings. The council continuously reviews its accommodation and service delivery needs but this is obviously a time-consuming task and will be spread over many years. In the meantime the council is unable to gain any benefit from the increasingly valuable assets in its ownership.
>
> 48. A method of realising this benefit has been developed. A package of properties has been put together, the use of which will need to be reviewed over the next twenty years. In order to obtain maximum flexibility, it is proposed that these properties could be disposed of

on a long lease of 75 years. The council would then lease the properties back on a shorter lease of twenty years. Investigations are being made as to whether [Council Co.], a private company wholly owned by the council, can be used for these transactions or whether a partially owned or totally independent company is necessary. Whichever route is followed, every effort will be made to ensure that there is no loss of control of these properties by the council.
49. It is hoped that the package of properties involved will have an estimated market value of £150m. In order to fund the purchase of the leasehold of these properties, the company used will need to borrow on the money market, supported by a council guarantee. The financing costs of this loan will be met by the payments made by the council under the lease-back arrangement.
50. The money raised by the sale of the long lease on these properties will be invested to earn the council income in the region of £15m in a full year. The payments by the council under the lease-back will be so structured as to grant the council a rent-free period for up to three years, after which a market rental will be charged designed to cover the financing costs. The estimated cash-flows of this arrangement are as follows.

	(£m)				
	87/8	88/9	89/90	90/1	91/2
Investment Income	12.0	15.0	15.0	15.0	15.0
Lease Rentals	0.0	0.0	0.0	27.2	27.2
Net Payments	–12.0	–15.0	–15.0	12.2	12.2

Virtually every aspect of this description has a context of *law* behind it, many of them touched upon in the extensive legal advice that the Deputy Solicitor provided as an Appendix to the Treasurer's report. The legal key to the entire venture was set by the opening paragraph of the passage above. This put the transaction in the context of the council's service delivery and accommodation needs, and reflected what lawyers had described as the 'Land Use' approach to the transaction – on which they had insisted. If the transaction was to be *intra vires* this must be because it was a sensible use of the council's property, and not because it bridged a short-term financial gap. It must therefore be based upon a genuine assessment of the council's long-term need for each of the properties involved (which included libraries, swimming pools, residential homes and possibly even the Town Hall), bearing in mind that at the end of the 20-year leaseback, which was the maximum period possible for prescribed expenditure purposes, there was a risk that for the remainder of the 75-year head lease, the council might lose occupation. That risk had to be finely judged. If it was too great, the entire scheme might be unlawful. But attempting to reduce the risk could itself result in the scheme 'not fully having its intended legal and financial effect', as the Deputy Solicitor's report put it, 'with consequent risk of disabling the Council's capital programmes for 1987/88 and future years'.

The Deputy Solicitor's advice concluded by saying that as long as legal advice, his and Counsel's, was sought and taken on such points of detail as which properties were included in the scheme and whether the company or companies involved were council-owned or semi-independent or wholly independent, he was 'reasonably satisfied that a scheme can be worked out' that would have the desired legal effect. He pointed out, though, that members still had the duty to decide carefully, in the context of their overall financial and budgetary responsibilities, whether to approve the scheme or not, and that this included 'taking a view as to the relative merits of the package of specific savings' the Treasurer had identified. He said there was little risk of the budget being unlawful if they adopted the package of savings, but:

> 41. The risk of unlawfulness is however substantially greater if you adopt instead the lease/lease-back proposals set out in paragraphs 47 to 50 of the main report. The chief reason for this is the argument that the adoption of the proposals is 'so unreasonable that no reasonable authority could ever have come to it' ...
> 42. I have to say that in my view such a challenge to a budget incorporating the Treasurer's lease and lease-back proposals would be unlikely to succeed if members approach their decision as I have advised. ... Nevertheless the risk is by no means negligible, and you are entitled to know about it.

A file note indicates, in fact, that there was a time when the Deputy Solicitor had wondered whether he should not just 'jump in with both feet and recommend the package of reductions as a better option than the lease/leaseback'. Ultimately, however, he did not, confining himself to the more usual role of ensuring that the relevant considerations were drawn to members' attention. Lease/leaseback was included along with the other proposed budget measures in the general comment in the Deputy Solicitor's report that:

> It is essential that in considering all these matters members should not look simply to immediate solutions but should consider the long-term consequences of any financial arrangements they propose to make. In this context particular attention should be paid to the figures set out in paragraphs 50 and 54 of the main report, each of which, notwithstanding immediate benefits, shows substantial shortfalls in the future. Members should question the Treasurer as to the way in which such shortfalls might ultimately be met.

The Deputy Solicitor was, in fact, contemplating questioning the Treasurer himself if members did not do so, in order to ensure that the 'relevant considerations' were properly addressed.

It is clear from reading the Deputy Solicitor's comments that some of the legal details of the transaction were still not settled and some of the arguments were finely balanced. At best, lease/leaseback offered a 'by no means negligible' risk of acting *ultra vires*, and even then, only if the council approached the decision in the way the Solicitor advised. If they did otherwise – if, for example, they failed to approach the matter on the basis that 'the possible requirement for continued occupation of the land after 20 years must not be subordinated to the immediate requirement for money' – the inference was that the transaction could not be saved.

The not-quite-finalized lease/leaseback arrangement was approved at the policy committee and council meetings in March 1987, despite the vigorous efforts of the Opposition. An unusually full minute of the discussions was kept, which could have acted as useful confirmation that the 'relevant considerations' had indeed been taken into consideration if the *vires* of the council's decision were ever questioned. The Deputy Solicitor confirmed that the budget proposals had been seen and approved by Leading Counsel. Specifics of the lease/leaseback transaction were left to be finalized by the Treasurer and the Deputy Solicitor, but for the purposes of the rate-making and budget of 1987 it was sufficient to proceed on the basis that the transaction would go ahead and would generate the £12m of investment income the Treasurer had indicated. This brought to a close, for that particular period, the second element of the council's response to the capital restrictions announced on 22 July 1986, the *policy*-driven probing of unfamiliar and complicated legal ground as the council struggled to find the legal *latitude* that would permit it to maintain its programmes until at least the general election.

G. The turning tide

The third strand of important consequences of the 22 July 1986 announcement was its effect on the intangibles. The announcement appears to have marked the beginnings of a changed sensibility in relation to the legal and financial environment that had evolved out of the *Local Government, Planning and Land Act 1980.* Until then there had been a more or less continuous stream of realizations that more was possible under the Act than had previously been thought; the *operative law* had continually expanded, building upon itself one block at a time. The 22 July announcement began to throw that process into reverse. If the announcement had stood alone its effect might perhaps have been more limited. After an initial period of readjustment, some new consensus would have emerged, and a sense of comfort with a different *status quo* might have come into being. 22 July 1986, however, was to be only the beginning. The government had said it would impose further restrictions if necessary; its subsequent actions in relation to leasing and housing subsidy proved its point.

The effect in the realm of the intangibles was to leave the council walking on legal eggshells, and with good reason. The announcement had not actually changed the law on deferred purchase, nor any other law for that matter; it had merely stated that at some point in the future (it was to take another ten months) the law would be changed with retroactive effect. This created uncertainty not only about what the *given law* was or might become in relation to future transactions, but also as to how the council should proceed in relation to the schemes already in place. The stakes were high. Depending on what the terms of the promised legislation turned out to be, one small false step might have enormous consequences.

Likewise with the lease/leaseback transaction people were evidently very aware that the dividing line between an *intra vires* transaction and an *ultra vires* one could be thin. The Deputy Solicitor's advice to the council shows fine lines being drawn at two levels: not only did the details of the scheme need to be carefully judged, but there also needed to be an ability to set aside the council's short-term financial need and approach the matter in terms of the council's long-term land use requirements. As to the details, lease/leaseback had always been recognized as having some difficulties that had to be overcome before its potential could be realized. Indeed, in notes that the Deputy Solicitor prepared for the Leader before the committee and council meetings in March 1987 the process was presented as having been almost an object-lesson in constructive legal problem-solving: with much input from Counsel and others – at least seven QCs' opinions were involved, though some were just written opinions prepared for other local authorities – the proposal had been progressively refined so that the problems were overcome and the potential could be realized. Another fine line was the distinction in terms of the *why* of the *ultra vires* rule between the council's land use requirements ('relevant') and its financial needs (which were potentially 'irrelevant' if they became 'dominant'). In cases that turn on such careful differentiation of the 'relevant' from the potentially 'irrelevant' there is always the possibility that the latter may loom larger in people's minds than legally they should. Preparing for decisions that seem likely to be *ultra vires* unless people can put out of their minds factors which, on any analysis other than a legal one, would obviously be extremely 'relevant' is always a delicate process.

Increasing the discomfort of the legal atmosphere in the wake of the 22 July 1986 announcement was the secretiveness with which the council was obliged to act. Included in the announcement was the warning that further restrictions might come if local authorities tried to find other means of outflanking the capital controls. Given its circumstances, this council was likely to make that attempt, especially when its application for redetermination ran into unforeseeable obstacles, so it had to be extremely discreet. As was said earlier, secretiveness, hiding things, easily shades into furtiveness, the sense that one has something to hide. This is an unfavourable climate in which to develop proposals that, at the end of the day, one wants to be able to proclaim to the world with a clear conscience as being *intra vires*.

Unfavourable, too, though in a subtler and unexpected way, was the more restrained financial *policy* of 'new realism' that was adopted following the 1986 local elections. Without this, the fact that the council needed to be secretive and was acting on the borders of its statutory powers might not have been exceptional; the council had certainly been there before. The difference this time, though, was that the council had little enthusiasm for the actions it felt constrained to take. These were now desperate measures rather than, as they might have seemed five years earlier, wonderful discoveries. In January 1987 the Leader was quoted in the local newspaper as saying 'Our purpose is to hang on until the General Election. We are in the business of providing a dented shield until then'. The image of the 'dented shield' had been used by Neil Kinnock, the leader of the Labour Party nationally, in the context of the first year of rate-capping to describe the moderate strategy 'for Labour councillors to stay in power and do their best to avoid cuts' (Lansley, Goss and Wolmar 1989: 45), as opposed to the confrontational strategy that had emerged despite his urgings. By March 1987 in our council this sense that the shield was indeed 'dented' pervaded not only the financial aspects of the council's position but also the legal ambience. The fact that the council's *disposition* was to edge back towards the financial mainstream meant that creative solutions required a heavier burden of legal justification. They no longer corresponded to the council's view of what its reasonable financial options ought to be; they were merely more reasonable than the alternatives. In circumstances such as these, forming the necessary conclusion that a financial decision is or can be *intra vires* becomes a more laboured process, an effort of the intellect rather than the intuition. That conclusion may still be reached, but it is reached less easily when it runs against the grain of the council's underlying *disposition*.

The result of all of this was that when, in March 1987, the council made its budget for the 1987/88 financial year, it was in a different situation financially, politically and legally than the year before. The tide was beginning to turn. Until then, events had proved reasonably manageable, as successive re-interpretations of what was permissible under the *Local Government, Planning and Land Act 1980* and related provisions such as ss.111 and 137 of the *Local Government Act 1972* had produced a growing sense of self-belief and an increasingly wide range of financial options that 'felt right'. Now, though, the government had removed the most effective of the devices that local authorities had developed, and a lack of self-assurance was beginning to affect what remained. The council was reduced to trying to hang on until the general election in an increasingly hostile legal environment.

11
'Policy-Capped': The 1988 Budget

The general election that had been the council's one faint hope of salvation for some time was called in May 1987 and held in June. The result was dismaying but not a surprise; again the Conservatives won. They promised, moreover, what Gyford, Leach and Game (1989: 315) describe as 'a massive and radical legislative programme, designed quite explicitly to emasculate local government and destroy all vestiges of "municipal socialism"'. The Queen's Speech included promises of legislation to replace domestic rates with the community charge (or 'poll tax'), to make the housing revenue account self-financing (or 'ring-fenced'), and to extend compulsory competitive tendering, to mention just a few. This was a challenging array of issues to confront the new Solicitor, who arrived in July 1987.

According to Lansley, Goss and Wolmar (1989: 176–7) 'The strategy of creative accounting ... came to an end' on the night of the general election, and 'Almost before the ballot papers had been counted, Margaret Hodge, leader of the Association of London Authorities and of Islington, was working on a strategy for the councils to survive another Tory term'. In our council this major shift in *policy* had occurred a year earlier, in the 'new realism' adopted immediately after the May 1986 local elections, and the Leader, according to the Treasurer (at interview) had been leaning that way even earlier. The strategy of creative accounting, nonetheless, was far from dead. It was instead an essential element in keeping the 'new realism' on a steady and palatable course during a year that was to prove, in the Treasurer's view (offered at interview), the hardest year of all.

Strikingly, though, the major restrictions under which he was working this year were of *policy*, not *law*. This chapter demonstrates, therefore, that *within* a government *policy* is potent, and a policy a government is determined to enforce can be far more effective than a *law* it is determined to avoid. This will be so whatever the public law resources of the government may be.

A. The general election and the mid-term review

The general election result immediately triggered the 'mid-term review' of *policy* that the council had discussed. The Leader presented to the policy committee in July 1987 a wide-ranging proposal addressing many parts of the government's agenda and also dealing at length with the council's troubling financial predicament. The committee's report of its meeting explained, in terms of masterly understatement:

> The council has always maintained that the funding of its programme was based on the hope of a political change in Government. This has not happened and the council now faces a situation of financial difficulty.

The daunting scale of that difficulty was set out in the Leader's report. For the current financial year, the £150m lease/leaseback had not yet materialized, which threatened a £12m shortfall in income. The proposed Company B.4 deferred purchase scheme of £19m for housing repairs and maintenance – now expanded to include a further £3m for painting – was also not finalized. Furthermore, no savings had yet been identified against the budgeted figure of £6m. The £30m gap the 1987 budget had projected for 1988/89 now looked as though it might increase, and for 1989/90 and 1990/91, identified as 'the two crunch years' (repayments under the large Company B.1 and B.2 deferred purchase schemes were due to begin), the gaps forecast were of £57m and £118m respectively.

Finally, despite a rearguard action among the more radical of the Labour group, the Leader was proposing that the council should do what it had struggled against so hard for so long: make major cuts in services. (Gyford, Leach and Game 1989: 317 note that 'fightback factions' determined to oppose cuts in jobs and services existed in various councils this time, but were 'outvoted in borough after borough by combinations of traditional Labour councillors and former radicals who had become convinced of the need for a change of strategy'.) The ever-controversial issue of rent increases was also in the air. In the council's mid-term review the Leader reported that 'the Treasurer feels we should start considering how we can reduce spending in 1988/89 with a package of £10m *in addition* to a rent increase'. For the two years to follow, the Leader added, 'we will have to look for further packages of savings in each of these areas of at least £15m in 1989/90 and £20m in 1990/91, as well as further rent increases in each year'.

Rejected, though, was the idea that the council might take immediate measures to reduce spending. The Leader commented that 'The council would not be panicked, as some other authorities had, into making hasty decisions'. After discussion by the policy committee and the council, this combination of cuts and a rent increase, but no panic, was approved as the council's general *policy*.

One of the major unknowns that the Leader's report mentioned was whether the council would be rate-capped again. In the short interval between the policy committee and the council meetings in July 1987 the news finally came. The answer was no. The Treasurer breathed a sigh of relief, and the council's rate-making process returned to a framework of *law* it had not experienced since 1984: no agonizing over redetermination; no debate about acceptance of the rate limit; and no judicial review of a rate-cap. Instead, echoing earlier years, the key decisions would be on rents, probably taken in time for the increase to take effect on 1 April 1988, and rates, on which, since the new *given law* of the *Local Government Act 1986*, the council's decision now had to be taken before 1 April. The rate decision, however, would be the council's, not the government's.

B. The best laid plans ...

Before the 1988 budget could be set, however, there was still the challenge of finding the resources to fund the 1987 budget. The £19m and £3m deferred purchase schemes were finalized in due course through Companies B.4 and B.5. The lease/leaseback transaction, on the other hand, gradually slipped out of reach. Some of the details that had been unsettled in March 1987 remained unsettled; the conveyancing work was massive and sometimes problematic; but most importantly, the banks lost interest after receiving public warnings from the government about the wisdom, though not the legality, of becoming involved (see *The Times*, 13 April and 24 June 1987). Lansley, Goss and Wolmar (1989: 178) quote the director of finance of Islington LBC complaining at the time that '... the banks have been scared off. They just will not do deals with us at this time, even though they know we are a blue chip investment. The Japanese, who set up many of the earlier deals, have dropped out entirely'.

The policy committee's minutes railed against this 'direct political interference by the Secretary of State for the Environment', but the government's message to the banks was presumably driven home in

July, when the Secretary of State for Education introduced emergency regulations prohibiting, as from midnight that night, 'important' asset disposals by local education authorities without his consent. The main objective was to block transactions that would complicate the government's plans at that time to remove polytechnics from local authority control. The effect for our council's lease/leaseback, even though educational properties were not involved, was that it simply could not do the deal, especially not at the £150m capital value that the 1987 budget had relied on for £12m of income. Whatever the council's *vires*, it lacked the *autonomy* to do it alone.

The missing £12m from the lease/leaseback, compounded by the fact that more than £3m of the necessary unidentified savings were proving hard to identify, put the Treasurer in a tight squeeze between the council's policies and his legal obligations. The *policy* was not to panic, to hold the line on spending this year in order to implement properly considered cuts and a priority based budgeting system for 1988/9. Its legal obligation, however, was to balance its budget, which required the Treasurer not only to prepare a proper budget at rate-making time, but also to take corrective measures during the course of a year if events overwhelmed the budgetary assumptions. This was not an express statutory duty, incidentally, but a somewhat open-textured obligation that *Butterworths* (2002/04: para. C[303]) calls the 'annual principle of finance', based on case-law and extrapolation from express provisions of statutes. Still, a discrepancy of more than £15m was clearly enough to demand action.

In October 1987 the Treasurer presented the financial package designed to straighten out the budget for the current financial year. The in-year gap was £15.5m. Half of this was covered by a combination of a revised estimate of attainable unidentified savings (£1.5m), a reduction in the allowance for price inflation (£2m), and by redirecting £4m of the provision that had been made in 1987 to smooth the transition to the government's new rules on the calculation of housing subsidy.

The rest of the missing millions was covered by a single item that, if the Treasurer had known then what we all know now about the *vires* of interest rate swap transactions, would not have happened. The Treasurer's report continued:

> **(B) ACTION I HAVE TAKEN SINCE 1ST APRIL 1987**
>
> (6) I entered into 7 interest rate swops, each of £25 million as it became more clear that it would not be possible to complete the lease/leaseback facility and receive the anticipated £12 million in 1987–88. Interest rate swops are an arrangement whereby the

> council receives a fixed rate of interest in return for paying a variable rate of interest. No element of principal is involved as the council either pays or receives the difference between the fixed and the variable rates. ...
>
> The interest rate swops entered into were different in that the council received an 'up front payment' in return for receiving a lower fixed rate of interest over the life of the swop. ...
>
> This arrangement resulted in the council receiving £19.36 million as an up front payment. This up front payment has been credited to the interest account of the council's Consolidated Loans Fund. After allowing for a reduction in housing subsidies (£11.62 million) on these transactions the result is a net saving in 1987/88 of £7,740,000.

The description of this as 'Action I Have Taken' means exactly what it says. There was no consultation with Counsel, or even with the council's lawyers, before the swaps were done. To all but a few leading members, the first they will have heard of them was the Treasurer's report. The Opposition voiced loud displeasure. The policy committee's minutes record that:

> In response to criticisms of the officers the Chair [Leader] informed the Minority Party that if it had any objections to the handling of the budget these should be directed to the Majority Party and that personal attacks should not be made on individual officers who carried out instructions in accordance with committee decisions and Standing Orders.

Those decisions and Standing Orders, though, were of the most general nature. The Treasurer had relied on his general delegated authority to enter financial transactions on the council's behalf. The *autonomy* with which he acted, without seeking legal advice, indicates that it was clear to him that he had the authority, and the council had the power, to do these deals. For the Treasurer, interest rate swaps were not a new idea. They had been on offer for some time, and though he had never felt inclined to enter one, the hesitation was not for any legal reasons, but because better financial options were available. In mid-1987, however, it seemed there were none. Financially, he considered the details of the swaps *meticulously*. Legally, however, he simply *intuitively* accepted them as *intra vires*, and did not contact the lawyers because there was nothing to ask them about – or so it seemed at the time. It was to be another three years before *Hazell v Hammersmith and Fulham LBC* (1991) said otherwise, in a decision that Loughlin (1996: 339–54), for one, has criticized vigorously.

When the district auditor became aware of the interest rate swaps, apparently some time in July, he responded in no uncertain terms – not to the swaps themselves, but to the 'up-front payment' element, which was unusual, though evidently not unique. (See Loughlin 1996: 340–2; *Westdeutsche Landesbank Girozentrale v Islington LBC* 1996; *Kleinwort Benson Ltd v Sandwell BC* 1993). The auditor wrote:

> Interest rate swaps are, of course, not uncommon as part of the management of loan debt (although great care is needed in their operation) but the present swaps are unusual. ...
>
> You will no doubt be aware that the auditor for the London Borough of Haringey has already reported to that council on a similar transaction entered into by the Borough. He has indicated that the unusual features of the interest rate swaps as carried out will require him to consider whether such interest swaps were within the powers of the council, and if so, whether the taking of the whole of the premium payment to the credit of the CLF [Consolidated Loans Fund] in the year in which it was received was lawfully open to the council.
>
> It goes without saying, of course, that I will have to consider the lawfulness of the transactions by the council during the course of my audit of the council's accounts. I am bound to say that I too have considerable doubts about the arrangements as I understand them. Certainly they raise serious issues of reasonableness and prudence and whether there has been a proper exercise of discretion.
>
> I understand that no report at all has been made to the council on this matter or information given to show that the short term gain would be at a cost to future ratepayers; nor has legal advice been obtained as to the swap or as to the proposed use of the £19.36m. There must be doubt whether the transaction has been properly authorised. My purpose in writing is to formally draw to your attention my serious doubts about this transaction and to ensure that there is proper authority for it, that any risks have been recognised and that decisions are only made by the council after full advice (both legal and financial) has been received and proper consideration been given to all the issues.

The district auditor's letter emphasized issues of *law* that were, of course, extremely familiar to the Treasurer in other contexts, but had simply not seemed germane to this particular decision. It now emerged, however, that the district auditor's approach to interest rate swaps was legally *meticulous* in its reference to relevant considerations, balancing of interests, and the like. Even so, the Treasurer was unusually assertive in defence of the swaps in his report to policy committee in October 1987. In substance, he rejected the district auditor's financial criticisms, and members had little difficulty in agreeing, at least those in the majority party.

Law, in the form of Counsel's opinion obtained after the district auditor wrote, also supported the Treasurer, but injected some unfamiliar tentative tones. Counsel had been asked to comment on the Legal Department's draft advice to the policy committee, which said that interest rate swaps were authorized by s.111 and s.151 of the *Local Government Act 1972*, that those provisions could empower the taking of the up-front payments, and that members should balance the advantages and disadvantages of the transaction and the proposed use of the consolidated loans fund, bearing in mind the alternatives, the council's extremely difficult situation, and the impact on future years. Counsel agreed, but added some cautionary comments:

> 5. We would wish merely to highlight three of the matters adverted to in the Solicitor's report which, in this context, appear to be of such significance that they should be drawn specifically to the attention of members.
> 6. The first is the general point made by Counsel advising Haringey in a similar context that 'creative accountancy (whilst it may be legitimate) can be no more than a possible temporary solution to the council's revenue budget problems. It does not produce any additional resources. It merely shifts the problem from one year to another (or others). Indeed, reliance on one off measures to finance a gap inevitably makes the position for future years worse, especially if expenditure continues to increase. They must, in prudence, be used only as a last resort when all other possible measures have been considered and must be used as sparingly as possible'.
> 7. The second point is to apply the above general point to this specific situation. ... As envisaged by the Treasurer, the present application of the interest rate swap arrangement is one part only of a comprehensive package of measures to bring the Borough's finances into balance. It is very important, in our opinion, that these proposals should be considered in this light and that they should not be considered in isolation. Accordingly, it follows that if and to the extent

> that other elements in the package of measures were either not adopted at all or were diluted then the larger would loom the interest swap proposals in the overall package and the more difficult it would be to justify its adoption as a reasonable exercise of discretion.
>
> 8. The third point concerns the impact of the proposals on future years and, in particular, on the discharge of the council's fiduciary duty. ... In this context where rates for this year are capped but next year's will not be, it is all the more important for the councillors to consider their fiduciary duty as well as the possible impact for services in future years of the deferred cost of obtaining this one off benefit. It seems to us that it is of the greatest importance that the full future costs and impact on rates and finances be spelt out clearly, unambiguously and with as much detail and precision as possible by the Treasurer.

The negative undertones of this advice are symptomatic of a change in the legal climate, of a shifting in the common ground of legal opinion. Expressions such as 'last resort', 'used as sparingly as possible', 'one part only of a comprehensive package of measures to bring the Borough's finances into order' had not been the common currency of recent years. Despite the fact that interest rate swaps were *intra vires* according to the *operative law* of the day (though these particular ones admittedly had some unusual features), a more tentative tone was creeping into the *operative law* as Counsel now expressed it, and as the council would begin to accept it.

Another important new element was the forceful early intervention of the district auditor, which took the Treasurer by surprise. Until this point, discussion of such matters tended to take place after the passage of time, and quite possibly in the less charged atmosphere of the audit of the accounts. But now there was a change, inspired no doubt by the Audit Commission's conclusion, in the wake of the 1985 'rates rebellion', that it should intervene earlier in events that it considered inappropriate, and needed new legal powers for this purpose (Audit Commission 1987: 6).

Backing up this more assertive posture of the district auditor was an extremely important, though seemingly innocuous, change of *organization* at the Audit Commission. In 1987 it set up an in-house legal department, initially one solicitor, the former Borough Solicitor for Greenwich LBC (who was presumably well versed in the mysteries of revenue and capital transactions, and had lived through the miseries of the 'united strategy of non-compliance' as solicitor to a rate-capped authority). The Commission's previous practice had been to rely on auditors' own legal knowledge for most practical purposes, and to obtain advice on specific matters from a firm of solicitors and from Counsel as and when needed.

Superficially, the establishment of an in-house legal service changed nothing in terms of *law* or the *ultra vires* rule: the legal powers of both the district auditor and local authorities remained the same. In terms of the dynamics of the relationship between auditors and local authorities on questions of *law*, however, it altered the balance. The Audit Commission's internal advice became an important counterweight to the internal advice of the local authority, and the two would tend to differ since they would view the law from two different perspectives. Both would start with the standard lawyer's objective of giving the best advice they could to their client – in one case the local authority, in the other the Audit Commission. For a local authority, however, *law* is an instrument for the achievement of practical results; a lawyer's 'best advice' will be alert to the client's *policy* objectives and will attempt not to put unnecessary legal obstacles in their way. A lawyer to the Audit Commission, by contrast, has a client whose *policy* should be to be entirely even-handed and dispassionate. For such a client the 'best advice' will focus more on accuracy of interpretation as an end in itself. A local authority lawyer, faced with two equally plausible interpretations of a statutory provision, will probably not be inclined to advise his or her council that it *must* adopt the one that is problematic in terms of *policy* rather than the one that is not. By contrast, a lawyer for a structurally dispassionate organization such as the Audit Commission, faced with exactly the same provision (which will apply, of course, to hundreds of local authorities, each of which may have a different *policy*), will probably be more inclined to advise that one meaning is correct and the other is not, letting the chips fall where they may. That advice, moreover, will be influential. Whether auditors agree with it or disagree, it is the advice they will have to live with.

In any organization, establishing an in-house legal service *organizes law in* in a way that does not happen when the legal advice is external and non-legal professionals only seek it as and when *they* recognize that they need it. When the Audit Commission created its in-house legal department it put into play, backed up by the powers and authority of the district auditors, a body of legal opinion which would have a different orientation than that of local authority lawyers, and would therefore tend to produce different *operative law*. For the remainder of the story told in this book, a more active Audit Commission, informed by its own internal view of the *operative law* of the *Local Government, Planning and Land Act 1980* and related statutes, was to be an important player. It became a significant counterweight to the *autonomy* of the council in deciding what its various statutory powers meant.

C. The 'policy-cap'

The council's grant related expenditure assessment ('GREA' below) for the coming financial year, 1988/89, was announced on 27 October 1987, and showed an increase of £3m over the previous year. The Treasurer's report to policy committee in November gave a clear indication of the Leadership's thinking on *policy*. The aim was to avoid being rate-capped again, and the Treasurer explained that, based on recent experience, rate-capping could be expected if the budget was more than 12.5% above GREA and increased the previous year's budget by either 6% or 4%. The calculations were, respectively, £116m, £113m and £110.5m. The report made no specific recommendations, but said that if the council wished to avoid rate-capping, a budget set at one of the two lower figures was the highest the council could safely go.

The report was merely 'noted' by the policy committee, but the decision was a tacit acquiescence in the policy of budgeting to avoid rate-capping. This *policy* was to become ever more solid as the year progressed, though its implications in terms of cuts and rent increases were to be controversial. Its effect was that the council, though not rate-capped, had 'policy-capped' itself by reference to the rate-capping system. Its rate would be the maximum that the Treasurer advised could be adopted while avoiding rate-capping, and in fact the council opted for the extra safety of the £110.5m figure, only 4% over the 1987 budget.

A rent increase would be an important part of this. In November the Labour group agreed to consult with tenants on the basis of a £2, £3 or £4 rent rise. Later that month, at the tenants' liaison committee the Treasurer's report went further, suggesting that 'savings of at least £10m and a £5 per week rent increase will be required in order to implement a reasonable rate increase and avoid the likelihood of becoming rate capped in 1989/90. For every £1 per week increase less than the above £5 per week it will be necessary to increase the level of savings by £2m'. Note that the entirely legal *policy* alternative of increasing rates was not even mentioned.

By the time the rent decision reached the policy committee in February 1988, the proposal under discussion was for a £3 rent rise on 1 April 1988 and a further rise of £3 on 1 October 1988, but no further increase until October 1989. Despite vigorous opposition by Labour dissenters to the second £3, the committee approved this in principle, subject to final confirmation in March. In the meantime the dissenters circulated an 'alternative budget' that aimed to reduce the rent increase. The Leader responded dismissively, characterizing it as 'not an alternative, nor a budget'.

D. Last minute reprieve

As budget day approached, lease/leaseback was abruptly back on the Legal Department's table. The Treasurer, who had never entirely given up on the idea, received word that a bank was now willing to do the deal, thus curing the council's lack of *autonomy*, and in February the Legal Department received instructions to proceed with the transaction as quickly as possible. Describing it as 'a matter of life and death', the Treasurer wanted it approved at the council meeting in March 1988, and completed the next day. Much had changed since last year. Only a £50m package of properties was now involved, with a lease period of only 20 years and a leaseback of 20 years less a day. The intent was to bank the £50m payment and receive £5m interest from it each year. There was to be a rent-free period of two years, then three years in which the rent would exceed the investment income by £5m, then 15 years when the rent would be only £500,000 more than the income. The Treasurer wanted to proceed with as little publicity as possible. The government had not yet acted on its musings the previous year about changing the law, and he did not want this transaction to slip from his fingers, as last year's larger one had.

Proper legal authorization for the transaction was essential if it was to remain *intra vires*, and in the wake of the district auditor's intervention in relation to the interest rate swaps, the standard of a 'proper' authorization had been raised. Obviously the best form of authorization would be a decision by council, hence the Treasurer's mention of the March council meeting. There was, though, also an existing authorization for the £150m lease/leaseback deal, approved in March 1987, but never acted upon. When its terms were examined – and they were examined closely, along with all other aspects of this new proposal – it was decided that they were broad enough to accommodate the transaction envisaged a year later. The 1987 decision had left the

Treasurer and the Solicitor considerable flexibility in finalizing the details, and the council's officers felt, and Counsel agreed, that the March 1987 resolution for a much larger transaction gave officers all the legal authority they needed to conclude the much smaller transaction now. In terms of the *who* of the *ultra vires* rule, therefore, the Treasurer now had two options. The £50m lease/leaseback could be approved by the council at its meeting on 15 March. Or it could be entered into by officers, relying on the delegated authority established 12 months earlier, but never acted upon, and never revoked.

As it turned out, delegated authority was exactly what the situation demanded. A lease/leaseback involving another local authority received publicity in early March, and on 9 March 1988, the Treasurer's fears that the government might step in were realized. A conference with Counsel to consider the revised lease/leaseback was interrupted by a telephone call from the Legal Department to say that the Secretary of State for the Environment had just made the dreaded 'as from midnight tonight' announcement. In what *The Times* the following day called an 'unexpected statement', Mr. Ridley announced in the House of Commons that at midnight on 9 March new temporary regulations were to come into effect to deal with local authorities acquiring capital assets on terms that were outside the letter of existing capital controls. 'The sheer breadth of the restrictions imposed by the announcement caught local authorities by surprise' (Loughlin 1996: 335), and lease/leaseback arrangements were specifically affected. Mr. Ridley said of the transactions that were to be covered by the new regulations that 'This is borrowing in fact though it may not be borrowing in law. In effect, money is being borrowed by disposal of capital assets in order to finance deficits on revenue account' (*The Times*, 10 March 1988). He said he would consult later on the regulations, which were described as temporary, but that they would come into effect that night:

> I have adopted this procedure to avoid any repetition of the events of 1986–87, when consultation preceded a change in the regulations and when nearly £2bn worth of deals were rushed through in the interim.

'Swift move by Ridley halts council lease deals' was the headline the next day in *The Times*. Not quite so. At 11.50 p.m. on 9 March, with ten minutes in hand before the new regulations came into force, the Deputy Solicitor formally entered the £50m lease/leaseback deal on behalf of our council. As a memento of the occasion, and until he left the council two years later, he kept a card on a shelf in his office – he has it still – headed 'Thoughts ... at Midnight on 9th March 1988'. Quoting some words attributed to the Duke of Wellington after the Battle of Waterloo, it reads: 'It has been a damned nice thing ... the nearest run thing you ever saw in your life ... By God! I do not think it would have done if I had not been there.' Indeed, it probably would not have.

E. An almost old-style budget

A week later came the council's budget day. The last-minute 'life and death' sprint for the lease/leaseback transaction had saved the day, and an *intra vires* balanced budget had been attained without the council being 'panicked into hasty decisions'.

On the capital side, the Treasurer's report was largely a demonstration of the cumulative financial impacts of the council's decisions over the recent years, set in a context of diminishing legal *latitude*. The capital programme for 1988/89 showed two-thirds of the available resources as being committed to projects that were already under way, and over the following two years, payments under the Company B.1, B.2 and B.3 arrangements were to build up to a level at which they would exhaust all of the council's available capital resources, leaving nothing for new schemes. The Treasurer had been advising members for the past two years that such a time would come. Also, with limited capital resources available and new legal restrictions in place, several of the initiatives of recent years were to be thrown into reverse. Capitalized housing repairs were to revert back to revenue in order to preserve housing subsidy. Non-housing repairs were to remain capitalized, but would not now be put into a deferred purchase arrangement because, under the new regulations, there was no advantage in doing so. Some capitalized salaries would also revert back to revenue because there were no capital resources available to cover them. Covenants relating to the new municipal offices and to the neighbourhood offices were due for renegotiation under one of the predetermined breaks in the arrangements, but the company the council had initially dealt with had been taken over by a bank which was unlikely to want to extend them; the Treasurer suggested that they should probably be paid off completely in 1989/90 in order to protect capital resources for the large deferred purchase payments that would become due the year after that.

Another problem was that some of the finely judged legal intricacies of the council's leasing arrangements might be unravelling. The Treasurer reported that the Inland Revenue had questioned the leasing of such items as heating systems, lifts and entryphones, and that the council would probably have a tax liability to meet. This called the whole viability of leasing this type of asset into question and could create real difficulties for the future. The dénouement, however, would come later, and will be described in the next chapter.

The advice from the (new) Solicitor that accompanied the Treasurer's report on the capital programme was brief. The main point it made was that

> In relation to the capital programme generally, the council is required to contain capital expenditure within the limits imposed by the controls under the Local Government, Planning and Land Act 1980.

Note, here, the reference to 'capital' expenditure rather than to 'prescribed' expenditure, as well as the bald statement that the council was 'required' to contain its expenditure within the statutory limits. This was the kind of brief overview of the law that would seem adequate at a time when the council's *policy* was to move back towards the financial solid ground, but which, as seen previously in this study, could well be considered an over-simplification at times when *law* was any more than *peripheral* to the decisions the council was contemplating. It was also a reflection of the fact that, with a new Solicitor in position, the *operative law* was being partially renewed, with a new perspective arriving that was not entirely based on our council's past experiences.

Similarly, on the revenue side, the *policy*-led move towards the safer financial ground meant that the *vires* of specific initiatives did not emerge as a major factor in either the Treasurer's report or the Solicitor's. The Treasurer proceeded from the delicately phrased premiss that 'Members may wish to take steps to ensure that the council is reasonably certain not to be brought back into rate-capping for 1989–90', and that a means to achieve this would be to adopt the 'most rigorous' of the criteria used so far for rate-capping, namely to exceed its 1987 budget by no more than 4%. Given the rent increase of £3 in April and a further £3 in October that had been approved in principle in February (the Labour dissenters were still trying to undo the second), this produced a budget of £110.5m, £60.5m in block grant and equalization payments, a 6.3% rate increase ... and still a £30m gap.

To bridge this the council had identified £10m in savings, and a further £2m of unidentified savings was considered to be realizable. Another £12m could be taken from the end-of-year provision for bad debts for 1987, though this time, for the first time in recent years, taking that amount still left almost £5m which could actually be used for writing off bad debts. Investment income of £5m was anticipated from the lease/leaseback that had been finalized in the nick of time the previous week, and £1m was still available from the early drawdown of funds from Company B.2 to Company B.3. There were to be reductions in staffing levels, but no compulsory lay-offs. There was to be no growth unless it was offset by additional savings beyond the £10m already identified. The budget was a mix of the thoroughly conventional – cuts and rent increases – with a variety of contributions from the financial transactions that had been identified over the past five years.

The legal advice that accompanied the Treasurer's report was different from that of recent years, yet nonetheless familiar. With the *given law* of the *Rates Act 1984* irrelevant this year to the council's decision, old faithfuls such as 'relevant considerations' and the 'trusteeship of the rate fund' re-emerged as the *law* that was explained, with a firm reminder that 'sound and prudent assessments are necessary'.

As for the 'relevant considerations', the Solicitor's report described what they were and confirmed that 'a desire not to be rate-capped in 1989/90' was 'among the matters which the council may properly take into consideration'. It spelled out that this 'should not be regarded as an overriding consideration but as one matter among all those which need to be taken into account'. In elaborating, however, the report did not mention a larger rate increase than the proposed 6.3% as an option, but only a smaller one, commenting that Members 'should, for example, give consideration to the setting of a rate at a lower level than that calculated to minimize the chances of rate-capping in 1989/90 if they are of a view that they could do so consistently with their assessment of required expenditure for the year'. The omission is striking, because a higher rate was possible, and the financial strain the 'policy-cap' created was considerable. Indeed, in purely financial terms, the council would probably have been better off risking a rate-cap.

F. And an almost old-style dissent

In its closing paragraphs the Solicitor's report set the scene for one last debate of *policy* that was anticipated in the policy committee and council meetings on 15 March. The report reminded members that:

> 21. Each member has a positive duty to ensure that the council complies with its duty to agree a balanced budget and to set a rate for 1988/89 on or before 1st April 1988. ...

> 22. In order to comply with these duties, members who are unable to support the recommendations in this report ought to put forward alternative proposals for a balanced budget provided that there is sufficient information available to them on which to do so.

That last paragraph prepared the ground for an exchange at the policy committee meeting, where, the minutes carefully record, the Leader asked whether the £2m figure for unidentified savings was the maximum the Treasurer would recommend this year and the Treasurer confirmed that it was.

The significance of this exchange became clear at the council meeting that immediately followed. Two Labour dissenters moved that the second £3 rent increase, scheduled for October, be deleted. The Leader, evidently well-prepared for this motion, raised a point of order, and the minutes pick up the story from there:

> This was that the proposition (not to agree the complete rent rise being recommended) in the absence of a proposal for alternative measures, would result in a budget which did not balance and that regard should be had to the legal implication in paragraph 21 [of the Solicitor's report, quoted above]. H.W. The Mayor, having sought the advice of the Chief Executive, ruled that in order for the amendment to be considered it must also contain measures to redress the balance proposed in the rent increase otherwise the council would not have a budget. A lengthy debate ensued on this ruling during the course of which [Councillor 2, the seconder of the motion] asked for the following addendum to be made to the amendment:
>
> > 'and that in order to balance the budget an item of £3m unidentified savings be included'.
>
> Following further advice the Mayor ruled that it would be unwise, even dangerous, to pass a budget on this basis. There was further debate on the issue at the conclusion of which the Chief Executive was asked to advise whether the amendment was legal. He stated that the advice of officials was that it would be imprudent for the amendment to be agreed since it was probably illegal. The Chief Executive, in order to assist members, quoted the following paragraph from a letter which had been sent to certain of the Members and former Members of another local authority by the District Auditor:
>
> > 'Members are not necessarily obliged to accept the advice of officers as to the legality of a proposed course of action but there

> was a strong inference of wilful misconduct if Members failed to act in accordance with that advice without advancing some cogent reasons for rejecting it'.
>
> H.W. The Mayor ruled, pursuant to Standing Order 63, that he was not prepared to accept the amendment proposed by [Councillor 1] and [Councillor 2] unless they were prepared to put forward concurrently specific proposals as to how the budget could be balanced in the event of their reduction in the rent increase being agreed. [Councillor 2] indicated that she felt the ruling was depriving her and [Councillor 1] of their democratic rights and they could not accept it. H.W. The Mayor enquired if there were any further amendments to the report of the policy committee.

'An impressive display of power politics', opined the local newspaper the next day, but 'outrageous'. 'The Labour rebels had every right to have their proposition debated'. The vice-chair of the finance sub-committee was obviously of the same opinion, and resigned:

> I would like to place on record that until yesterday, I believed that we as a council were fortunate to have some of the best financial and legal advice available to any council in this country. Unfortunately, yesterday ... these same officers were put under severe pressure to advise that an amendment to the budget, standing in the names of [Councillors 1 and 2] was illegal. ... This they could not do, because it would have thrown into jeopardy the 1987/88 budget [the previous year's budget, which had provided for £6m of unidentified savings]. The fact that the Treasurer and the Solicitor could only question the prudence of what was being proposed ... means that the amendment did not fall within the Standing Order the Leader referred to and hence a debate should have been allowed. ... Instead, yesterday the Mayor and officers were put under unwarranted pressure ... in order to ensure that the amendment to the budget was not subject to public debate.

Much of this complaint rings true. Clearly *law* had been used as a means of preventing debate, and in the light of the large budgetary uncertainties considered acceptable in previous years, it does seem surprising that the amendment should have been ruled out of order as proposing an *ultra vires* unbalanced budget this year. The proposed unidentified savings allowance was still smaller than in recent years.

There is, though, another side to the argument. Comparing, first, the unidentified savings figures, the £2m that the Treasurer considered the maximum in 1988 came on top of £10m of identified savings and after several months of effort to identify them. Finding even £2m more would be a very different exercise from finding £6m in 1987, after no previous concerted effort at finding savings. As for the *law*, furthermore, it is not necessarily the case that if a £6m allowance for unidentified savings is *intra vires* one year it is necessarily *intra vires* another. There are times, as has been mentioned before, when a council's *policy* is a determinant of its legal *latitude*, and a decision that was legally 'reasonable' one year becomes legally 'unreasonable' the next for no other reason than that the council has changed its mind. For dissenters who had not yet changed their minds the switch might seem bizarre. Indeed, if they were in the majority the switch would not even occur. Yet once the council collectively has changed its mind about what its financial situation can sustain, it becomes 'irrational' for it to continue along the path the dissenters continue to urge.

It is worth emphasizing once more, though, the very important point that in 1988 the council was not rate-capped. As a matter of *law*, there was nothing preventing it from taking a properly considered decision to increase rates by more than 6.3% in order to make a substantial improvement in its immediate financial position. It was 'policy-capping', not rate-capping, that had made this year, for the Treasurer, the hardest year of all. Indeed, one of the interesting things about the 1988 deliberations, especially given the public split in the Labour ranks over the rent increase, is that nobody, not even the Labour dissenters, suggested increasing the rates as an alternative to making the October rent increase. There was every likelihood that an additional £3m could be raised from rates in 1988 without serious risk of being rate-capped in 1989 – the Treasurer had explicitly made conservative assumptions about what the criteria for rate-capping would be – and it was also quite possible that, in purely monetary terms, the council might be better off rate-capped than not. Nonetheless, there does not seem to have been any serious opposition to the policy of budgeting to avoid rate-capping. So although the year had been a terribly difficult one financially, what had made it so difficult, and had generated all the same kinds of activities as legal constraints had in other years, was *policy*, not *law*.

12
Out With the Old, Again: The 1989 Budget and Beyond

Out of the dissension of the 1988 budget a leadership challenge developed. If it had succeeded, one consequence would very probably have been to throw the council's financial decision-making off the legally uncontroversial track it now seemed set to follow, and back into areas where issues relating to the legal limits of its powers would have become more prominent again. However, the challenge failed, and the major financial decisions for 1989 continued on a legally uneventful path. Fiscal self-restraint remained the order of the day, and issues of *vires* were not prominent in the council's decision-making. In the background, though, important changes of *law* were under way. The government was proposing to repeal the major financial provisions of the *Local Government, Planning and Land Act 1980*, replacing them with controversial and problematic new provisions: a new revenue support grant, new capital controls, the community charge (or 'poll tax') and ring-fencing of the housing revenue account. It was time, once more, for throwing out the old *law*, and preparing for the new, as the life-cycle of the *Local Government, Planning and Land Act 1980* began to draw to a close.

The council's actions at this stage are those of a government reluctantly but determinedly exerting internal financial control. In terms of public law this produced a year of little activity in relation to budget and rates, but more in other areas to which discretion was displaced as the council sought to sustain whatever it could of its policy agenda despite its financial restrictions. To cap it all off, when the details of the incoming *given law* were known there was a final mad dash of activity to make good use of the outgoing legislation in the short time available before a more unforgiving régime replaced it. Here again, therefore, there is a reminder that even in a single time and place, and within a single overall framework of *policy*, the art of the possible may be sustained in a variety of ways. The process is issue-specific, depending on some factors that are within a government's control and some that are not.

A. Running a tight ship

Shortly after agreeing its 1988 budget, the council put strict controls in place to ensure that its spending through the year remained within targets. Expenditure not provided for in the budget would not even be considered until November. New expenditure that *had* been provided for in the budget, but which had growth implications for the coming year, 1989/90, was not to be actually incurred without further approval. If a committee made savings it would no longer be able to spend them on other items within its mandate; instead they were to be accumulated centrally. There were to be regular reviews of committees' success in achieving the savings required.

The council decided to apply more extensively this year the priority based budgeting it had tried in 1988. Then it had been applied to refuse collection, street cleaning, vehicle maintenance and cleaning of buildings, areas where cost-effectiveness was a priority as the council prepared for the challenge of other impending *given law*: the compulsory competitive tendering provisions of the *Local Government Act 1988*. Savings of 10%, £700,000, had been realized. Some jobs had been lost, but service standards had been maintained. For 1989 the areas for priority based budgeting were housing management, residential care for the elderly, libraries and planning and valuation, and the potential savings were estimated at more than £13m. Again it was recognized that there would be some loss of jobs, but the council was beyond the stage now of hoping that both jobs and services could be maintained, and of the two, protecting services took precedence.

The broad financial strategy for the 1989 budget was adopted in June 1988. On the basis of existing spending patterns the projected shortfall was £31m in 1989/90, £58m in 1990/91 and £69m in 1991/92 – large gaps, though the first two were noticeably reduced from the previous estimates of £57m and £118m. The council decided to plan for a further £10m in cuts in 1989/90 and another £10m in 1990/91. The possibility of another rent increase was also mentioned, though the council reiterated that this would not take effect until October 1989.

In the period leading up to the 1989 budget, savings accumulated rapidly. The in-year targets of £10m identified savings and £2m unidentified savings were met. Prospective savings towards the coming year's £10m target were also being identified, and the council took the savings early when possible, thus obtaining part of the benefit in 1988. When asked during the course of the research for this book whether the scale of these savings did not give credence to the dissenters' argument at the 1988 budget-making that a smaller rent increase and a larger 'unidentified savings' figure could balance the budget, the Treasurer replied that the early savings during 1988/89 were fortuitous, and could not have been relied on as a reasonable expectation in March 1988. To this one might add that the proponents of the reduced rent increase were the very people who, if they had won the debate, would have been the hardest pressed to identify the increased unidentified savings. As has been observed before in this study, questions like what is a 'reasonable' savings figure to produce a lawful balanced budget may sometimes depend as much on the *disposition* of the councillors as on the arithmetic.

Comparing the overall process of the 1989 budget to that of 1988, two features particularly stand out. First, there was no specific *law*-based focus determining the budgetary plan for 1989. For 1988, it will be recalled, *policy* had been guided by the law and practice of rate-capping and by the council's clear determination to avoid the Secretary of State's clutches. For 1989, by contrast, though there was an equally clear and extensive programme of savings, this was predominantly based on a combination of financial considerations (the council's firm intent to bring its spending into line with its resources) and political considerations (what level of cuts, at the end of the day, the Labour group would tolerate). The council did, of course, wish to avoid charge-capping, but any efforts in this direction would have been speculative at this time, since there was no experience or government guidance as to what the charge-capping criteria would be.

The echoes here, both in terms of substantive *policy* and of the impact of the *ultra vires* rule, are of the early 1980s, before the Left gained ascendancy. Then, too, the key to the council's decisions on rents, rates and cuts had been a blending of financial necessity with political palatability, and the council's *policy* was such that difficulties of *law* were not likely to be encountered. In 1989, after years of crisis, and despite a far greater accumulated awareness of the relevance of the *ultra vires* rule to the council's financial decision-making, a similar stage had been reached. The council's general *policy* for its 1989 budget allowed legal factors, for the most part, to recede into the background.

The second notable feature this year is that few if any serious efforts were made to identify new financial devices. The council might still show interest if an opportunity presented itself, of course. For example, in mid-1988 preliminary discussions were held with Company B in relation to 'factoring', receiving a lump sum now in return for promising to pay over future capital receipts from such reliable sources as right-to-buy sales of council houses, and tentative approval was given for the arrangements to be made. However, they never proceeded. The Audit Commission, with its new and more assertive *disposition* towards policing the *ultra vires* rule, and equipped with a new statutory power under s.30 of the *Local Government Act 1988* to pre-empt unlawful financial transactions before they occurred, intervened in a proposed factoring arrangement elsewhere, and by March 1989 it had been declared *ultra vires* (*R v Wirral MBC, ex parte Milstead* 1989). As the Audit Commission became more active, local authorities' *autonomy* in relying on their own internal *operative law* was reduced. Conveniently for our council, though, its *policies* by now meant that its legal obligation to develop a balanced budget did not generate the need to seek actively for new financial means to reconcile the irreconcilable.

In his rate-making report in March 1989 the Treasurer referred to the financial devices of previous years, commenting that 'the scope for finding such devices is now for all practical purposes exhausted'. That was intended as a statement of fact based on the government's restrictions of local authorities' legal *latitude* (the acid test was that even Company B had not identified effective counter-measures). There were, though, two intangible reinforcements that deserve mention. One is that the council's *policy* orientation at this time made it very easy for the Treasurer to hold and express this opinion; it did not have to be rigorously cross-checked against countervailing political and financial imperatives. The other was that the change in the tide of professional opinion that has been mentioned in recent chapters was causing some of the imaginative uses that had been made of the existing legislation to lose their rosy glow. As confidence in some of those devices began to wane, it became that much easier to acknowledge the scope for finding them as being 'exhausted'.

B. Playing it safe

Symptomatic of this disposition to vacate the field of financial controversy was the evolving sorry tale of the council's advance leasing arrangements. In mid-July 1988 the Treasurer described the position as follows:

> Leasing and Fixtures 1988/89
>
> (14) The council entered into a series of advance leasing arrangements for five years commencing in 1987/88. However, the leasing of such items as heating systems, lifts and entryphones was called into question by the Inland Revenue. The result of this investigation

> caused the banks to withdraw their support from these arrangements unless they were converted into Hire Purchase agreements which have the Inland Revenue's approval. The council agreed to make a once off payment of tax to the Revenue and enter into HP arrangements. District Audit on the advice of their legal adviser have now argued that the Hire Purchase Agreements are a charge against the council's allocations and though they have indicated a willingness to look favourably on the existing commitments would view any new commitments as prescribed expenditure. This effectively rules out any further expenditure on these items.

One of the interesting features of the advance leasing problem was that Counsel advised that there were good grounds for arguing that both the Inland Revenue and the district auditor were wrong – that the Inland Revenue was wrong in denying the scheme its intended tax effect, and that the district auditor was wrong in treating the transaction as involving prescribed expenditure. In relation to the Inland Revenue, papers requesting authority to launch a legal challenge were prepared, but this approach was dropped, as the alternative of converting to a hire purchase agreement seemed preferable. In relation to the district auditor a challenge was also considered but not pursued, partly for practical reasons – given the council's duty of annual accounting, the legal challenge could not have produced results quickly enough – but partly also because in the more tentative legal climate of the day, there was an inclination to let sleeping dogs lie, a concern that more might be lost by losing a judicial review action than could be gained by winning it, especially given that the Audit Commission was allowing a concession for existing transactions. The council's key objective now was to get control of its finances; it preferred a quiet life if possible, and better a financially tolerable fudge than an unpredictable legal tussle with the Audit Commission.

C. The ghost of budgets past

The budget documents that emerged at the end of this year of little budgetary creativity and large conventional savings were very different in tone from their recent predecessors. They read as an exercise in financial management rather than in the implementation of statutory powers. They bore numerous echoes of the recent past, but all with the ring of something that was indeed becoming the past. Capitalized repairs and maintenance were to be funded, but only £3m of this was by way of existing deferred purchase arrangements, with the remainder coming from mainstream resources. The covenant schemes for the municipal offices and for the neighbourhood offices, trailblazers for the subsequent Company B.1 and B.2 arrangements, were to be paid off early. New computers were to be acquired, and until recently this would have been done under leasing arrangements. This year, however, capital receipts were to be used, with payments being made under the *de minimis* exception that treated expenditure under £6,000 on plant and equipment as not being 'prescribed expenditure'. Leasing was now less viable, and using up existing capital receipts had become important because the proposed new *given law* of the *Local Government and Housing Bill* imposed a 'retroactive removal of the right to spend 100 per cent of previously accumulated capital receipts' (Gibson 1992: 74). 'After the change in the Capital Control procedures', said the Treasurer's report, in a passage that the Solicitor specifically reinforced, 'it is likely that unused capital receipts at 1/4/90 will have to be used to repay debt. It would thus be advantageous to use as much as possible of the unused balance on this type of expenditure'.

On the revenue side, too, the pendulum was swinging back towards the uncomplicated legal days when estimates and provisions were less strained by the need to 'balance' conflicting realities. Another rent increase was also adopted – £3, some 13.5%, to take effect in October as previously promised. The Treasurer advised that this was the absolute minimum, but the political climate was now such that he was prepared to 'strongly recommend' in the budget papers that the increase should be more than £7, an increase of over 30%.

Other major items in the 1989 budget included cuts of £10m, adjustments reflecting the revenue costs or savings of unwinding deferred purchase and similar arrangements of recent years, an allowance of £2m for unidentified savings, and a further amount of, in effect, £1m of savings anticipated from early implementation in 1989/90 of cuts which the council would identify for 1990/91.

What is missing from these reports – at least, as seen through the eyes of the past several years – is the climax, the point at which the Treasurer, having detailed the council's financial predicament, pulls the carefully crafted *intra vires* rabbit out of the hat, and the Solicitor advises that as long as members carefully take into account all relevant considerations, as identified in the report, the budget has been made to balance. In place of this, the calculation with which the report ended was stunningly simple and entirely uncluttered by all the paraphernalia of the foregoing years. The Treasurer set out the approved committee estimates, adjusted them for block grant (£51.5m), for precepts, and for the various measures described in the report, and calculated the net income still required:

> 63. This would produce a general rate levy of 242.90p, an increase of 19.8%.
> 64. If some or all of the above measures were not to be adopted then a higher level of rate would be required.

Not for many years had budget-making seemed so legally prosaic, and so close to the archetype under the *General Rate Act 1967*, under which a council determines its income from sources other than rates, determines its expenditures, and levies a rate to make up the difference.

D. Internally displaced discretion

To say, though, that *the budget* proceeded relatively free of legal complications is not to say that legal creativity was dead. In non-financial areas new issues were being explored, and the tightness of the council's overall budgetary *policy* was an important factor in this. It was displacing the council's discretion from its financial powers to other areas of potential *latitude*.

Planning gain, for example, was something that the council had decided the previous year to seek more actively, and this year it became a point of controversy. Planning gain involved developers providing on-site benefits to serve the area of the development, but the developer had the option of providing the benefits by way of a 'commuted payment'. At the July 1988 council meeting an Opposition member complained to the Chair of the development and planning committee:

> Don't you see that soliciting planning gains, either in cash or in kind, and in effect selling planning consents is every bit as corrupt as the old Spanish custom your profession used to go in for of selling indulgences.

The Chair did not agree that the council was selling planning permissions and presented the rationale in planning law for planning gain and the commuted payments. He played an equally straight bat in December when, after a report in the national press that the council would 'facilitate planning consents for cash', the Opposition member again railed against what he called the council's 'extortion racket'.

Imaginative housing initiatives are also referred to several times in council documents of this period. One was a scheme under which housing associations would get sites developed by private developers on the strength of a so-called 'put option' under which the association could require the council to take a lease of the property when developed. The council could then use the property for housing, while its lease payments to the housing association would, in effect, fund the development. A housing committee report in March 1988 mentioned that a number of these 'special initiatives' were being investigated, mostly aimed at reducing the numbers of households in bed and breakfast accommodation, but some involving the disposal of sites to organizations that would offer the council substantial nomination rights. These initiatives, the report continued,

> are new ones for local authorities and would not be necessary but for the Government's hostile attitude towards conventional public housing provision. Nevertheless we are determined to explore all possible ways of continuing to make provision in response to the needs of those residents who are still dependent on the council to provide decent housing.

A particularly large venture at the time (though it eventually stalled, partly because of problems with the title to the land) aimed to combine a council-owned site with a neighbouring privately-owned site, and to develop, in combination with a consortium of housing associations, community groups and private companies, a major scheme involving housing, light industrial use, open space and a few small shops or other services. As described in December 1988, the housing element included 84 dwellings for sale and 111 housing association and shared ownership units in which the council was to receive 50% nomination rights. The financial viability of the scheme depended heavily on the blend of dwellings and uses and the number of properties for sale.

The Treasurer has commented (at interview) that the period from which the kinds of initiatives described above emerged was an interesting one. Line departments were not only coming up with suggestions for original measures, but, unusually, they were making more effort to follow through and bring the ideas to fruition.

This change makes perfectly good sense in terms of the dynamics of the interplay between a government's *policies* and the *ultra vires* rule. In the current financial year, 1988/89, the council remained committed to its political and social objectives, but now accepted that its overall financial *policy* had to be more restrictive than it would have liked. The result was that the pressure for innovation was diverted away from the council's general financial decision-making into other areas, and line departments had the additional incentive that, if they could not find imaginative ways of operating in accordance with the new financial imperative, the likely alternative was cuts. In some ways this was a replication, within the council, of what had gone on between the council and the government in earlier years. Then it had been the government that imposed the financial pressure and the council that explored any *latitude* in its statutory powers to find ways of avoiding the pressure. Now it was the council that was imposing the pressure and the line departments that were trying to find ways out. An important difference, of course, was that the council, unlike the government, was only too willing to go along with the departments' ideas if they worked. The expression 'displaced discretion' comes to mind, of course, but with the rider that now it was the council's *policy*, rather than *law*, that was the cause of the displacement.

E. Going out with a bang

The 1989 budget was the last to be prepared under the *Local Government, Planning and Land Act 1980*; with it this tale is drawing to a close. To bring the story full circle, though, a brief review of activities during the 1989/90 financial year is necessary. This was a year of transition between the 1980 Act and the new scheme that was to become operative on 1 April 1990. Transitions, like so many other features of local government activity under the *ultra vires* rule, have some features that are immutable and others that vary considerably, depending on the *disposition* of each individual council and on the relative merits, as the council sees them, of the old *given law* as against the new.

For 1990, the two governing Acts were to be the *Local Government Finance Act 1988* and the *Local Government and Housing Act 1989*. Between them they established a complete new framework of *given law* for local government finance – new capital controls, a new revenue support grant, the uniform business rate, the poll tax and the extremely important requirement of 'ring-fencing' of the housing revenue account so that it became self-financing. This was all very different, and a major task to be completed before the 1989/90 financial year ended was that of reconfiguring the council's financial position, which had evolved over ten years of budgeting under the 1980 Act, so that the council was properly placed to function under the replacements.

There were three major areas in which preparedness for the new scheme was crucial: poll tax, rents and capital financing. All were extremely important financially, and in each case the new *given law* was anathema to the council. But in terms of the specifically legal dimension of the council's preparations they generated very different chains of events.

The simplest legally, though the most controversial in terms of national politics, was the poll tax, that 'bizarre mistake of the Thatcher era' (MacGregor 1991: 445; see generally Midwinter and Monaghan 1993; Butler, Adonis and Travers 1994). This performed essentially the same function as rates under the old system: it was a tax that a local authority could levy if its other anticipated revenues were insufficient to meet its estimated expenses. There were many difficulties associated with it, but in terms of *law* the basic idea was straightforward. By the time of the 1989 budget the council had worked itself back into a position in which the final rate-making component of the annual budget was not particularly problematic from the point of view of the *ultra vires* rule. The poll tax in 1990, subject to the fact that the possibility of charge-capping might arise under circumstances that the government was not prepared to specify, was likely to be the same.

The rent decision was more legally interesting. 'Ring-fencing' under the *Local Government and Housing Act 1989* made the council's rent decision a very different exercise from before. Previously the key legal question had been of the 'balance' between the interests of rentpayers and ratepayers, this being largely reflected in the size of the contribution from the rate fund to the housing revenue account – roughly 30% in our council. Under the new legislation, however, no such contribution would be possible, and this would make the rent decision a more mechanical exercise of simply determining the level of rents that would avoid a deficit in the housing revenue account. Mathematically, this threatened to generate a rent increase of £7.45 for 1989, substantially more than even the £4.50 that the government had established as its guideline figure for the council. The council had to find some way of containing the increase. The government's guideline figure was the most it would countenance as a matter of *policy*.

Its legal *latitude* in this case lay in the fact that the government had not yet specified by regulation (as it was entitled to do) which items had to be charged to the housing revenue account and which would be borne by the general fund. The Treasurer reported that the government had intended to do this, but had been unable to manage it in the time available because of the complexity and variety of local authority practice. This left it open to the council to decide that some of the costs previously borne by the housing revenue account should be charged to the general fund instead. By chance, this built onto a well-established local disagreement in which a councillor who was a tenants' advocate of long standing had argued that council rents were providing a disguised subsidy to the rate fund, since tenants' rents were partly applied to services that, elsewhere in the borough, were paid for out of the rates. The council had analysed its rent-borne expenditure closely in response to that criticism. With the advent of 'ring-fencing' the work came to serve a different purpose. Items relating to 'non-tenant services' were carefully identified and transferred out of the housing revenue account, thus reducing the total cost of the items to be covered by rents so that a rent increase of only the government's guideline figure, £4.50, was sufficient. There was, of course, still potentially a 'balance' argument to be made in relation to this new allocation of costs as between council tenants and poll tax payers (the latter included council tenants, of course), but questions of *vires* relating to this 'balance' were not a major preoccupation. Financially, the new 'balance' was not unfavourable to poll tax payers by the standards of previous years. Greater legal concerns were whether the government might introduce regulations which invalidated the allocation the council had adopted, and, much more so, whether the £39 increase in poll tax it produced might create a danger of charge-capping.

Far more significant, though, in terms of the legal adjustments required in anticipation of the new *given law* of 1 April 1990 were those relating to the council's capital commitments. The new rules on capital controls, especially the way they treated existing transactions and capital receipts, led to a major exercise in winding up commitments under the old legislation as far as possible and finding good uses for capital receipts before the new legislation required them to be used for retiring debt. As a deliberate act of *policy*, moreover, the council went one step beyond merely straightening out its existing commitments. Faced with the prospect of new *given law* that would be more restrictive than the existing rules, the council decided not only to use up its existing capital receipts but also to generate new ones as long as these, too, could be used before the new régime took effect. Here, then, was one final 'pre-implementation licence' to be grasped.

Much activity flowed from this, particularly as the end of the financial year approached. Outstanding covenant arrangements were paid off early where possible. Frequent use was made of the *de minimis* exception to the definition of 'prescribed expenditure': many things that could be bought either in small amounts or in bulk were therefore bought in small amounts, among them £750,000 of school catering equipment which the council decided in early March 1989 should be ordered, supplied and installed under contracts of £6,000 or less by the end of the month. The advance leasing arrangements needed to be restructured again, and were renegotiated where possible to become 'operating leases', which would not use up any of the council's capital resources under the new scheme, as opposed to 'finance leases', which would. The council was also advised to use up the 'planning gain' money from previous years under the pre-1990 statutory regime, so as to avoid any of it having to be applied to debt repayment.

Sales of land were also a noticeable feature of the period. When the council drew up its 1989 budget it included an estimate of £11.5m to be received from right to buy sales, a large amount by previous years' standards. By the end of the year, this figure had grown enormously; the council was now expecting to have completed £28m of sales, with a further £30m in 1990/91. There was also pressure to complete the sale of several major development sites in 1989/90 so as to bring the receipts into the more advantageous legal context of that year. As capital receipts from sales of land grew, so also did the council's 'non-prescribed capital expenditure'. An estimate of £8.5m at the start of the year had grown to an enormous £21m by January 1990, and to an even more enormous £40m in March, as the Treasurer made every effort to both generate and mop up as much as possible of the council's available capital spending capacity before the new *law* took away its ability to do so. The concept of 'notional capital expenditure' also finds its way into council documents during this period. Just as, in the past, some transactions had been structured to generate 'notional capital receipts', so other transactions produced 'notional capital expenditure' which reduced the council's accumulated capital receipts without actually requiring it to spend money.

Among the most important items attended to in the preparations for the new legislation were the £50m lease/leaseback that had been entered into in the nick of time for purposes of the 1988 budget and the very large Company B.1 and B.2 deferred purchase transactions. As for the lease/leaseback, agreement was reached with the banks and the suitably congenial *ad hoc* private company with which the lease/leaseback had been concluded (it was jointly owned by Company B and a financial institution) for the transaction to be reversed in 1993. As for the deferred purchase arrangements, the Treasurer worked long and hard to pay these off before 1 April 1990 with the proceeds of a proposed

£200m bond issue, and came close ... but unfortunately the council lacked the legal *autonomy* to do this without the approval of the Secretary of State for the Environment, and this was not forthcoming. The refinancing of the deferred purchase arrangements, therefore, was one large and problematic item of unfinished business that the Treasurer would have to attend to under the new, and more awkward, *given law* of the incoming legislation.

F. And so to bed

All things considered, though, and despite all the convolutions associated with the new financial régime, the picture emerging from the 1989 budget and the 12 months it covered was not all that bad. The package of savings planned for the following year was a modest 3%–5%, and during 1989/90 there appeared to be more scope for accommodating new spending initiatives than had been seen for some time. Two very similar quotations from council documents summarize the feeling that the corner had been turned, that the worst was over financially. In June 1989, when the council was just beginning its planning for the 1990 budget, a joint report from the Treasurer and the Solicitor commented:

> 41. The 1989/90 budget includes provision for the repayment of [Company B] principal and interest. Lease/leaseback arrangements will be terminated in 1993. If everyone acts sensibly in 1989/90 and 1990/91 therefore, the council can look forward to a more stable financial position in the 1990's.

At the end of the financial year, in the budget report for 1990/91, the Treasurer's comment was similar:

> The financial future although bleak does offer some prospects of stability rather than the hand to mouth existence the council has had to operate during recent years of stringent government controls and ratecapping.
>
> There are several reasons for believing this, firstly [and remarkably, one must interject] the council's base budget now incorporates all expenditure resulting from previous financing decisions that were taken in the past to balance the budget in the short term. Secondly, the re-financing of the [Company B] deferred purchase arrangement result is a fixed and known commitment for future

years which has been incorporated in the base budget. Lastly, the operation of the safety net for block grant will work in the council's favour for 1991/92 onwards as the contribution it is required to make of £41 per chargepayer will cease in 1991/92.

Poll Tax rises should be kept near the level of inflation from 1992/93 onwards.

As things stood in March 1990, then, the turmoil of the 1980s seemed to be coming to a close. The council's finances seemed in tolerable order, and the new *law* of local government finance was such that the events of the previous ten years seemed unlikely to be repeatable, even if the council's *disposition* had been to try, which at that time it was not.

G. Postscript

In fact, life was to prove less simple. First came retroactive charge-capping for the 1990/91 financial year; the council was caught. Then came the House of Lords's decision in *Hazell v Hammersmith and Fulham LBC* (1991), which declared local authority interest rate swaps *ultra vires* and cast a cloud of uncertainty over a wide variety of local authority financial transactions, both past and future, for a number of years. This, in turn, substantially complicated the Treasurer's attempts to refinance the Company B.1 and B.2 transactions, but finally, after much effort and many Counsels' opinions, routinely shared by now with the Audit Commission, the refinancing occurred. Counsel was satisfied that there was nothing in the new *given law* of *Hazell* that made the refinancing *ultra vires*. Mission accomplished, the Treasurer retired soon afterwards.

A few years later his successor was in a similar predicament. The Company B.1 and B.2 arrangements were due for refinancing again, and there was another large new fly in the legal ointment. The recent court decision in *Crédit Suisse v Allerdale BC* (1995) had raised concerns that virtually any transaction that had been deliberately structured to be outside the capital controls of the *Local Government, Planning and Land Act 1980* might be *ultra vires* on that ground alone. Counsel, though, told the Treasurer and the Solicitor what they needed to hear. The Company B.1 and B.2 arrangements had been *intra vires* when entered into, and nothing in either *Hazell* or *Allerdale* changed that; the arrangements had been valid exercises of the council's power as a housing authority to improve the properties it owned, and the fact that the council had done this through deferred purchase arrangements rather than by other lawful means was immaterial. Thus the refinancing could proceed, sleeping dogs could be left to lie, and the Treasurer and Solicitor were not confronted with the awkward question that may often arise when a tide of professional opinion that once flowed vigorously forward begins to ebb: 'But if *that* one was *ultra vires*, what about these others?'

13
Conclusion

> The history of the Government's attempts to control the capital, and indeed the current, spending of local authorities in England and Wales since 1979 fits neatly into the escalation theory familiar to most militarists. A gradual buildup of punishment is matched by growing ability and determination on the part of the victim to soak it up. Eventually, either the punishment has to be abandoned or the victim dies.
>
> (Davies 1987: 25)

Well, the punishment was not abandoned; the victim did not die. Instead, Pyrrhic victories could probably be claimed on all sides as local government moved forward, in April 1990, into the brave new financial world of the *Local Government Finance Act 1988* and the *Local Government and Housing Act 1989*.

The events of the previous 11 years, wide-ranging and tumultuous though they had been, had at their heart the most basic of public law stories: that of the introduction, settling in, maturity and eventual replacement of a particular statutory régime. In this case the core legislation was the controversial *Local Government, Planning and Land Act 1980*, as supplemented in its mid-life by the even more controversial rate-capping framework of the *Rates Act 1984*. These two Acts set the legal scene for one of the epic sagas of English local government, the long-running clash of wills between the Thatcher government and a number of determined Labour local authorities, of which our council was one. Yet when one peels off the outer coating of conflict and controversy, the process of sustaining the art of the possible was really no different here than in countless other situations. The council simply attempted to understand the legislation so far as necessary for its purposes at any particular time, and to use that understanding, along with the other statutory powers at its disposal, to achieve the best possible outcomes as it saw them.

Governments and agencies of all kinds perform that task, though with different legal resources. Our council was better equipped than some, but worse than others. By comparison with many other local governments (see Denters and Rose 2005b: 9–11) it was a large organization with a wide range of functions. This gave it more legal avenues of response to centrally imposed pressures than would probably be available to many of the nearly 90,000 local governments, often special purpose, that exist in the United States (Valente *et al.* 2001: 6–7; Savitch and Vogel 2005: 213). On the other hand, it did not have the additional range of options that governments with an inherent capacity to act or legislative powers would have, even granted that both of these typically come with constitutional and public law restrictions on their exercise. As compared with a government with legislative powers, moreover, our council was more constrained by *law* that was not of its choosing than any of them would be.

Whatever a government's legal resources, however, *policy* is the force that determines what issues of *law* it confronts as it pursues its vision of how the world should be. Thus within our council, in the early days when the Labour Right held sway and aimed to minimize rate increases, *policy* ran with the grain of the *law*, and *law* was largely *peripheral* to the action. After 1982, however, when the Left gained control, with their *policy* of modest increases in services and large expansions of capital programmes, new issues of *law* became prominent: the balance between ratepayers and the beneficiaries of services, the maximization of grant by lawful means, the development of new *intra vires* means of achieving old ends but in ways that put as little strain as possible on the rate fund.

Then came rate-capping and the council's active participation in the 'united strategy of non-compliance' – a wholly exceptional *policy* that brought to the fore its own range of legal issues. These included technical questions about what a 'balanced budget' really was, novel applications of familiar rules like the need to avoid party political motivations and fettered discretions, and a once-in-a-lifetime (at most, one would hope) close analysis of the nature of 'wilful misconduct'.

For the next three years the key problem of finance and *law* was to find ways of 'bridging the gap' between the council's spending plans and its available revenue, but the *policy* leading to this recurrent problem was different each time. In the first year it was to hold out until the next general election in the hope of a Labour victory and easier financial times. Then, with that hope dashed, it was to avoid being panicked into hasty cuts. Finally, when the council came free of rate-capping for the first time since the *Rates Act 1984* had been enacted, it was to avoid being rate-capped again. Most striking was the last of these years, when the 'gap' was entirely generated by *policy*, yet the financial and legal 'bridging' measures were no less desperate than the ones before.

Then came 1989, the last year of the *Local Government, Planning and Land Act 1980*. The council's main financial *policy* now led it back to a legally unproblematic budget like those of the early years, but as the unenticing prospect of the new *given law* drew ever closer, the council made one additional choice of *policy*, launching into a flurry of activity and taking as much advantage as possible of the legal *latitude* that was still briefly available until the new legislation lowered the boom.

If the council's *policy* had been of grudging acquiescence from day one of this saga, very little of the *law* the council actually addressed would have needed exploration.

As *policy* interacts with *law*, of course, *law* does not stand still. In our council's case the *given law* of Acts and regulations changed regularly, and was supplemented by further *given law* in the form of court decisions. The council could not decide what any of these said. A government with legislative power would never be in quite as difficult a situation, since it can at least decide the content of its own Acts and regulations, and can reverse some court decisions it dislikes. Even then, though, a government has to adapt its behaviour to the laws it enacts, which is not always easy, and sometimes these are laws that some or all of the bureaucrats involved think ill-advised, but still have to work with (or around).

Changes in the *given law* are clear cut – one day the law says one thing, the next it says another. With legislation and regulations there is typically, though not always, advance notice and time to prepare. Case-law, by contrast, operates instantaneously, and is in effect retroactive. The moment the court says what the *law* is, that is what the law has been from the day the legislation was first enacted. The practical challenge is therefore to adjust after the event.

Operative law, on the other hand, is internally generated, and is continually evolving. It develops not in fits and starts, as the *given law* does, but in a process of continuing adaptation as people work through their daily lives with a knowledge of what is legally certain and what is not, yet having to take decisions regardless of how certain or uncertain the *law* is. As each decision is taken it becomes part of the foundation upon which future decisions will build, a phenomenon most clearly demonstrated in this council in the 1980s by the continuing ability of the deferred purchase concept, once accepted as *intra vires* by the council's own particular *operative law* (and only afterwards by the government and later the *given law* of court decisions) to adapt into various different forms within the confines allowed by Acts and regulations as they existed at different points in time.

In the 11 years examined here of the evolving interaction of *law* with *policy*, every step was logical, many of them were predictable, yet none of them was inevitable. They were logical in the sense that at every step along the way, the words of Acts and regulations, combined with the *what*, the *why*, the *who* and the *how* of the *ultra vires* rule, established a matrix of possibilities into which all outcomes had to fit. They were predictable in the sense that, given the *disposition* of the council at any particular point of time, particular issues of *law* would naturally come to the fore as the ones where the presence or absence of legal *latitude* mattered. They were not inevitable, though, for the *policy* never had to be as it was, nor did the specific engagements of *law* with *policy* have to turn out in the way that they did. Even within the well-defined conceptual framework that the *ultra vires* rule establishes for local authority decision-making, there are always choices.

Some of these are obvious. They are the major decisions of *policy*, recited earlier in this chapter, that determined the main course of the action. Others, however, are more discreet yet still influential, and must be highlighted now. These are the choices that advisors make in their own minds as they decide what advice to give or not to give.

Many examples have been seen in this book. In 1981, for instance, if the Deputy Solicitor had continued to feel and express the 'considerable doubts' that he initially had about Company B's proposed covenant arrangements for the new municipal offices, this precedent-setting project might not have occurred, and others could not have developed so swiftly and smoothly out of it. In 1985, the year of the 'rates rebellion', if the Solicitor's soul-searching about whether 'certainty' was the correct standard to apply in deciding when and whether the council was acting *ultra vires* had resolved itself differently, he would have felt obliged to give advice that would have backed the council into an even more uncomfortable legal corner than the one it eventually faced. In 1987 the Deputy Solicitor could have decided that he should indeed 'jump in with both feet' and advise against the lease/leaseback transaction that the council was then considering, which would not only have made it very much harder for the council to bridge its budgetary gap in 1987, but would also have meant, as things turned out one year later, that the council's officers did not have delegated authority to sign a smaller lease/leaseback just in the nick of time, with ten minutes to spare before the government's new emergency regulations took effect.

On all of these occasions, of course, the Treasurer was also making professional judgments about the council's financial situation and about the viability of particular initiatives. What the Treasurer did or did not say as a matter of *finance* would influence what the Solicitor or Deputy Solicitor felt compelled to say as a matter of *law*. In all such cases it is the exercise of individual professional judgment that determines what legal *information* decision-makers have to deal with, and these inputs in terms of *information* condition the outputs that the eventual decisions represent.

In relation to the specific story played out in this book, different exercises of professional judgment on issues like these would have changed at least some of the features of our council's journey through the 1980s, and could well have reshaped it considerably. Indeed, the entire saga of local government finance in the 1980s would have been very different if enough local authority lawyers and their Counsel had reached slightly more restrictive conclusions on some of the central issues of professional judgment, or *operative law*, arising under the 1980 Act. A clear and narrower professional consensus on these issues would have been a major obstacle to the *dispositions* of councils like ours.

Equally plausible, but more complex, would have been a scenario in which our council's lawyers gave more restrictive advice than they did, but it emerged that less restrictive advice was being given at the time in other local authorities that were similarly situated in terms of *policy*. In this case members would quickly have become aware of the discrepancy; they would therefore have *contested* the opinions provided to them subsequently, and those opinions might well have been reconsidered in the light of the advice that was being given elsewhere. It is hard in any organization, local authorities among others, for a lawyer to adhere to an opinion that is not only problematic and disadvantageous from the point of view of the organization's *policy* but also out of line with the developing consensus of professional opinion, as expressed elsewhere. This is not just a matter of *realpolitik* – 'local government lawyers often inhabit the uncomfortable area between the hammer and the anvil' (Dobson 2002: 48) – but also because there is a natural tendency to defer to the collective professional wisdom of one's peers, accepting it as reflecting at least a reasonable point of view even if, personally, one thinks it is mistaken. The reality of the day, though, was rather the opposite of this. Especially in the early years of the 1980s, opinions of the kind that our council's lawyers were providing were the ones that were creating the new professional consensus, as the *operative law* of the *Local Government, Planning and Land Act 1980* developed rapidly in response to the pressures of circumstances. Other councils, therefore, were the ones who faced the choice of either adopting the emerging consensus, perhaps against their better judgment, or finding themselves financially disadvantaged if they did not.

What this underscores is, of course, that whereas *given law* is a matter of fact, expressed in statutes and in case law, *operative law*, which is the application of *given law* to the facts of particular situations, is always a matter of opinion. Opinions differ; each one is, in a sense, unique. Though they are shaped and constrained by common elements – in our case the four 'W's of the *ultra vires* rule as applied to the wording of particular statutes – every interpretation of every statute is potentially a source of diversity, since the subtly different shades of nuance or understanding that are the product of each individual exercise of professional judgment may open, for some local authorities, avenues that remain closed to others.

Here, then, let us expand the analysis, both in time and in place. Stewart (2000), writing at around the time the *Local Government Act 2000* introduced 'executive arrangements' into the statutory framework of English local government, identified the themes of 'diversity of locality, but yet within uniformities' (5) and 'continuity and change' (8) as key to the past and future understanding of the system. Leach (2006: 8), looking back at the new arrangements after their first five years, adopts the framework of 'new institutionalism' in observing that new structures like these are always mediated by local factors, and Berg and Rao (2005b: 1–2) explain that the new institutionalism embraces 'constitutional institutionalism', which is the framework of formal rules and structures under which a government operates, and 'sociological institutionalism', which is concerned with practical applications and behaviours in relation to the formal rules. This combination of perspectives provides a useful vantage point for looking at the functioning of public law both in local government specifically and in government more generally.

We begin with the 'continuity' and the 'uniformity' in the local government context. According to *Butterworths* (2002/04: para. A[48]), 'despite its unsatisfactory legal foundations, and its extreme consequences, the ultra vires principle must be regarded as permanently entrenched as the basis of the system of judicial control'. It is hard to disagree. Although Valente *et al.* (2001: 264) are right to point out that a judge-made rule, Dillon's Rule in their case, 'may be abrogated by judicial action as well as by a state constitutional amendment or legislative command', judicial abrogation of the *ultra vires* rule is unlikely, and becomes increasingly so as legislatures enact broad enabling provisions like s.2 of the *Local Government Act 2000*. If legislatures have decided that local authorities should have wide general powers, and have carefully chosen both the nature of and restrictions on those powers, judges are unlikely to turn the flank of the legislative exercise by creating a wide-ranging and amorphous non-statutory capacity for action like the Crown's or that of the old municipal corporations.

As for a legislature, if it tries now to change the underlying principle that local authorities can only do what statute permits it is faced with a logical conundrum. The only way that Parliament can change the law is by statute. But how can Parliament change the rule that local authorities can only do what statute permits if its only legal instrument is a statute that says what local authorities can do? Take, for example, the outline of a 'general competence' provision that the Ministry of Housing and Local Government (against its better judgment and not expecting it to be accepted) prepared for Labour Ministers in November 1969. This was a proposal that local authorities should have the power 'to do any thing and to incur any consequent expenditure which in their opinion would be in the interests of their area or their inhabitants' (see Rattenbury 1984: 346). The Ministry added that there would be a qualifier designed to prevent local authorities from flouting the intentions of Parliament, but even if one removes the qualifier the power described is still a statutory power to act. Under it, local authorities would still be doing what statute permitted.

A legislature that was determined enough to find its way out of this conundrum might possibly be able to do so. The idea to work with would be the establishment of 'natural person powers', as are mentioned in s.6 of the *Municipal Government Act* of Alberta, Canada. The full Alberta package, however, contains a variety of elements that show the phrase itself is not enough. The legislation contains statements of municipal 'powers', 'duties' and 'purposes' which interconnect, partially counteract each other, and leave lots of room for argument about what the legislature intended or accomplished (see Wakefield 2007: 15–19). In *Passutto Hotels (1984) Ltd v Red Deer (City of)* (2006; paras 17–21) the Alberta Act was described as giving broad authority, which was intended to be interpreted generously, but the overall framework of the judgment was still that municipalities are statutory bodies whose only powers are those that are expressly conferred, necessarily implied or indispensable to municipal operations. Ontario's more recent *Municipal Act* also provides for natural person powers, but in a framework which shows even more clearly that there is no magic in the words themselves. In Ontario 'A municipality has the capacity, rights, powers and privileges of a natural person' but only 'for the purpose of exercising its authority under this or any other Act' (s.8).

Elements of the *ultra vires* rule beyond the underlying principle that local authorities can only do what statute permits are equally resistant to legislative change. As a matter of legal theory, the *what*, the *why*, the *who*, and the *how* all revolve around statutory interpretation. Parliaments can change the content of statutes, but it is harder to change by legislation the way that judges approach the task of interpreting them. Indeed, it is a feature of public law generally, not just of the purely statute-based version that applies to local authorities, that it is resistant to legislative change. If, for example, one of the substantial foundations for judicial review is a constitutional provision such as 'the famous "due process" clause of the Fourteenth Amendment' (Carter and Harrington 2000: 68), there is little an individual government or legislature can do about what the courts decide the provision means. If a government relies on its 'inherent capacity' it is entirely in the hands of the courts, since the legal attributes of inherent capacity are determined by judge-made law, not by governments or by legislation. Courts themselves, of course, can develop new principles to apply in the judicial review of government action – the ongoing tales in England of 'proportionality', 'substantive legitimate expectations' and 'conspicuous unfairness amounting to an abuse of power' as potential bases for judicial review spring to mind as examples – but legislatures, for the most part, cannot do much about it. In New Zealand McLean (2006: 137–41) describes an intriguing attempt. There in the 1990s the government altered its legislative drafting practices so that the Crown relied more on its 'natural person' capacity and less on statutory provisions. This did have some effect, but primarily in adjusting which elements of public law would be the bases for judicial review.

Public law's power as a force for 'continuity', to return to Stewart's term, is thus reflected in the fact that it is relatively impervious to legislative change. Its relevance to 'uniformity', another of Stewart's terms, is best shown in a context like English local government, where several hundred local authorities are subject to many of the same statutes and exactly the same *ultra vires* rule at the same time. Even when one makes allowance for the different groups of functions performed by unitary, county and district councils, this is a thoroughly uniform structure.

This also makes it, of course, a perfect testing ground for 'diversity', the term with which Stewart counterbalances 'uniformity'. The identical nature of the formal legal rules, of the 'constitutional institutionalism' in other words, means that the 'sociological institutionalism' of government behaviour is revealed in the different ways in which local authorities apply the same rules. 'Diversity' will be harder to observe in one-of-a-kind governments that do not easily lend themselves to external comparisons, though even here it can be identified through internal studies over time or in different fields of activity.

Here, then, let us inject the human element in the form of the government lawyer, to whom falls the primary role of turning the *given law* of Acts and cases into the *operative law* of decisions and actions. The role combines both uniformities and diversities.

The uniformities begin with this. The basic professional task of government lawyers is to inform their governments of what the law is whenever the circumstances require it, or, as this has been formulated before in this study, to provide legal inputs so that outputs can be legal. In the particular case of English local government the law is that local authorities can only do what statute permits, and statute determines not only *what* local authorities can do, but also *why* they may do it, *who* can do it, and *how*. Whatever legal *information* a lawyer feeds into local authority decision-making must be in one way or another a reflection of that theme. If, furthermore, as was seen in Chapter 2, the combined effect of these four 'W's is that local authorities are better seen from the legal point of view as being entities concerned with the impartial and disinterested discharge of conceptually independent statutory responsibilities, rather than as free-standing 'political institutions for local self-government' (Stewart 2000: 26), the former is the direction in which legal advice will inevitably lead. This is not because lawyers either individually or collectively prefer the former vision to the latter as a matter of political philosophy. It is not, either, because the former represents the legally binding product of what McAuslan (1980: xii) might call the judiciary's collective 'ideology' of local government, their 'set of values, attitudes, assumptions, "hidden inarticulate premises" that may not be well thought out and are usually disguised rather than spoken out loud'. Though there may be elements of 'ideology' at play, particularly in concepts such as the trusteeship of the rate fund, the forces at work here are far more mundane. It is simply a matter of how statutes are interpreted, with the starting point being the text, and with the statute itself providing the answers as to *what* may be done and *why*, to *who* may do it and *how*. If one starts from that premiss, as the *ultra vires* rule does, the idea that the business of local government is the impartial and disinterested discharge of statutory responsibilities emerges as a consequence rather than as an ideology. It is not so much a vision of what local government *should* be but a reflection of what it will *in fact* be if local authorities follow all the rules they must if they want their actions to be *intra vires*. In applying the screen of the four 'W's to all local authority action the lawyer is simply doing what he or she is paid to do.

Where diversity arises is in the way that task is performed. As this book has shown, a lawyer may allow *law* to take a back seat or a front seat in decision-making; may rely on an *intuitive*, a *reasoned*, or a *meticulous* mode of analysis of particular issues; may be willingly or unwillingly, or by accident or by design, *organized into* or *organized out of* particular decisions; may find more or less *latitude* in the wording of particular statutes. The individual lawyer will probably do all of these things at different times, and different lawyers will do them differently. There are many ways, all equally justifiable, of performing the lawyer's role.

This diversity will then both generate and be influenced by the similar diversities in the behaviour of other actors. Charlton and Martlew (1987: 196), writing in fact of the budget process in Stirling District Council in 1986 but in terms that are probably true of much government decision-making at all times, observe that

> the term 'budget process', implying as it does the logical progression of one activity developing from one stage of creation to the next, is misleading. In fact there are several 'budget processes' in Stirling District Council going on side by side and often connected only in a vague sense which many of those involved do not fully understand.

The legal contribution to decision-making is one of those many processes, and diversity in the manner of its performance will produce variety in when, how and to what effect the legal process interconnects with those others. At the same time, the manner in which those other processes are conducted will determine when, how and to what effect *law* has an opportunity to interconnnect with them. Diversity, therefore, abounds, even while the 'continuities' and the 'uniformities' shape its dimensions.

Then comes 'change', the last of Stewart's four terms. Change, of course, can be both internally and externally generated, and much of this study has highlighted the former – change in the *operative law*, change in informal *organization*, and so on – since it is the less self-evident. But there has also been much change imposed externally by legislation in recent years, touching virtually every aspect of local government – functions, powers, structures, finance, management, organization and more – and some of it deserves comment both in its own right and as a reflection of more general public law themes. Change will continue, of course. Stoker and Wilson (2004b: 262), acknowledging 'that many people in the local government world feel that they have, since the 1980s, been on the roller-coaster from hell', had suggested that the ride should soon become less bumpy, because 'the managerial revolution ... has reached its zenith, and the limits of its capacity to deliver worthwhile change'. No such luck. The recently enacted *Local Government and Public Involvement in Health Act 2007*, while scaling back at least some of the excesses of things like inspection schemes and the local government Code of Conduct, also contains revised provisions on 'executive arrangements' that, when implemented over the next few years, will put the vast majority of local authorities through the disruption of revisiting their 'executive arrangements' and casting them into a somewhat different form. Another major upheaval in the making is the potential establishment of unitary authorities in several areas that currently have two-tier local government arrangements.

Among the numerous legislative changes of the recent past, one that deserves additional comment from the public law perspective is s.2 of the *Local Government Act 2000*, the power to promote economic, social or environmental well-being. Like some of its counterparts in other countries, this is a broad power and creates welcome freedoms. The point to be added here, though, is that when viewed through the optic of the *ultra vires* rule it may also impose unwelcome responsibilities. In some cases claimants have persuaded the courts that since this is a wide-ranging statutory power that *can* be exercised in their favour, local authorities have a public law obligation to consider properly whether they *should* do so (*R (Theophilus) v Lewisham LBC* 2002). *R (J) v Enfield LBC* (2002) took this even further, suggesting that s.2, when combined with s.6 of the *Human Rights Act 1998*, could generate a positive obligation for a local authority to act when an individual's rights under the European Convention were not being secured by other means. Arden (2002: 53–4) considered this interpretation 'akin to an absurdity ... wrenching the power out of an altogether different quality of legisation, distorting it and diverting attention from its intended application', and in *Westminster CC v Morris* (2005) the Court of Appeal seems to have substantially restricted the *Enfield* approach. S.2 remains double-edged, however, and sometimes local authorities will have a vested interest in showing that it *cannot* be used, as in *R (Saima Khan) v Oxfordshire CC* (2004), where the council successfully argued that other legislation prevented it from assisting Ms Khan under s.2.

Whether, against this background, s.2 will ever become the 'power of first resort' that the government described but that practice has not yet delivered (Office of the Deputy Prime Minister 2005: 118) remains to be seen. It is not impossible, but from a government lawyer's perspective there is good reason to be wary of both statutory powers and inherent capacities that are *intuitively* accepted as meaning that 'it goes without saying that we can do this'. For English local government, the cautionary tale of s.111 of the *Local Government Act 1972*, *Hazell v Hammersmith & Fulham LBC* (1991) and interest rate swaps shows how badly things can sometimes go wrong when statutory powers are too easily taken for granted. Government lawyers in other jurisdictions probably have comparable cautionary tales of their own.

Another legislative change that is directly related to public law is the establishment of the 'slightly bizarre' (Sharland 2006: 52) mandate of the local authority 'monitoring officer'. This is an internal enforcement role, often assigned to a council's senior solicitor, that was established by the *Local Government and Housing Act 1989* as part of the Thatcher government's reaction to the controversies of the 1980s. Keith-Lucas (2002) provides a thorough account of the role, which was designed to reinforce the principle of legality in local authority behaviour and has been expanded since. Its central element in this respect is the monitoring officer's duty to issue a report on any 'proposal, decision or omission' that 'has given rise to or is likely to or would give rise to ... a contravention ... of any enactment or rule of law' (ss.5 and 5A, *Local Government and Housing Act 1989*). The monitoring officer's report blocks the action in question until the report has been considered. A comparable but narrower duty to report unlawful financial items had been placed on a local authority's chief financial officer a year earlier.

Leigh (2000: 269) comments that the monitoring officer post is 'unique within British government'. However, the broader idea it reflects of giving government officials a statutory responsibility to police the legality of some part of their own governments' actions does have some counterparts. Under New Brunswick's *Financial Administration Act*, for example, an official called the Comptroller, with statutory security of tenure (s.11), has the duty to reject requisitions for payments if they are not a lawful charge against an appropriation or if they would result in an expenditure in excess of the appropriation (s.39).

Internal controls like these, of course, involve both *given law* and *operative law*, and in the case of the monitoring officer, whose duties are expressed in very general terms, *operative law* looms especially large. 'The performance of these duties is hardly calculated to enhance officer-member relations', Sharland (2006: 55) comments, and whether the duties are a continual thorn in the side or a relative nonentity depends entirely upon how one interprets open-ended expressions such as 'likely to' and 'any ... rule of law'. Keith-Lucas (2002) writes that 'Some selectivity is clearly required' in applying the section, and goes on to list 'a set of circumstances in which it is customary for the Monitoring Officer not to make a statutory report, despite the fact that the duty to report may strictly apply' (18). He had earlier noted in passing, writing after the legislation had been in force for more than ten years, that there had only been 'the occasional statutory report' (1). In this way the *operative law* of the monitoring officer's powers can tame their enormous disruptive potential. It would not take much, though, possibly just a few words by a judge in a court case, to shift the balance of professional opinion to a position in which monitoring officers would consider that this duty was one they had to perform much more frequently.

Another recent legislative change that directly relates to the functioning of the *ultra vires* rule, this one affecting an external rather than an internal control on the legality of local authority action, is the recent repeal, long wished for by local government, of the district auditor's power (actually, duty) of surcharge. When the events described in this book began, surcharge was a potential *consequence* to be borne in mind in certain circumstances. Later amendments added the power to serve prohibition notices, thus adding an explicit ability to restrict local authorities' *autonomy*. The *Local Government Act 2000* repealed the surcharge provisions and replaced prohibition notices with advisory notices under which auditors could delay, but not prohibit, action, and could apply to the court for a declaration if necessary (see Supperstone 2003).

The point to remember about powers like these – other governments, too, may operate under some element of binding supervision by an external agency – is that however relaxed or accommodating their 'sociological' application may be most of the time, they still have their 'constitutional' core, and at whatever time an issue erupts, both the government and the other agency must play the hand the *given law* has dealt them. At the time of the 1985 'rates rebellion', for example, the district auditor had a duty to surcharge if loss was caused by 'wilful misconduct'. Several years earlier, the statutory trigger had been the broader expression 'negligence or misconduct', and there was also a duty to surcharge if an item of account was 'contrary to law'. A few years later, the district auditor acquired the power to intervene to prevent the wrongful action, rather than, as in 1985, simply to warn what the *consequences* would be if, on subsequent examination, he determined that wilful misconduct had in fact occurred.

Clearly, during the 'rates rebellion', the district auditor was far from trigger-happy. Nonetheless a duty is a duty, and even a discretion must be expected to be exercised when the circumstances cry out for it. One cannot know, of course, how events in 1985 would have played themselves out if the auditor's responsibilities were still expressed in their earlier, less forgiving, terms of 'negligence or misconduct' and 'contrary to law', or in their later interventionist form allowing for different versions of prohibition. One thing that one can say, however, is that in any confrontation between a statutory body and a statutory regulator there will be an element of inevitability to the terms and the nature of their encounter. With both bodies having identifiable public law powers (whatever these may be) and both being subject to public law rules about how those powers are exercised, it should not be hard to identify how and where the crunch will come. Just as the public law conditions of early 1985 steered the 'rates rebellion' in the direction they did, other conditions at other times would lead in other directions.

The last of the recent legislative changes to be mentioned here is the introduction of 'executive arrangements' by the *Local Government Act 2000*. Unlike the previous examples, executive arrangements are not concerned with the substance of local authority powers nor with their internal or external enforcement, but they are a major change in the internal organization of most English local authorities, and *organization* is a key element in the functioning of public law. During the events described in this book, our council was operating under the traditional local government model, with all functions vested in the council collectively and discharged through committees and staff. This system still survives in most of the smaller English local authorities, with a population under 85,000, that were permitted to retain it (also in Scotland – see McConnell 2004; McFadden 2004), but larger ones must operate under a three-way internal split, with some functions vested in the council, most functions vested in an executive, and an overview and scrutiny committee having the task of holding the executive (primarily) to account.

The executive itself can take one of three forms. Two involve elected mayors (a new departure for English local government), and have not been widely adopted. The large majority of local authorities have chosen the so-called 'leader and cabinet' executive, in which the elected councillors select the leader (House of Commons 2007: 29). The *Local Government and Public Involvement in Health Act 2007* is now eliminating one mayoral model and revising the leader and cabinet model with the objective that, under both remaining forms of executive 'All executive powers will be vested in the mayor or leader who will have the responsibility for deciding how these powers should be discharged – either by him or herself or delegated to members of cabinet individually or collectively' (House of Commons 2007: 31–2). References to 'cabinet' in this local government setting, incidentally, should not be confused with the traditional cabinet of Westminster-style governments. The local government cabinet is a body with formal executive powers within a highly regimented legal framework. By contrast, the essential role of a traditional Westminster cabinet is simply as the body through which the Crown makes up its mind on matters it chooses to decide this way.

Local government did not welcome the prescriptive nature of executive arrangements, nor the specific and limited range of options (Wilson and Game 2006: 101, 103). The literature on their early years refers to some administrative benefits (not surprisingly: cabinet government *is* convenient to cabinets), but also to 'dynamic conservatism' (Ashworth, Copus and Coulson 2004: 465) and to 'passive as well as active resistance' (Cochrane 2004: 492) blunting their effect on the roles of members, so that, initially at least, 'many local authorities implemented the 2000 Act with little real change to their ways of going about business' (John 2004: 53). The party political structure is also mentioned as an important factor in this (Copus 2006; Leach 2006), with councillors' shared political loyalties tending to join back together what the 'council', 'executive' and 'scrutiny' roles attempted to put asunder.

It should come as no surprise that local government practice under executive arrangements may look very different from the vision that inspired the legislation – and this regardless of the fact that many local authorities thought the legislation misconceived. Under the council and committee system, too, it was often pointed out that the legal theory and the political reality of local authority decision-making made an odd couple (Leigh 2000: ch. 6), and the Crown is even more notorious as a government in which 'The theory and history ... cannot always be reconciled with contemporary constitutional structures and practices' (Lordon 1991: 1). From the public law perspective, nonetheless, the point to emphasize here is that despite the reality of the 'sociological institutionalism' that writers describe in various governmental contexts, formal rules matter. Much of the time, admittedly, one can behave as though they do not; people can go with the 'sociological' flow, and no legal harm is done. Sometimes, however, the 'constitutional' is critical, and an internal legal opinion on whether a particular issue is or is not an 'executive responsibility' or a 'key decision', to use some of the legal terminology of executive arrangements (see *Cross* 2004: 105, 115) will determine who, if anyone, has the authority to enter a $50m lease/leaseback at ten minutes to midnight on the last day it is possible to do so. The amended executive arrangements under the *Local Government and Public Involvement in Health Act 2007* will throw up their own set of issues. Vesting executive authority in leaders personally not only reshapes the *who* of the *ultra vires* rule in ways yet to be determined but also raises tangential issues such as how the rule against 'bias' will apply and whether leaders may be 'fettering their discretion' or considering 'irrelevant considerations' if they pay too much attention to the views of colleagues.

It is hard to imagine any government benefiting from internal rigidities of *organization* that, like executive arrangements, are not of its own making (and therefore unmaking). Old style local government, though not always convenient, was structurally simple. Everything flowed back to the council, and a broad power of delegation, though it 'fosters an undue legalism', as Rawlings writes in his intriguing analysis of the first incarnation of the Welsh Assembly, nevertheless 'allows great flexibility' (2003: 117–18). Executive arrangements involve no less legalism, and revolve around an internal separation of powers that creates what Keith-Lucas (2002: 3) calls issues of 'internal vires' – of 'whether a particular decision is within the powers of a particular part of the authority' – based on what he considers an 'arbitrary and confused division of functions' (2002: 71).

Even rigid separations of powers can, of course, be made to work, and the courts may sometimes acquiesce in this. Writers on American administrative law sometimes indicate that if the courts applied constitutional separation of powers theory strictly, modern public administration could not exist, since it depends on 'Congress's questionable delegation of quasi-legislative and quasi-judicial powers to administrative agencies' (Warren 2004: 3–4). Rosenbloom (2003: 11) says that 'the constitutional separation of powers *collapses* ... into administrative agencies'. Nonetheless specific separations of powers like those required by local authority executive arrangements have huge potential for dysfunctionality. However manageable 'sociological institutionalism' may make them, government lawyers cannot afford to be ignorant of the 'constitutional institutionalism' that underpins them.

But what if there are no government lawyers? This question is prompted by Keith-Lucas's passing comment that 'a number of principal authorities do not employ any legally qualified staff' (2002: 6). This is the result of a non-statutory change that has occurred in England in recent years, externalization of legal services, though in some other countries, especially when local authorities are very small, it would probably be the norm.

Having no lawyers is a very significant step in *organizing law out* of decision-making, though that is no doubt not the purpose of the arrangement. Though officers in those authorities will have a good working knowledge of the *law* relating to their responsibilities, they will not be alert to all of the issues that a lawyer should be. From the point of view of the application of the *ultra vires* rule, there is a big difference between obtaining legal advice (from outside the council) only when non-lawyers recognize they need it and having the source of legal information *organized into* the council's structure, with a mandate that includes averting problems as well as responding to them. This is not to say that the one is necessarily better than the other. Even in large local authorities cost/benefit analyses of the two approaches can presumably be conducted, and it is tempting, in fact, to have a sneaking sympathy with an 'ignorance is bliss' philosophy for dealing with the all-pervasive four 'Ws' of the *ultra vires* rule. Nevertheless, in terms of this book's preoccupation with the relationship between public law and government practice, what must be said is that the extent to which lawyers are *organized in* will always be important, and if they are *organized out* so comprehensively that there are no lawyers on staff at all, the dynamics of the relationship between *law* and *policy* would probably play themselves out rather differently from the way described in this book.

Where lawyers are *organized in*, however, one can be confident the relationship between law and practice will involve both the *given law* of Acts and regulations and the *operative law* that evolves when people try to put them into practice. But much more will also be found, for these are just some of the elements in the cooperative human endeavour, with all its complexities, that government represents. Decision-making structures also partly determine when, whether, and to what effect *law* filters into the consciousness of decision-makers, and equally important will be the familiar variables of intra-organizational human behaviour. There are formal and informal working arrangements which will determine who says what to whom about what. There are less concrete factors such as the office culture or 'the way we do things here'. Personal factors are also important – who knows what, who is good at what, who gets on with whom. People will take day-by-day decisions about which internal battles are worth fighting and about when it is time to back off and when to step forward. The possibilities are myriad, and will determine what legal *information* decision-makers have, which will in turn affect what *latitude* they perceive themselves as having and how free they are to achieve the outcomes that suit their *disposition*. These behavioural factors are among the sources of the many diversities (to use Stewart's terms again) that emerge, and as has been demonstrated by this study's examination of the twists and turns of one local authority's encounter with a particular set of legal issues, it should not be thought for a moment that *law* lacks the capacity for diversity, either in itself or in its interactions with the other component parts of government decision-making.

On the other hand, *law's* dominant characteristic is undoubtedly as a force for uniformity, and especially in the case of public law rules, which are relatively impervious to legislative change, for continuity. Though legislation can readily alter the details of *what* governments can do, *why* they can do it, *who* can do it, and *how,* it is inherently less capable of altering the public law framework within which the legislation operates. For an English local authority and many others in the world, the basic proposition is that all of these things are determined by legislation. While statutes change, therefore, the process of working with them on the terms established by the *ultra vires* rule continues, held together by the underlying principle that local authorities can only do what statute permits, and mediated through the professional duty of the local authority lawyer to tell his or her local authority client what the law is whenever circumstances require it. Other governments may have additional legal resources along with their statutory powers, subject to additional public law constraints, but within them, too, sustaining the art of the possible will revolve around the familiar process of providing legal inputs, in accordance with their own particular public law rules, so that outputs can be legal.

This is why the events described in this book, though obviously firmly anchored in their own particular time and place, nevertheless illustrate themes that are perennial and widely generalizable. *Law* and *policy* continue to interact in the contexts determined by *organization. Disposition, information, latitude, autonomy* and *consequences* continue to be key factors in the relationship between public law and government practice. Government lawyers will still act in an *intuitive*, a *reasoned* or a *meticulous* fashion as they convert the *given law* of Acts, regulations and cases into the *operative law* that will be, at different times or from different people's points of view, a *subliminal, peripheral, explicit, determinative* or *contested* factor in their governments' decision-making processes.

Thus one council's experiences in the 1980s, though obviously unique in one way, are archetypal in another. With their extraordinarily wide range of occurrences, from the mundane to the momentous, they provide an unusually complete picture of the many ways in which governments can address the enduring and preordained task that public law presents: to do the best they possibly can for their communities, using only the resources their public law allows.

Bibliography

Andenas, Mads, and Duncan Fairgrieve (eds) (2000). *Judicial Review in International Perspective*. The Hague: Kluwer.

Arden, Andrew (2002). 'Whose Well-Being: Central or Local Government?' [2002] *Journal of Local Government Law*, issue 3: 51.

Arnold-Baker, Charles (1973). *The Local Government Act 1972*. London: Butterworths.

Ashworth, Rachel, Colin Copus and Andrew Coulson (2004). 'Local Democratic Renewal: An Introduction.' *Local Government Studies*, vol. 30, no. 4: 459.

Audit Commission (1984). *The Impact on Local Authorities' Economy, Efficiency and Effectiveness of the Block Grant Distribution System*. London: HMSO.

—— (1985). *Capital Expenditure Controls in Local Government in England*. London: HMSO.

—— (1987). *Annual Report*. London: HMSO.

Aulich, Chris (2005). 'Australia: still a tale of Cinderella?' In Denters and Rose (2005a): 193.

Baldwin, Robert (1994). 'Governing with Rules.' In Richardson and Genn (1994): 157.

Berg, Rikke, and Nirmala Rao (eds) (2005a). *Transforming Local Political Leadership*. Basingstoke: Palgrave Macmillan.

—— (2005b). 'Institutional Frameworks in Local Government: A Comparative Framework.' In Berg and Rao (2005a): 1.

Black, Julia (1997). *Rules and Regulators*. Oxford: Clarendon.

Black, Julia, and Peter Muchlinski (1998). 'Introduction,' in Black, Muchlinski and Walker (1998): 1.

Black, Julia, Peter Muchlinski and Paul Walker (1998). *Commercial Regulation and Judicial Review*. Oxford: Hart.

Boddy, Martin, and Colin Fudge (eds) (1984). *Local Socialism? Labour Councils and New Left Alternatives*. London: Macmillan.

Boynton, John (1986). *Job at the Top: the Chief Executive in Local Government*. Harlow: Longman.

Branson, N. (1979). *Poplarism, 1919–25*. London: Lawrence & Wishart.

Bridges, L., C. Game, J. McBride, O. Lomas and S. Ranson (1987). *Legality and Local Politics*. Aldershot: Avebury.

Briffault, Richard (2004). 'Home Rule for the Twenty-first Century.' *The Urban Lawyer*, vol. 36, no. 2: 253.

Buck, Trevor (ed.) (1998a). *Judicial Review and Social Welfare*. London: Pinter.

—— (1998b) 'Judicial Review and the Discretionary Social Fund: The Impact on a Respondent Organization.' In Buck (1998a): 114.

Bush, Graham W. A. (2005). 'New Zealand: a quantum leap forward?' In Denters and Rose (2005a): 174.

Butcher, Hugh, Ian G. Law, Robert Leach and Maurice Mullard (1990). *Local Government and Thatcherism*. London: Routledge.

Butler, David, Andrew Adonis and Tony Travers (1994). *Failure in British Government: the Politics of the Poll Tax*. Oxford: Oxford University Press.

Butterworths Local Government Law, 2nd ed., looseleaf (2002) (eds) Patrick Elias, QC, and James Goudie, QC. London: Butterworths. [Continued as Elias and Goudie (2004).]

Byrne, Tony (1994). *Local Government in Britain: Everyone's Guide to How It All Works*, 6th ed. London: Penguin.

Carmichael, Paul (1995). *Central-Local Government Relations in the 1980s: Glasgow and Liverpool Compared*. Aldershot: Avebury.

Carter, Lief, and Christine Harrington (2000). *Administrative Law and Politics*, 3rd ed. New York: Longmans.

Charlton, Jacqueline, and Chris Martlew (1987). 'Stirling District Council.' In Elcock and Jordan (1987): 181.

Cheetham, Terry (1981). 'The Local Government Act. How the New System of Capital Controls will Operate.' *Local Government Chronicle*, 16 January 1981: 39.

Cochrane, Allan (2004). 'Modernisation, Managerialism and the Culture Wars: Reshaping the Local Welfare State in England.' *Local Government Studies*, vol. 30, no. 4: 481.

Cochrane, Allan, and Alan Clark (1990). 'Local Enterprise Boards: The Short History of a Radical Initiative.' *Public Administration*, vol. 68, no. 3: 315.

Committee on the Management of Local Government (1967). *Management of Local Government*. London: HMSO.

Cooley, Sumil F. A. (2001). *Principles of Administrative Law in Sri Lanka*, 2nd ed. Colombo: Gunasena & Co.

Cooper, Davina (1998). *Governing Out of Order: Space, Law and the Politics of Belonging*. London: Rivers Oram Press.

Cooper, Phillip J. (2007). *Public Law and Public Administration*, 4th ed. Belmont: Thomson.

Copus, Colin (2006). *Leading the Localities: Executive Mayors in English Local Governance*. Manchester: Manchester University Press.

Craig, P. P. (2003). *Administrative Law*, 5th ed. London: Thomson.

Craig, Paul, and Adam Tomkins (eds) (2006a). *The Executive and Public Law: Power and Accountability in a Comparative Perspective*. Oxford: Oxford University Press.

—— (2006b). 'Introduction.' In Craig and Tomkins (2006a): 1.

Crawford, Colin, and Victor Moore (1983). *'The Free Two Pence.' Section 137 of the Local Government Act 1972 and Section 3 of the Local Government (Scotland) Act 1973*. Chartered Institute of Public Finance and Accountancy.

Cross on Principles of Local Government Law, 3rd ed. (2004), by Stephen Bailey. London: Sweet & Maxwell.

Daintith, Terence, and Alan Page (1999). *The Executive in the Constitution: Structure, Autonomy and Internal Control*. Oxford: Oxford University Press.

Davies, A. C. L. (2006). 'Ultra Vires Problems in Government Contracts.' 122 *Law Quarterly Review*: 98.

Davies, Harry (1987). 'Capital Spending.' In Parkinson (1987): 25.

Delaney, Hilary (2001). *Judicial Review of Administrative Action – A Comparative Analysis*. Dublin: Round Hall.

Denters, Bas, and Lawrence Rose (eds) (2005a). *Comparing Local Governance: Trends and Developments*. Basingstoke: Palgrave Macmillan.

—— (2005b). 'Local Governance in the Third Millennium: a brave new world?' In Denters and Rose (2005a): 1.
—— (2005c). 'Towards Local Governance?' In Denters and Rose (2005a): 246.
Department of the Environment and Welsh Office (1989). *Local Authorities' Interests in Companies in England and Wales. Consultation Paper in the Form of a Draft Circular*. London and Cardiff.
Department of the Environment, Transport and the Regions (2001). *Power to Promote or Improve Economic, Social or Environmental Well-Being*. London.
De Smith, Woolf and Jowell's Principles of Judicial Review, 5th ed., rev. (1999), by Lord Woolf, Jeffrey Jowell and A. P. Le Sueur. London: Sweet & Maxwell.
Dobson, Nicholas (2002). 'Forsaking Pride.' [2002] *Journal of Local Government Law*, issue 2: 40.
Dukhira, C. (1999). 'Mauritius: A Review of Democratic Decentralisation in an Island State.' In Reddy (1999): 129.
Duncan, Simon, and Mark Goodwin (1987). *The Local State and Uneven Development: Behind the Local Government Crisis*. New York: St. Martin's Press.
Egeberg, Morten (1999). 'The Impact of Bureaucratic Structure on Policy Making.' *Public Administration*, vol. 77, no. 1: 155.
Elcock, Howard, and Grant Jordan (1987). *Learning from Local Authority Budgeting*. Aldershot: Avebury.
Elcock, Howard, Grant Jordan and Arthur Midwinter, with George Boyne (1989). *Budgeting in Local Government: Managing the Margins*. Harlow: Longmans.
Elias, Patrick, and James Goudie, QC (eds) (2004). *Local Government Law*, 2nd ed., looseleaf. London: Tottel.
Elliott, Michael (1983). 'Constitutional Continuity and the Position of Local Government.' In Young (1983a): 35.
Fennell, P. (1986). '*Roberts v. Hopwood*: The Rule against Socialism.' *Journal of Law and Society*, vol. 13: 401.
Finer, Herman (1933). *English Local Government*. London: Methuen.
Galligan, D. J. (1986). *Discretionary Powers: A Legal Study of Official Discretion*. Oxford: Clarendon Press.
Game, Chris, and Chris Skelcher (1983). 'Manifestos and Other Manifestations of Local Party Politics – The Spread of Party Politics since Reorganization.' *Local Government Studies*, vol. 9, no. 4: 29.
Gibson, John (1982). 'The Block (and Target) Grant System – Theory and Evidence.' *Local Government Studies*, vol. 8, no. 3: 15.
—— (1992). 'British Local Government Finance under the Conservatives.' *Local Government Studies*, vol. 18, no. 4: 55.
Gordon, Richard (1996). *Judicial Review: Law and Procedure*. London: Sweet & Maxwell.
Grant, Malcolm (1984). *Rate Capping and the Law*. London: Association of Metropolitan Authorities.
—— (1986). *Rate Capping and the Law*, 2nd ed. London: Association of Metropolitan Authorities.
Griffith, John (1993). *Judicial Politics since 1920: A Chronicle*. Oxford: Blackwell.
—— (1997). *The Politics of the Judiciary*, 5th ed. London: Fontana.
Gyford, John (1985). *The Politics of Local Socialism*. London: Allen & Unwin.
Gyford, John, Steve Leach and Chris Game (1989). *The Changing Politics of Local Government*. London: Unwin Hyman.

Halliday, Simon (2000). 'The Influence of Judicial Review on Bureaucratic Decision-Making.' [2000] *Public Law*: 110.

—— (2004). *Judicial Review and Compliance with Administrative Law*. Oxford: Hart.

Halsbury's Laws of England, 4th ed., reissue (2001). Vol. 29(1), *Local Government*. London: Butterworths.

Harris, B. V. (2007). 'The "Third Source" of Authority for Government Action Revisited.' 123, *Law Quarterly Review*: 225.

Hart, W. O. (1968). *Introduction to the Law of Local Government and Administration*, 8th ed. London: Butterworths.

Head, Michael (2005). *Administrative Law: Context and Critique*. Sydney: Federation Press.

Hertogh, Marc, and Simon Halliday (eds) (2004). *Judicial Review and Bureaucratic Impact: International and Interdisciplinary Perspectives*. Cambridge: Cambridge University Press.

Himsworth, Chris (2006). 'The Domesticated Executive of Scotland.' In Craig and Tomkins (2006a): 192.

Hogg, Peter W. (1997). *Constitutional Law of Canada*, 4th ed., looseleaf. Scarborough: Carswell.

House of Commons (2007). *The Local Government and Public Involvement in Health Bill*. Research Paper 07/01. Online.

Humes, Samuel, and Eileen Martin (1969). *The Structure of Local Government: A Comparative Survey of 81 Countries*. The Hague: International Union of Local Authorities.

Hutter, Bridget (1997). *Compliance: Regulation and Environment*. Oxford: Clarendon Press.

Jacobs, Brian (1984). 'Labour Against the Centre: the Clay Cross Syndrome.' *Local Government Studies*, vol. 10, no. 2: 75.

John, Peter (2004). 'Strengthening Political Leadership? More than Mayors.' In Stoker and Wilson (2004a): 43.

Jones, David P., and Anne S. de Villars (2004). *Principles of Administrative Law*, 4th ed. Scarborough: Thomson Carswell.

Kaunda, J. M. (1999). 'Malawi: Local Government Democratisation and Decentralisation – an Uncertain Future.' In Reddy (1999): 113.

Kay, Jane (1999). *Administrative Law*. London: Blackstone.

Keith-Lucas, B. (1962). 'Poplarism.' [1962] *Public Law*: 62.

Keith-Lucas, Peter (2002). *Monitoring Officer: The Role of the Monitoring Officer following the Local Government Act 2000*. Association of Council Secretaries and Solicitors.

Kleinmann, Mark, Richard Eastall and Emilie Roberts (1990). 'What Determines Local Authorities' Capital Expenditure on Housing? An Evaluation of Various Models.' *Urban Studies*, vol. 27, no. 3: 401.

Laffin, Martin, and Ken Young (1990). *Professionalism in Local Government: Change and Challenge*. Harlow: Longman.

Lansley, Stewart, Sue Goss and Christian Wolmar (1989). *Councils in Conflict: the Rise and Fall of the Municipal Left*. Basingstoke: Macmillan.

Leach, Steve (2006). *The Changing Role of Local Politics in Britain*. Bristol: Policy Press.

Leach, Steve, and John Stewart (1992). *The Politics of Hung Authorities*. Basingstoke: Macmillan.

Leigh, Ian (2000). *Law, Politics, and Local Democracy*. Oxford: Oxford University Press.

Lewis, Stephen, and Anthony Harrison (1983). 'Capital Spending in the Public Sector: 4 Paradoxes.' *Public Money*, vol. 3, no. 1: 60.

Lordon, Paul (1991). *Crown Law*. Toronto: Butterworths.

Loughlin, Martin (1983). *Local Government, the Law and the Constitution*. London: The Local Government Legal Society Trust.

—— (1985). 'The Restructuring of Central-Local Government Legal Relations.' *Local Government Studies*, vol. 11, no. 6: 59.

—— (1986). *Local Government in the Modern State*. London: Sweet & Maxwell.

—— (1990). 'Innovative Financing in Local Government: The Limits of Legal Instrumentalism – Part I.' [1990] *Public Law*: 373.

—— (1996). *Legality and Locality: the Role of Law in Central-Local Government Relations*. Oxford: Clarendon.

Loveland, Ian (1995). *Housing Homeless Persons: Administrative Law and the Administrative Process*. Oxford: Clarendon Press.

Lukes, Stephen (1974). *Power: A Radical View*. London: Butterworths.

MacGregor, Susanne (1991). 'Poverty, the Poll Tax and Thatcherite Welfare Policy. Part I: How the Poll Tax Axed Mrs. Thatcher.' *Political Quarterly*: 443.

Marsh, David, and R. A. W. Rhodes (eds) (1992). *Implementing Thatcherite Policies: Audit of an Era*. Buckingham: Open University Press.

Mason, Nigel, Roger Turner and Michael Dodd (1999). *Local Authority Activity Under Section 137, Local Government Act 1972*. London: Department of the Environment, Transport and the Regions.

McAuslan, Patrick (1980). *The Ideologies of Planning Law*. Oxford: Pergamon Press.

McBarnet, Doreen (2004). *Crime, Compliance and Control*. Aldershot: Ashgate.

McBarnet, Doreen, and Christopher Whelan (1999a). 'Challenging the Regulators: Strategies for Resisting Control.' In McCrudden (1999a): 67.

—— (1999b). *Creative Accounting and the Cross-Eyed Javelin Thrower*. Chichester: John Wiley.

McCarthy, David J., and Laurie Reynolds (2003). *Local Government Law in a Nutshell*, 5th ed. St. Paul: Thomson/West.

McConnell, Allan (2004). *Scottish Local Government*. Edinburgh: Edinburgh University Press.

McCrudden, Christopher (ed.) (1999a). *Regulation and Deregulation – Policy and Practice in the Utilities and Financial Services Industries*. Oxford: Clarendon Press.

—— (1999b). 'Social Policy and Economic Regulators: Some Issues for the Reform of Utility Regulation.' In McCrudden (1999a): 275.

McFadden, Jean (2004). *Local Government Law in Scotland: an Introduction*. Edinburgh: Lexis Nexis.

McLean, Janet (2006). 'New Public Management New Zealand Style.' In Craig and Tomkins (2006a): 124.

Merry, Allan (1999). 'Transparency, Confidentiality and Freedom of Information.' In McCrudden (1999a): 185.

Midwinter, Arthur (1985). 'Setting the Rate – Liverpool Style.' *Local Government Studies*, vol. 11, no. 3: 25.

Midwinter, Arthur F., and Claire Monaghan (1993). *From Rates to the Poll Tax: Local Government Finance in the Thatcher Era*. Edinburgh: Edinburgh University Press.

Mullen, Tom, Kathy Pick and Tony Prosser (1996). *Judicial Review in Scotland.* Chichester: John Wiley.
Munro, Jane (2003). *Public Law in Scotland.* Edinburgh: Thomson.
Newton, Keith (1976). *Second City Politics.* Oxford: Clarendon Press.
Obadina, Derek (1998). 'Judicial Review and Gypsy Site Provision.' In Buck (1998a): 244.
Office of the Deputy Prime Minister (2005). *Formative Evaluation of the Take-Up and Implementation of the Well-Being Power, 2003–2006.*
Parkinson, Michael (1985). *Liverpool on the Brink: One City's Struggle against Government Cuts.* Hermitage: Policy Journals.
—— (ed.) (1987). *Reshaping Local Government.* Hermitage: Policy Journals.
Pasteur, D. (1999). 'Democratic Decentralisation: a Review of the African Experience.' In Reddy (1999): 31.
Paying for Local Government (1986). Cmnd. 9714. London: HMSO.
Rattenbury, T. P. B. (1984). *Ultra Vires and the Powers of Local Government.* D. Phil. thesis, Oxford University.
Rawlings, Richard (2003). *Delineating Wales: Constitutional, Legal and Administrative Aspects of National Devolution.* Cardiff: University of Wales Press.
Reddy, P. S. (ed.) (1999). *Local Government Democratisation and Decentralisation: A Review of the Southern African Region.* Kenwyn: Juta & Co.
Rhodes, R. A. W. (1984). 'Continuity and Change in British Central-Local Relations: "The Conservative Threat", 1979–83.' *British Journal of Political Science,* vol. 14, no. 3: 261.
—— (1986a). Review of *Between Centre and Locality,* by Stewart Ranson, George Jones and Kieron Walsh. *Public Administration,* vol. 64, issue 2: 231.
—— (1986b). *The National World of Local Government.* London: Allen and Unwin.
—— (1992). 'Local Government Finance.' In Marsh and Rhodes (1992): 50.
—— (1999). *Control and Power in Central-Local Government Relations,* 2nd ed. Aldershot: Ashgate.
Richardson, Genevra, and Hazel Genn (eds) (1994). *Administrative Law and Government Action. The Courts and Alternative Mechanisms of Review.* Oxford: Clarendon Press.
Robson, W. A. (1954). *The Development of Local Government,* 3rd rev. ed. London: Allen & Unwin.
Rogers, Ian MacFee (1971). *The Law of Canadian Municipal Corporations,* 2nd ed., looseleaf. Toronto: Carswell.
Rosenberg, David (1989). *Accounting for Public Policy: Power, Professions and Politics in Local Government.* Manchester: Manchester University Press.
Rosenbloom, David H. (2003). *Administrative Law for Public Managers.* Boulder: Westview.
Sarma, B. C. (2004). *The Law of Ultra Vires.* Kolkata, New Delhi: Eastern Law House.
Savitch, Hank W., and Ronald K. Vogel (2005). 'The United States: executive-centred politics.' In Denters and Rose (2005a): 211.
Sbragia, Alberta (1986). 'Capital Markets and Central-Local Politics in Britain.' *British Journal of Political Science,* vol. 16, no. 3: 311.
Schwartz, Bernard, and H. W. R. Wade (1972). *Legal Control of Government: Administrative Law in Britain and the United States.* Oxford: Clarendon Press.

Scott, Colin (1998). 'The Juridification of Regulatory Relations in the UK Utilities Sector.' In Black, Muchlinski and Walker (1998): 19.
Sedley, Sir Stephen (2000). 'Policy and Law.' In Andenas and Fairgrieve (2000): 259.
Sharland, John (1997). *A Practical Approach to Local Government Law*. London: Blackstone.
—— (2006). *A Practical Approach to Local Government Law*, 2nd ed. Oxford: Oxford University Press.
Smellie, K. B. (1949). *A History of Local Government*, 2nd ed. London: G. Allen & Unwin.
Smith, K. (2006). 'Are We On Track? Issues of Organizational Structures in South Africa.' Institute for Local Government Management of South Africa. Accessed online at http//www.ilgm.co.za/page.asp?PageID=135 on 3 January 2007.
Smith, Peter (1983). 'Local Authority Budgets 1983: No Reduction of Services.' *Public Money*, vol. 3, no. 2: 47.
Smith, Peter, and John Stewart (1985). 'Local Authority Expenditure Targets.' *Local Government Studies*, vol. 11, no. 4: 21.
Stewart, John (2000). *The Nature of British Local Government*. Basingstoke: Macmillan.
Stoker, Gerry, and David Wilson (eds) (2004a). *British Local Government into the 21st Century*. Basingstoke: Palgrave Macmillan.
—— (2004b). 'Conclusions: New Ways of Being Local Government.' In Stoker and Wilson (2004a): 247.
Sunkin, Maurice (2004). 'Conceptual Issues in Researching the Impact of Judicial Review on Government Bureaucracies.' In Hertogh and Halliday (2004): 43.
Sunkin, Maurice, and Kathryn Pick (2001). 'The Changing Impact of Judicial Review: The Independent Review Service of the Social Fund.' [2001] *Public Law*: 736.
Supperstone, Michael (2003). 'Local Authorities and Audits: Challenges to Auditors: New Frontiers.' [2003] *Journal of Local Government Law*, issue 3: 62.
Thompson, Helen, and Chris Game (1985). 'Section 137: Propaganda on the Rates?' *Local Government Studies*, vol. 11, no. 2: 11.
Travers, Tony (1982). 'The Block Grant and the Recent Development of the Grant System.' *Local Government Studies*, vol. 8, no. 3: 3.
Valente, William D. (1980). *Local Government Law: Cases and Materials*, 2nd ed. St. Paul: West.
Valente, William D., David J. McCarthy, Richard Briffault and Laurie Reynolds (2001). *Cases and Materials on State and Local Government Law*. St. Paul: West.
Wade, Sir William, and Christopher Forsyth (2004). *Administrative Law*, 9th ed. Oxford: Oxford University Press.
Wakefield, Kim (2007). *Alberta Municipal Law & Commentary*. Markham, Lexis Nexis.
Wallis, M. (1999). 'Lesotho: Seeking Local Democracy in the Mountain Kingdom.' In Reddy (1999): 91.
Warren, Kenneth F. (2004). *Administrative Law in the Political System*, 4th ed. Boulder: Westview.
Webb, Sidney, and Beatrice Webb (1922). *English Local Government*. London: Longmans, Green and Co.

Wilson, David, and Chris Game (2006). *Local Government in the United Kingdom*, 4th ed. Houndmills: Palgrave.

Widdicombe, David (Chair): Committee of Inquiry Into the Conduct of Local Authority Business (1986). *The Conduct of Local Authority Business*. London: HMSO.

Young, Ken, ed. (1983a). *National Interests and Local Government*. London: Heinemann.

—— (1983b). 'Introduction: Beyond Centralism.' In Young (1983a): 1.

Cases Cited

[Note: The dates listed below may not match the dates in the text. The text uses the year of the court decision, in order to preserve chronology; the citation below is the date of the report.

Cases marked as BAILII are publicly accessible on the website of the British and Irish Legal Information Institute. Cases marked as CANLII are publicly accessible on the website of the Canadian Legal Information Institute.]

A-G, ex rel. Tilley v Wandsworth LBC, [1981] 1 WLR 854.
A-G v Great Eastern Railway Co., (1880) 5 App. Cas. 473.
A-G v Wellingborough BC, (1974) 72 LGR 507.
Akumah v Hackney LBC, [2005] UKHL 17 [BAILII].
Allsop v North Tyneside MBC, (1992) 90 LGR 462.
APPH v Wednesbury Corporation, [1948] 1 KB 223 [BAILII].
Belcher v Reading, [1950] Ch 30.
Bovis New Homes Ltd v New Forest DC, [2002] EWHC 483 (Admin) [BAILII].
Bromley LBC v GLC, [1982] 2 WLR 62 [BAILII].
CCSU v Minister for the Civil Service, [1985] AC 374 [BAILII].
Chertsey UDC v Mixnam's Properties Ltd, [1965] AC 735.
Condron v National Assembly for Wales, [2005] EWHC 3007 (Admin) [BAILII].
Crédit Suisse v Allerdale BC, [1997] QB 306.
Crédit Suisse v Waltham Forest LBC, [1997] QB 362.
Hall & Co. Ltd v Shoreham-by-Sea UDC, [1964] 1 WLR 240.
Hazell v Hammersmith and Fulham LBC, [1992] 2 AC 1.
Khadr v Canada, 2006 FC 727 (CANLII).
Kleinwort Benson v City of Glasgow Council, [2002] ScotCS 132 [BAILII].
Kleinwort Benson Ltd v Sandwell BC, [1994] 4 AER 890.
Kruse v Johnson, [1898] 2 QB 91.
Larocque v Canada, 2006 FCA 237 (CANLII).
Lavender v MHLG, [1970] 1 WLR 1231.
LCC v A-G, [1902] AC 165.
Leeds Corpn v Jenkinson, [1935] 1 KB 166.
Luby v Newcastle-under-Lyne-Corpn, [1964] 2 QB 64, Div Ct; [1965] 1 QB 214, CA.
Manchester City Council v Greater Manchester Metropolitan County Council, (1980) 78 LGR 560.
Meade v Haringey LBC, [1979] 2 AER 1016.
Newbold v Leicester CC, [1999] EWHC Admin 670 [BAILII].
Passutto Hotels (1984) Ltd v Red Deer (City of), 2006 ABQB 641 (CANLII).
Pickwell v Camden LBC, (1982) 80 LGR 798.
Porter v Magill, [2001] UKHL 67 [BAILII].
Prescott v Birmingham Corpn, [1955] Ch 210.
R v Brent LBC, ex parte Gladbaum, (1989) 88 LGR 627.
R v Broadland DC, ex parte Lashley, [2001] EWCA Civ 179 [BAILII].
R v Bromley LBC, ex parte Lambeth LBC, The Times, 16 June 1984.

R v Ealing LBC, ex parte Times Newspapers Ltd, (1987) 85 LGR 316.
R v GLC and Another, The Times, 31 December 1984.
R v GLC, ex parte Bromley LBC, The Times, 27 March 1984.
R v Greenwich LBC, ex parte Governors of the John Ball Primary School, The Times, 27 December 1989.
R v Hackney LBC, ex parte Fleming, (1985), see Loughlin 1996: 190.
R v Hammersmith and Fulham LBC, ex parte Beddowes, [1987] 1 QB 1050.
R v Lewisham LBC, ex parte Shell UK Ltd, [1988] 1 AER 938.
R v Liverpool CC, ex parte Secretary of State for Employment, The Times, 12 November 1988.
R v Merseyside CC, ex parte Great Universal Stores, (1982) 80 LGR 639.
R v Port Talbot BC, ex parte Jones, [1988] 2 AER 207.
R v Secretary of State for the Environment, ex parte Birmingham CC, (1986), see Loughlin 1996: 291.
R v Secretary of State for the Environment, ex parte Brent LBC, [1982] QB 593.
R v Secretary of State for the Environment, ex parte Hackney LBC, The Times, 26 March 1984.
R v Secretary of State for the Environment, ex parte Hackney LBC, [1984] 1 WLR 592.
R v Secretary of State for the Environment, ex parte Hammersmith and Fulham LBC, The Times, 18 May 1985.
R v Secretary of State for the Environment, ex parte Hillingdon LBC, [1986] 1 WLR 807.
R v Somerset CC, ex parte Fewings, [1995] 1 AER 513 [BAILII].
R v Wirral MBC, ex parte Milstead, [1989] RVR 66.
R (Bancoult) v Secretary of State for Foreign and Commonwealth Affairs, [2007] EWCA Civ 498 [BAILII].
R (Capenhurst) v Leicester City Council, [2004] EWHC 2124 (Admin) [BAILII].
R (Chief Constable of West Midlands Police) v Birmingham JJ, [2002] EWHC (Admin) [BAILII].
R (Comninos) v Bedford BC, [2003] EWHC 121 (Admin) [BAILII].
R (Godfrey) v Conwy BC, [2001] EWHC Admin 640 [BAILII].
R (Island Farm Development Ltd) v Bridgend CBC, [2006] EWHC 2189 (Admin) [BAILII].
R (J) v Enfield LBC, [2002] EWHC 432 (Admin) [BAILII].
R (Nadarajah and Abdi) v Secretary of State for the Home Department, [2005] EWCA Civ 1363 [BAILII].
R (Saima Khan) v Oxfordshire CC, [2004] EWCA Civ 309 [BAILII].
R (Theophilus) v Lewisham LBC, [2002] EWHC 1371 (Admin) [BAILII].
R (Western Riverside Waste Authority) v Wandsworth LBC, [2005] EWHC 536 (Admin) [BAILII].
Roberts v Hopwood, [1925] AC 578.
Shell Canada Products Ltd v City of Vancouver, 1994 CANLII 1115 (SCC).
Westdeutsche Landesbank Girozentrale v Islington LBC, [1996] 2 AER 961 [BAILII].
Westminster CC v Morris, [2005] Civ 1184 [BAILII].
Wheeler v Leicester City Council, [1985] AC 1054 [BAILII].

Index

www.ingramcontent.com/pod-product-compliance
Ingram Content Group UK Ltd.
Pitfield, Milton Keynes, MK11 3LW, UK
UKHW041909040925
462611UK00003B/166
* 9 7 8 1 3 4 9 3 6 2 8 1 3 *